Democratic Foreign Policy Making

DEMOCRATIC FOREIGN POLICY MAKING: PROBLEMS OF DIVIDED GOVERNMENT AND INTERNATIONAL COOPERATION

Edited by
ROBERT PAHRE

DEMOCRATIC FOREIGN POLICY MAKING
© Robert Pahre, 2006.

First published in 2006 by
PALGRAVE MACMILLAN™
175 Fifth Avenue, New York, N.Y. 10010 and
Houndmills, Basingstoke, Hampshire, England RG21 6XS
Companies and representatives throughout the world.

PALGRAVE MACMILLAN is the global academic imprint of the Palgrave Macmillan division of St. Martin's Press, LLC and of Palgrave Macmillan Ltd. Macmillan® is a registered trademark in the United States, United Kingdom and other countries. Palgrave is a registered trademark in the European Union and other countries.

ISBN-13: 978–1–4039–7457–0
ISBN-10: 1–4039–7457–8

Library of Congress Cataloging-in-Publication Data is available from the Library of Congress.

A catalogue record for this book is available from the British Library.

Design by Newgen Imaging Systems (P) Ltd., Chennai, India.

First edition: November 2006

10 9 8 7 6 5 4 3 2 1

Printed in the United States of America.

In memory of
Michael Wallerstein, 1951–2006
teacher
scholar
friend

Contents

List of Tables

List of Figures

Chapter 1

Divided Government and International Cooperation: An Overview

Robert Pahre

"Democracy" plays a central role in foreign policy today. Both abroad and at home, this is true in two senses. First, democracy is often the subject of U.S. foreign policy, as it is in many nations. President George W. Bush, like President William Clinton before him, has made the spread of democracy abroad an explicit goal of U.S. foreign policy.

Second, democracy at home shapes foreign policy making. For example, both Clinton and Bush have confronted challenges of democratic foreign policy making at home. Clinton faced an increasingly hostile Congress in which Republicans ultimately enjoyed a majority in both chambers. Though the younger Bush has enjoyed the luxury of a Republican Congress (with a brief exception), he has had to deal with a polarized public as well as significant political and legal challenges to his foreign policy. The leaders of other democracies have faced analogous domestic political constraints, perhaps most notably in Spain, where the Popular Party was turned out of office largely over the issue of the Iraq war.

Democracy raises many questions for analyzing foreign policy making. Though many people analyze foreign policy in terms of a unified state pursuing a single "national interest," others have been open to examine the messier world of democratic policymaking. Even so, most discussions of democracy and foreign policy have overlooked two important facts. First, democracies differ not only from autocracies but also from one another.

Our understanding of democratic foreign policy making must therefore be built on variation across democratic institutions. Second, democracy is a process by which groups make decisions when they disagree with one another. Our analysis of democratic foreign policy making should therefore address these differences of opinion both theoretically and normatively, and be built explicitly on cases of domestic disagreement over policy.

Because disagreements among citizens play such an important role in democracy, many observers have argued that democracy is somehow bad for foreign policy. These critics argue that national unity—rallying behind the president in time of crisis or war, for example—is essential for effective policymaking, and that internal critics operating within democratic procedures inhibit this unity. For example, G.W. Bush has regularly made claims that "defeatism" among his Democratic opponents harms the national interest, most recently in his 2006 State of the Union address.[1] In peacetime, too, some maintain that democracy makes it harder to cooperate with other nations because special interests will block otherwise advantageous treaties in the legislature.

At a more abstract level, our understanding of democratic foreign policy making is limited because relatively few studies of democracy examine several countries at the same time. What happens when a parliamentary democracy like the United Kingdom interacts with a presidential democracy like the United States? Is this different than two parliamentary democracies or two presidential democracies? Or, how does a single political system such as the United States vary over time from "bipartisan" periods such as the 1950s to the polarized system of today?

This book addresses these questions in theoretical terms. It focuses first on the division of powers that is found in any democracy. We analyze this division of powers as a "divided polity," in which some powers may be held by different actors. Second, this book examines the extent to which people in a democracy disagree with one another, an idea that we operationalize through the concept of "the degree of divided government." Though most research to date has suggested that such divisions make foreign policy more difficult, the contributors to this volume develop more subtle arguments in which the degree of divided government may make the pursuit of international cooperation easier as well as more difficult. Third, we analyze theoretically the rules under which people who disagree will struggle over policy, which we examine in terms of "agenda-setting." We give special attention to (1) those actors who control negotiations with other countries and (2) the status quo (or reversion point) if those negotiations fall through. Viewed differently, we use "divided government" as a form of analytical leverage to examine the democratic foundations of international cooperation, and then we make this concept more complex as a way to gain a richer and more nuanced understanding of how democracy affects foreign policy.

This introduction lays out the theoretical foundation for this choice of focus. The conclusion summarizes our findings and then discusses the substantive and normative implications of these findings for our understanding of democratic foreign policy making. We give particular attention to two questions. First, the existing theoretical literature has tended to argue (1) that democracies are less likely to cooperate with other countries because of the many actors who can veto such cooperation; and (2) that when they do cooperate, democracies often obtain favorable outcomes because the other side has to make concessions to satisfy these "veto actors"[2] (this latter claim is often called the "Schelling Conjecture"). Empirical studies have tended to support (1). At the same time, empirical tests tend to call (2) into doubt as a systematic claim about foreign policy, while finding anecdotal evidence for it under some conditions.

The contributors to this volume make refined claims on both points. Democracy may make cooperation more likely under some conditions but less likely under others. Some democracies can use their veto actors as leverage for obtaining concessions, while others cannot. Specifying the precise conditions under which each of these claims holds, and examining still further claims about democracy, is the central task of this volume. This richer set of claims then informs our normative evaluation of democracy and foreign policy making in the conclusion. Blanket statements that democracy makes foreign policy more difficult—or easier, for that matter—are not supported by the theory and evidence in this volume. Instead, particular features of democracy have specific effects on foreign policy.

Democratic Foreign Policy Making as a Matter of Rules

Because we are interested in the nitty-gritty of democratic foreign policy, the contributors to this volume give extensive attention to the rules of the democratic game. The study of these rules is grounded in a large body of theoretical research on politics in general and on foreign policy and international relations more narrowly. This theoretical literature allows us to specify abstractly the conditions under which the general claims described earlier do or do not hold.

Like other games, politics has both players and rules. Two or three decades ago, the discipline of political science gave most of its attention to the actors, their interests, and their values. Today the rules of the political game have become more interesting to the field.

While this focus on institutions has spread throughout all the subfields of the discipline, these rules look very different in the various spheres of politics. Domestic politics usually takes place in a highly institutionalized environment. Democracies choose representatives subject to electoral rules, and these representatives make policy in a rule-governed fashion. Administrative agencies are also highly rule-bound, both in democracies and authoritarian systems.

International relations occur in a different setting, which often goes under the label of "anarchy" (see Mearsheimer 2001; Waltz 1979 inter alia). States lack legal authority over one another unless they choose to create institutions that bind them. While such institutions are increasingly important in the international system—led by the European Union's pervasive influence in European politics—states retain the ability to secede from these organizations. This means that any grant of authority to international organizations is voluntary and subject to revocation.

These features make the study of international politics differ significantly from the study of domestic politics. Because there is no government to make and enforce rules, decentralized cooperation between the players poses a much more central problem in international relations than in domestic political systems (see inter alia Axelrod 1984; Keohane 1984; Oye, ed. 1986). As a result, theory development has often pursued different directions in the study of international relations than in the study of domestic political systems.

While domestic and international politics are analytically distinct, scholars are increasingly aware of their substantive interrelationships. Since the demonstrations at the Seattle summit of the World Trade Organization (WTO), for example, international trade policy has become more salient in the domestic politics of many countries (see Bhagwati 2004). Antiglobalization activists and their more traditional allies in labor and environmental organizations take the lead in battles that will likely shape the future of many international economic organizations. Though these domestic trade policy conflicts occur within rule-governed domestic political systems, each country negotiates with other states over these issues in an allegedly anarchic international system.

This volume explores the interrelationship between these two realms. While internal political conflicts over foreign policy occur in a rule-based political system, states negotiate their differences over policy in a more anarchic international society.[3] This tension between the international and domestic spheres makes modern international relations particularly interesting, both analytically and substantively.

To examine these connections more thoroughly, this volume focuses on cases in which there exist important domestic differences over foreign policy, or "divided government." This divided government normally reflects differences over opinion at home, and often reflects structural divisions of power. The concept arises from the literature in American politics (i.e., Alesina and Rosenthal 1996; Fiorina 1992; Lohmann and O'Halloran 1994), in which it refers to the differences in partisan control between the Congress and the president, but the contributors to this volume extend this concept to many other countries. Like most of that literature, the contributors build on a spatial theory of politics, in which policy is modeled as a point in space. For example, a policy might be more to the Left or the Right in terms of ideology, and this can be thought of as being to the Left or the Right along a line representing that ideological space.

The individual chapters explore the effects of this divided government on international cooperation. Differences of opinion between an executive and the legislature may certainly lead to visible foreign policy conflicts. Yet many countries, notably majoritarian parliamentary systems such as the United Kingdom, do not have strong divisions between the two branches of government. Even so, many parliamentary systems have other actors—such as coalition partners in a multiparty government, upper chambers of the legislature, supramajoritarian coalition requirements for some policies, or rules for public referenda—that force us to reconsider the concept of "divided government." Examining this variety is a central task of this volume.

Theories of International Cooperation

So far we have considered only the foreign policy problem in a single country, and the relationship between different branches of government there. However, understanding more fully the effects of divided government on international cooperation also requires that we understand why cooperation represents a significant problem in international relations. The field of international relations has largely agreed on a common definition of cooperation, which occurs when "actors adjust their behavior to the actual or anticipated preferences of others, through a process of policy coordination" (Keohane 1984: 51–52). In other words, cooperation requires a conscious choice by which states change their behavior. The game of Prisoners' Dilemma (PD) provides an essential point of reference here. In this game, two players must decide whether to cooperate with each other or not. Both prefer to cooperate, but there is some advantage to cheating on your partner, that is, not cooperating while your partner cooperates.

While domestic politics takes place within some institutional framework set by a state with a monopoly over the legitimate use of force, international cooperation occurs between sovereign nations not subject to any legal authority. For this reason, states must both monitor and enforce cooperation themselves, without recourse to third party enforcers. A threat to punish any cheater requires that the game be played repeatedly, so that today's would-be cheaters can be deterred by tomorrow's punishments. As a result, study-ing enforcement became central to cooperation theory (Axelrod 1984; Keohane 1984; Lipson 1984; Martin 1992; Oye, ed. 1986; Pahre 1994b, 1995, 1998: Chapters 7–9; Stein 1983; Yarbrough and Yarbrough 1986). This research looks at how states monitor compliance, and how they improve information about compliance and about one another's preferences.

The literature in international relations finds that three variables explain the success or failure of cooperation: "mutuality of interest, the shadow of the future, and the number of players" (Axelrod and Keohane 1986: 227; see also Axelrod 1984; Keohane 1984; Koremenos, Lipson, and Snidal 2001; Lipson 1984; Oye, ed. 1986). Each variable makes enforcement easier, or the incentive to cheat less. Mutuality of interest raises the benefits from cooperation; any punishment that would take those benefits away therefore gains force and makes cooperation more likely. The shadow of the future is the degree to which the players value the future. Increasing this value makes players want to avoid future punishment, again making cooperation more likely. Finally, increasing the number of players makes cooperation harder because there are more would-be cheaters to monitor, and there is an incentive to pass the buck when it is time to punish them.[4]

Existing theory seems not to have appreciated the extent to which these hypotheses depend on the valuation of the status quo. Research suggests that a high shadow of the future might make cooperation less likely by mag-nifying the distributional effects of a bargain (Fearon 1998). A state will negotiate harder for a good deal if it believes this bargain will affect its pay-offs for a long time to come. Its willingness to hold out will depend in part on its valuation of the status quo, that is, the utility of doing nothing. Moreover, as Hammond and Prins argue at length, existing theories of domestic politics have given inadequate attention to the status quo.

Taken on their own terms, existing theories of cooperation present further problems. The first independent variable in cooperation theory, "mutuality of interest," is simply another way of saying that states' preferences affect their willingness to cooperate (cf. Koremenos, Lipson, and Snidal 2001; Moravcsik 1998). It is notoriously difficult to specify these preferences independently of the outcomes they are trying to explain (Snidal 1985), though Thomas König and Simon Hug (2000; also Hug and König 2001 and chapter 5) have developed some techniques for inferring political parties' evaluations of specific policies.

Perhaps most surprisingly, cooperation theory has failed to study variation between cooperation and noncooperation. By looking overwhelmingly at successful cooperation, cooperation theory has avoided asking whether the reversion point—the outcome that results if cooperation breaks down— might affect the likelihood of cooperation. Hammond and Prins examine this question systematically in chapter 2. Both Rosendorff and Pahre also examine reversion points in their respective chapters, giving particular attention to the domestic politics of trade policy. For example, Rosendorff shows that having a divided polity will shape cooperative tariffs even when executives have equally liberal tariffs, that is, the same reversion point. In chapter 5, Hug and König explicitly define all players' preferences relative to the status quo. Drawing on a different tradition in conflict studies, Todd Allee and Paul Huth give explicit attention to variation between cooperative settlements and escalation to war in chapter 6.

It is often forgotten that rational choice theory rests on preferences for one option over another, so that one must study the roads not taken if one wants to understand the choices actually made. I have emphasized the reversion point in this section because this leads naturally, if surprisingly for most people, to the subject of domestic politics. First, when domestic political actors have different preferences we may think of this as a different evaluation of the status quo relative to international cooperation. This role of the reversion point in divided government is most evident in chapters 2 and 5. Second, the very existence of divided government affects the status quo. This problem is emphasized in chapters 3 and 4. We see both of these effects in the following section.

Two-Level Games, Divided Government, and International Cooperation

While the effects of the international system on international cooperation remain a dominant concern in the discipline, theoretical research has not rested with traditional cooperation theory. Recent years have seen substantial research on how domestic politics affects international relations, increasingly using theories from comparative politics to explain trade policy and cooperation (Gilligan 1997; Hug and König 2002; Lohmann and O'Halloran 1994; Mansfield et al. 2000; Milner 1997; Milner and Rosendorff 1997; O'Halloran 1994; Pahre 1997, 2001a, 2001b; Verdier 1994).

The literature on two-level games has gained the greatest prominence in this area. Robert Putnam (1988) first distinguished between the "Level I" game between two governments and the "Level II" game between each government and any relevant domestic actors. Since Putnam, much of the literature has developed typologies of the behavior by which foreign policy affects domestic politics or vice versa. For example, the nonformal literature has examined bargaining tactics such as mobilizing foreign interest groups, changing foreign domestic political agendas, making side payments, or using international negotiations to avoid blocking actors at home (Evans, Jacobson and Putnam 1993; Friman 1993; Moyer 1993; Paarlberg 1993; Schoppa 1993).

Instead of cataloguing forms of influence, formal theorists have focused on how rational negotiators can anticipate domestic actors' reactions and respond by changing their bargaining behavior. These arguments only make sense if the legislature's preferences differ from the executive's. This difference between executive and legislative preferences has become known as either "divided government" or the "degree of divided government," two terms that I define more explicitly later in this section.

The existing literature has explored two distinct effects of divided government on international cooperation. First, the presence of a legislature that can veto treaties makes cooperation harder for the executive to negotiate. Many claim that domestic politics normally makes international cooperation less likely (Iida 1993; but Karol 2000; Milner and Rosendorff 1996, 1997; Mo 1994, 1995; Schneider and Cederman 1994).[5] The need for the American president to take into account the problems of Senate ratification provides a classic example of this problem. For example, President Jimmy Carter had to negotiate several changes to the Panama Canal Treaty in order to achieve narrow ratification by a vote of 67–33 in the Senate. Trying to satisfy an unpredictable legislature under uncertainty may also force an executive to maintain a hardline stance abroad, preventing cooperation with foreigners (Milner 1997).

The second effect of divided government goes by the name of the "Schelling Conjecture." In *Strategy and Conflict*, Thomas Schelling (1960: 19–23) conjectured that an executive whose hands were tied would be able to negotiate more favorable outcomes than an unconstrained executive. For example, the president may successfully make demands of Japan in trade negotiations, reminding his interlocutors that he must satisfy a hardline Congress if any bargain will stick. The core notion is older, dating at least to E.H. Carr's (1939: 38) observation that

It became a commonplace for statesmen at Geneva and elsewhere to explain that they themselves had every desire to be reasonable, but that public opinion in their countries was inexorable; and though this plea was sometimes a pretext or a tactical manœuvre, there was often a solid substratum of reality beneath it.

A substantial formal literature has grown up around this claim (Iida 1993, 1996; Mo 1994, 1995; Schneider and Cederman 1994), evaluating the conditions under which it may or may not be true.

The contributions to this volume call both of these arguments into question, though each hypothesis may be true under certain conditions. To specify these conditions more precisely, we develop more exact definitions of the various terms entailed in the argument. First, a *divided polity* has two or more actors whose choices affect the outcome of the policy game. Some examples include the president and Congress in the United States, the two parties in the coalition of the Christian Democratic Union, Christian Socialist Union, and Socialist Party behind Chancellor Angela Merkel's government in Germany, or the federal structure of Switzerland. This term refers to the mere existence of multiple relevant actors, and says nothing about their preferences.[6] Allee and Huth provide one operationalization of this concept in chapter 6, the percentage of seats controlled by the governing coalition in a democracy.

This division in the polity is a necessary condition for *divided government*, or the difference in preferences between the politically relevant actors. This is sometimes measured dichotomously, if crudely, as present if the American presidency and Congress are controlled by different parties (Lohmann and O'Halloran 1994; Mayhew 1991; O'Halloran 1994). It is hard to know how to translate this to multiparty or parliamentary systems. In addition, the mere existence of institutional divisions does not imply that all veto players are relevant for the outcome. The contributors to this volume demonstrate this point both theoretically (Hammond and Prins, chapter 2) and empirically (Hug and König, chapter 5).

We can develop more precise hypotheses by moving beyond dichotomous variables. In conventional usage, the *degree of divided government* is a continuous variable referring to the variation in this difference in domestic preferences, usually the distance between the legislative and executive ideal points in a spatial model. In chapter 5, Hug and König measure these distances using factor analysis of public opinion data. They emphasize differences in preferences over the differences in resources controlled by the government and its opponents. Pahre's chapter 4 uses largely institutional criteria, supplemented by case study evidence of preferences in a few countries.

Important as these concepts are, neither the presence of a divided polity nor the degree of divided government suffices to characterize a political system. For that we also need to give attention to the rules of the policy making process. We focus particularly on the distribution of agenda-setting powers, that is, the identity of the actor who proposes a new policy to other decision makers. Agenda-setting matters at two stages. First, an actor may have controlled the agenda that determined the location of the present status quo. Second, an actor may control the negotiating agenda and/or the substance of international treaties that are submitted to legislatures for ratification.

To understand the importance of agenda-setting, consider several examples. In the United States, domestic legislation is proposed by Congress, subject to a presidential veto that is itself subject to override by a two-thirds majority of both chambers. Foreign policy is made under quite different procedures, in which the president proposes international treaties to the Senate for approval by a two-thirds majority. Most two-level theory, as analyzed systematically by Hammond and Prins in chapter 2, focuses on this latter procedure.

This difference in procedure has important theoretical implications when we consider the status quo. In domestic policy, any new law changes the old law, which was originally passed by Congress. Thus, the agenda-setter today was also the agenda-setter for yesterday's legislation. In contrast, many foreign policy decisions allow the executive to modify policies previously chosen by Congress. In trade policy, for example, the president negotiates downward a tariff that Congress had originally set. Here, today's agenda setter was the ratifier of yesterday's policy, while today's ratifier was yesterday's agenda setter (see Pahre 2004a for full analysis of this example). Thus, American policy domains differ in terms of who the agenda-setter and ratifier are, and who controls the reversion point.

Such institutional differences grow in importance when we turn to other political systems. Most American studies of European parliamentary politics (Alesina and Rosenthal 1995; Fiorina 1992: 112–125; Laver and Shepsle 1991; Martin 2000: Chapters 6–7; Milner 1999 but Pahre 1997) use the term for both minority governments and coalitions made of parties with differing preferences. Grouping these two kinds of governments together is an error because they are institutionally different in agenda-setting terms. A minority government proposes legislation to a parliament with a different median ideal point for approval. In a coalition government, two or more parties jointly set the agenda and ratify the deal; because a majority coalition will control a majority in the parliament, passage is normally a mere formality. The coalition government and the legislature may even have the same ideal point. As Hug and König show in chapter 5, European political systems vary considerably along these dimensions.

Agenda-setting and control over the reversion point also vary across issues in the European Union (Pahre 2001a, 2004b). The Commission negotiates with foreigners on behalf of the Union in trade policy and, where negotiations are appropriate, competition and antitrust policy. Reversion points come from various sources, from the member states' original tariffs in 1957 to target prices for agricultural commodities set by the Commission each year. The European Central Bank sets the reversion point in monetary policy, and sets the agenda in negotiations with outsiders such as the U.S. Federal Reserve when agreeing on joint open-market operations. In contrast, the president of the European Council conducts negotiations for expansion, while the European Council and the European Parliament both ratify any accession treaty.

In other cases, earlier treaties might provide the reversion point. In this case, neither the executive nor the legislature "controls" that reversion point. The Amsterdam Intergovernmental Conference (IGC) analyzed in chapter 5 is one example, while the preexisting territorial disputes analyzed in chapter 6 may or may not have been established by previous agreements. In the case of an IGC, negotiating governments act as agenda setters, while chapter 6 examines cases in which a "challenger" sets the agenda by making an initial territorial demand on the "target."

As this discussion suggests, then, the concept of divided government encompasses not just the existence of two relevant actors whose preferences may vary, but also various patterns of agenda-setting and ratification. *Even if both the executive and the legislature must assent to any treaty*, we can distinguish four ideal types, shown in table 1.1. The table also provides some illustrations of each. For example, central bank agreements on joint intervention in currency markets reflect bank control over existing monetary policy as well as bank agenda-setting powers in international negotiations. In some sanctions cases, such as U.S. sanctions against South Africa in the 1980s, the executive branch set foreign policy while Congress proposed joint action with other countries against apartheid. EU enlargement negotiations represent another case, in which the Council of Ministers controls both the status quo and oversees negotiations with potential members.

These three cases are relatively infrequent, however. By far the most important in both theoretical and empirical studies is the case in which the legislature controls the status quo while the executive negotiates international

Table 1.1 Possible Agendas, with Illustrations

	Executive proposes treaty	Legislature proposes treaty
Executive proposes status quo	Central bank cooperation	Unusual, but perhaps some sanctioning cases
Legislature proposes status quo	Trade negotiations	EU expansion (Council is "legislature")
Status quo is previous treaty	Amsterdam IGC	(None found)

treaties (see especially chapter 3). This is the pattern in trade negotiations for most countries, for example (see chapter 4). However, table 1.1 shows clearly that we need to consider alternative configurations of agenda-setting and control over reversion points as well as this canonical trade policy problem.

These rules affect both a veto player's power to reject international cooperation and the validity of the Schelling Conjecture. They also determine the reversion point, the outcome that occurs in the absence of cooperation. Whenever divided government produces a sufficiently bad reversion point, governments become more likely to cooperate with each other. By looking at these additional issues, the contributors to this volume show that the conventional wisdom on divided government may or may not hold. Whether divided government makes cooperation less likely depends on institutions (divided polity), preferences (degrees of divided government), and agenda-setting.

In contrast to much of the formal two-level literature, information does not play an important role in the contributors' analyses. Hammond and Prins argue forcefully that including uncertainty complicates inference problems considerably in the kinds of analyses found in this volume. It is difficult to determine whether a particular outcome is best attributed to a combination of institutions (divided polity and agenda-setting), preferences (degree of divided government), or uncertainty if the analyst allows all of these factors to vary in a particular model. For this reason, the contributors here assume that governments have good information about one another and their domestic politics.

As this point suggests, the framework here provides a foundation for analysis and is not intended to be an exhaustive list of all the features of democratic foreign policy making. Our goal is to clarify and extend existing theoretical and empirical analyses, expecting research into divided government and foreign policy making to continue in the coming years.

Methodological Diversity in the Study of Democratic Foreign Policy Making

The contributors to this volume employ a variety of methods to use this framework. Some chapters explicitly test hypotheses, such as Allee and Huth's chapter. Others, such as Hammond and Prins's or Rosendorff's, engage more explicitly in theory building. Pahre's, and Hug and König's chapters use a more interactive strategy combining comparative case studies with theory building and testing. The chapters also vary in terms of the methodological debates of the discipline around formal theory, quantitative methods, and qualitative research.

We can characterize these differences in terms of two aspects of science, discovery and justification (see Pahre 2005). Justification, which consists of the problems of testing and attempting to falsify hypotheses, has dominated methodological debates since the publication of King et al.'s *Designing Social Inquiry* (1994). Discussion has focused on the relative strengths of quantitative methods for testing hypotheses, that is, "justifying" a scientist's claims to the rest of the community. This is normally treated as a purely methodological problem but, rightly conceived, also includes questions of rhetoric (McCloskey 1985).

This literature has set aside the question of how scientists think up hypotheses in the first place, that is, the problem of discovery (or heuristics). Discussions of qualitative methods, especially the comparative case study method, have given this heuristic question much more attention (Collier 1993; Eckstein 1975; Ragin and Becker 1992). Heuristics also play an important role in the analysis of formal theory, which usually rests on a Lakatosian epistemology (see especially Diermeier 1996; Green and Shapiro 1994, 1996).

Though the contributors to this volume have taken pragmatic approaches to each of their chapters, the project as a whole rests on a Lakatosian epistemology. This means that each chapter takes as given a coherent body of theory and then proposes and explores a different set of additional assumptions (for a similar argument about applied formal theory, see Pahre and Papayoanou 1997). In chapter 2, Hammond and Prins elaborate this common foundation, systematizing and regularizing the foundations of the spatial theory of two-level games.

From these shared elements, the chapters build in different directions, often distinguished by methods. Like Hammond and Prins's, Rosendorff's chapter relies on formal theories on foreign policy. However, he extends the theory in a different direction, connecting spatial theory to economic theory in order to provide economic and political foundations for a theory of democratic foreign economic policy. Unlike the other chapters, his also brings elections explicitly into the analysis, instead of discussing elections solely as a background condition yielding the executive and legislative office-holders that we analyze. Rosendorff also supplements his formal analysis with some empirical illustrations that establish the plausibility of the model.

Pahre's and König and Hug's chapters draw from these traditions but their motives are more empirical than theoretical. Each seeks to explain a particular cluster of empirical problems (nineteenth century trade treaties and bargaining outcomes in the Amsterdam IGC, respectively) in light of theory. Each finds both successes and limitations in existing theory, which induces them to extend received theory in the direction of new hypotheses. In this way they combine the heuristic strengths of case study research with the underlying logical strengths of formal theory.

Allee and Huth take a different approach, focusing on hypothesis-testing (justification) drawn from the theory, an approach recommended by many (Morton 1999). Rather than examining conditional claims as an on/off switch (as implied by Hammond and Prins) they assume a probabilistic world in which there exists random factors that can confound any attempt at theory testing. In this setting, some claims that are discretely conditional in theory may take smoother functional forms. To capture this, they propose a novel operationalization of the concept of the degree of divided government, a continuous one.

As a contrasting example, a conditional operationalization of divided government is most strongly evident in König and Hug's chapter. By looking at the preferences of specific actors within concrete institutional settings, they can specify when a ratifier may want to block a treaty and when it will not. This connects very nicely to Hammond and Prins's emphasis in chapter 2 on conditional claims. Pahre's chapter 4 also demonstrates the conditional nature of theoretical claims about divided government but finds more difficulty in precisely stating those conditions.

Several methodological lessons follow. First, the volume shows the advantage of a nondogmatic, more pragmatic approach to methodology. Simply put, different problems require different methods, and neither the "statistical worldview" (McKeown 1999) nor dogmatic formalism (as found in Morton 1999) can solve all scientific problems. The contributors use all three legs of the methodological stool in contemporary political science, formal theory, quantitative methods, and case studies. Though the volume as a whole is grounded in the formalized spatial theory of two-level games, chapters 4–6 all draw from original data sets to evaluate their claims, and various kinds of qualitative evidence play an important role in chapters 3–5.

Second, and perhaps more unusual, the contributors accept the theoretical and methodological consequences of working with indeterminacy. Hammond and Prins provide the strongest example in their claim that "anything can happen" when one examines the effects of divided government on foreign policy. However, under well-defined conditions divided government has well-defined effects, as chapters 4–5 show. As a result, the apparent indeterminacy at the most general level is consistent with much more specific results under well-specified conditions. This finding is central to the volume's emphasis that divided government has more complicated effects that the previous literature has suspected.

This indeterminacy presents some empirical challenges. One key concept in Hammond and Prins's chapter, which is also found in some other chapters, is the "win-set," the set of points that governments would rationally negotiate when they anticipate the challenges of domestic politics. Most of the chapters analyze these win-sets as sets of possible outcomes and do not try to whittle down their predictions to a single unique point. These win-sets therefore include many outcomes that did not happen, that is, many counterfactual outcomes. Such counterfactuals cannot be tested directly in a quantitative study, which takes as observations only the reality that we observe.

However, some counterfactuals can be analyzed in a qualitative study. For example, in an intergovernmental negotiation, a scholar might reasonably claim that the UK would have accepted certain outcomes that did not in fact occur. Some of these would have been better for the UK, in which case it is axiomatic that the UK would have accepted them. Some of these counterfactual outcomes would have made the UK worse off, but internal documents and interviews might reveal that they would have been acceptable nonetheless. Qualitative evidence in chapters 4 and 5 provides illustrations of this kind of reasoning from counterfactuals, which is one way to deal with the indeterminacy of win-sets.

The third methodological point that emerges from this volume is the variety of ways that they combine theoretical work with empirical studies. One challenge in this work is trying to match the functional form of a formal model with the equations used to estimate regression models (see Pahre 2005). In some cases, these are identical. For example, Rosendorff's chapter derives linear, probabilistic hypotheses. Though their hypotheses differ slightly, this is exactly the functional form tested by Allee and Huth in chapter 6.

Other chapters emphasize nonprobabilistic, conditional hypotheses. For example, Hammond and Prins demonstrate quite generally, and are echoed by Pahre in a more narrow theory, that many results of spatial theory take strongly conditional (if-then) forms. In one case, divided government has a particular effect, while it may have the opposite (or no) effect across a particular threshold. One empirical analysis informed by conditional theoretical claims is discussed in Hug and König's chapter.

Perhaps paradoxically, then, the volume shows the advantages of methodological breadth along with a focus on theoretical narrowness when deriving and testing hypotheses. Particularly when taking advantage of the analytical rigor of formal theory, as do many of the chapters, it pays to be specific about the claims being made.

Overview of the Contributions

Using these methods, the contributors to this volume use the general framework of the book—divided polity, divided government, and agenda-setting—to understand the effects of domestic politics on international cooperation. Chapters 2 and 3 provide overviews of the central analytic and substantive topics of two-level theory: the spatial theory of politics and the effects of democratic government on foreign policy.

In chapter 2, Thomas Hammond and Brandon Prins develop a model of divided government and international cooperation. Their unidimensional spatial model captures the various possible patterns of divergent interest between the executive, legislature, and foreign negotiator. While the claims of the literature do hold under some conditions, they hold in only a minority of the entire universe of possible preferential orderings. They also argue that theory must explicitly account for the reversion point (or status quo), the policy outcome that occurs in the absence of cooperation. These findings call into question both of the conventional claims about divided government, the veto player effect, and the Schelling Conjecture.

The theory of divided government is not necessarily limited to the study of democratic regimes. Nonetheless, the major focus of the theory remains modern democracies, for whom the effects of democratic governance on foreign policy is central. In chapter 3, Peter Rosendorff examines an important part of this problem, the effects of democracy on trade policy. As in Hammond and Prins's analysis, the reversion point plays an important role in the analysis. Unlike Hammond and Prins, Rosendorff considers two policy dimensions, one for the policy of each state. Rosendorff argues first that democracies have a greater tendency to unilateral liberalization. Democracy also affects the ability of governments to improve on this reversion point. Rosendorff argues that democracies are more likely to cooperate in the form of preferential trading arrangements. Finally, democracies are more willing to offer concessions when negotiating with another democracy. As a result, Rosendorff shows us how two-level theory analyzes the differences between democratic and autocratic foreign policy making.

Chapters 4 and 5 present empirical studies of the relationship between divided government and international cooperation. Both the chapters move beyond the Hammond–Prins framework in explicitly considering two policy dimensions. Pahre follows Rosendorff in assuming two dimensions, while Hug and König allow for more than two dimensions in practice.

In chapter 4, Pahre examines both the problem of ratification and the reversion point. He shows that ratification has rarely been a problem for most polities, a fact that suggests that the two-level literature has emphasized ratification problems too strongly.[7] Ratification obstacles constrained a few countries but do not explain intertemporal variation. To remedy this, he focuses on agenda-setting and reversion points. He argues that under conditions of divided government, it matters whether the executive or the legislature controlled the agenda establishing the reversion point. When the executive controls the reversion point, for example, divided government can make cooperation more likely by threatening an outcome that the legislature will not accept. Substantively, he moves beyond the traditional focus on contemporary democracies to consider nineteenth-century democracies, semidemocracies, and autocracies in Europe and the Western hemisphere.

In chapter 5, Simon Hug and Thomas König explore the democratic polities of the European Union in detail. They give particular attention to the ratification problem, showing why the degree of divided government— and not merely the existence of a divided policy—presents the central problem for ratification. Though most countries had a divided polity, only a few exhibited a significant degree of divided government. In short, variation in institutions alone cannot explain variation in cooperation. Closer attention to preferences is essential. When theory is properly operationalized in this way, they argue, divided government does yield bargaining advantages consistent with the Schelling Conjecture. They illustrate how two-level theory can provide a systematic analysis of a large number of countries even while recognizing the unique features of each case.

While the other chapters emphasize relatively cooperative realms, Todd Allee and Paul Huth examine the more conflictual sphere of territorial disputes in chapter 6. Divided government affects the absence of cooperation, and the likelihood of escalation. They find that divided government does not influence the decision to initiate a territorial dispute, but does make states considerably less likely to make concessions to end territorial disputes cooperatively. By focusing on foreign willingness to *make* concessions, instead of home government willingness to *resist* concessions, they also find strong evidence contradicting the Schelling Conjecture. State leaders are considerably less likely to make concessions to an adversary whose government is divided. Instead, leaders prefer to make concessions when their opponent is in a stronger position domestically and is therefore better able to reciprocate concessions. One implication of their study is that we can use two-level theory to examine reversion points, or noncooperative outcomes, systematically, thereby extending the theory into the study of conflict.

All five chapters share a common theoretical framework: they assume rationality, treat collective institutional actors (parties, legislatures, executives) provisionally as unitary actors, use a spatial model of policy, and examine rule-governed behavior domestically combined with international negotiations under anarchy. All use the common framework of divided polity, divided government, and agenda-setting. Yet the chapters also differ within this framework, ranging from pure theory to a mostly empirical exercise. Some are interested in the foundations of preferences (Rosendorff and, to a lesser extent, Pahre), while others assume that preferences are exogenous (Hammond and Prins, Hug and König, Allee and Huth). Most focus on cooperation, though Pahre and Rosendorff each consider both single-play (noncooperative) and the repeated-play (cooperative) outcomes in their analysis. In this way, the contributors collectively show how this common framework can be extended into a variety of concrete foreign policy problems.

Conclusion

Divided government is a central feature of most democracies, and of many other systems. If politics is the process by which people make collective choices when they disagree (Riker and Ordeshook 1973)—or more pithily, who gets what, when, how (Lasswell 1902)—then we should expect differences in preferences to be a key part of any theory purporting to explain how domestic politics affects foreign policy.

Analysis of the Schelling Conjecture provides a good example of these concerns. Under some conditions, preferences and institutions combine to give a country considerable bargaining leverage over its interlocutors.

We should also expect variation in institutional structures to play an important role in any theory of democratic foreign policy making. Not all democracies are alike, and they should not be treated as a homogenous type to be differentiated solely from nondemocratic (or "autocratic") states. Instead, looking at the nature of agenda-setting in any polity helps us better characterize democratic polities in this volume and in future research.

The analyses found in this volume have important implications for democratic theory. One conventional indictment of democracy is that it makes the conduct of foreign policy more difficult. For example, Henry Morgenthau (1973: 530–531) argues that

> If nations who are sovereign, who are supreme within their territories with no superior above them, want to preserve peace and order in their territories, they must try to persuade, negotiate, and exert pressure upon each other.

The new parliamentary diplomacy is no substitute for these procedures. On the contrary, it tends to aggravate rather than mitigate international conflicts and leaves the prospect for peace dimmed rather than brightened. Three essential qualities of the new diplomacy are responsible for these unfortunate results: its publicity, its majority votes, and its fragmentation of international issues.

From this perspective, domestic divisions make these problems more severe, and make a stronger executive attractive. If this diagnosis is wrong, then so is the prescription. Divided government at home, under some conditions, makes it easier for nations to cooperate. If this is true, then the arguments of many chief executives that they should be given greater powers in foreign policy—especially in time of war—become less compelling. After the contributors have examined these questions theoretically and empirically in the coming chapters, I turn to this final, normative question in the conclusion.

Chapter 2

Domestic Veto Institutions, Divided Government, and the Status Quo: A Spatial Model of Two-Level Games with Complete Information

Thomas H. Hammond and Brandon C. Prins

The role of domestic institutions and politics has long been of interest to students of international politics and foreign policy formulation (Corwin 1917). Of course, some theories of international politics—especially the various strands of Realism (Layne 1993, 1994; Mearsheimer 2001; Morgenthau 1949; Waltz 1979)—assert that domestic politics has no impact at all on the politics among nations; instead, what matters almost exclusively are national power, especially the nation's economic and military capabilities. Other schools of thought, however, do allow some room for domestic politics to play a role. For example, arguments have long been made (see Lippman 1922, 1925), and empirical studies appear to demonstrate (Baum 2002; Graham 1989; Holsti 1996; Mueller 1973; Nincic 1992a; Page and Barabas 2000) that public opinion influences foreign policy decisions. More recently, some scholars have suggested that domestic economic conditions can affect a nation's propensity to use military force abroad (Davies 2002; James and Oneal 1991; Morgan and Bickers 1992; Ostrom and Job 1986; Russett 1990a) as well as its propensity to engage in cooperative international ventures (Lindsay, Sayrs, and Steger 1992). Some studies have even inverted this "diversionary" theory of conflict, suggesting that domestic political vulnerability may increase the probability of becoming a target of aggression (Chiozza and Goemans 2004; Gelpi 1997;

Huth and Allee 2003; Leeds and Davis 1997). Evidence also suggests that domestic institutional constraints may influence the likelihood of conflict between states (see Bueno de Mesquita et al. 2003; Dixon and Senese 2002; Morgan and Campbell 1991; Pickering and Kisangani 2005; Prins and Sprecher 1999; Schultz 1998; Schultz 2001).

While the relative importance of international versus domestic factors has been a matter of dispute with regard to questions of war and peace, there is more agreement that domestic factors often have a major impact on bargaining over international trade (Hansen 1990; Henning 1994; O'Halloran 1993; Patterson 1997; Rogowski 1989; Simmons 1994), over the role of international organizations (Botcheva and Martin 2001; Goldstein 1996; Oye 1986), and over the allocation of foreign aid (Apodaca and Stohl 1999; Bacchus 1997; Blanton 2000; Carroll 1966; Meernik, Krueger, and Poe 1998; Montgomery 1962; Ruttan 1996). Problems of international trade, for example, often evoke domestic conflicts due to distributional inequities stemming from national trade policies; as the former chair of the House Ways and Mean Committee, Dan Rostenkowski (D-Ill.), once put it, "Trade is becoming very, very parochial. It's employment, it's our jobs" (quoted in Snow and Brown 1997).

As for international organizations, antipathy for the United Nations has long been evident in some congressional circles. For example, not only did Senator Jesse Helms (R-NC), as chair of the Senate Foreign Relations Committee (1995–2001), argue that the United Nations should be dismantled but he also found little value in international financial institutions as well. Furthermore, public opposition to American troops serving under a UN command, even for peacekeeping missions, remains strong (even though NATO remains quite popular with the American public).

Foreign aid has always been heavily influenced by domestic interest groups even though it was originally conceived as an arm of America's containment strategy for the cold war. For example, the agriculture and shipping industries were traditionally among the stronger supporters of international aid because the federal government bought domestically produced agricultural commodities and shipped them overseas on American freighters. And on particular regional issues the Israeli and Greek lobbies were important in sustaining funding levels and other supportive policies.

In addition to these broad issue arenas in which domestic interests and constraints have appeared to affect foreign policy decision making, there are several historic cases in which the Senate, due to its constitutional authority over the ratification of treaties, has played a major role in the making of foreign policy. The Senate's rejection of the League of Nations Treaty following World War I is perhaps the best-known example. More recent examples include the Carter administration's withdrawal of the draft SALT II treaty from Senate consideration after the Soviet Union invaded Afghanistan, and the Clinton administration's acceptance of a State Department reorganization plan drafted by Senator Helms that he demanded as the price for his acquiescence to the Chemical Weapons Convention.

For at least some important classes of foreign policy decisions, then, it is generally agreed that domestic politics can play a significant role. It is also agreed that there are important cases in which the U.S. Senate has had a substantial impact on the outcome of presidential negotiations with other countries.

Yet until recently, this understanding of the impact of domestic veto institutions and divided government has remained at a rather general level. Indicative of the unresolved status of thought here is the fact that two contradictory hypotheses have been advanced regarding the impact that domestic veto institutions can have on national leaders' negotiations with other countries. Indeed, these two hypotheses coexisted in the literature for over three decades without even much recognition of their incompatibility.

The more traditional hypothesis—we dub it the "unified government" hypothesis—is that domestic veto institutions weaken the President's ability to negotiate effectively with foreign powers. This assertion about the virtues of unified government, and about the negative impact of divided government, has been advanced not only by presidents, as one might expect, but also by journalists and other commentators on public affairs in the United States (Lippman 1922, 1925), by students and practitioners of the diplomatic arts (Kennan 1984), and by a variety of other analysts (see e.g., Blechman 1990; Cheney 1990; Crovitz 1990; Destler, Gelb, and Lake 1984; Martin 1998; Rostow 1989). Some critics assailed what they saw as the congressional micromanagement of foreign affairs in the aftermath of the Vietnam War. A former director of the Arms Control and Disarmament Agency, Eugene Rostow, even insisted that the President had become merely a "figurehead graciously presiding over the activities of an omnipotent Congress" (quoted in Lindsay 1994: 161). Blechman (1990: 108) likewise argued that

> From a national perspective, the struggle between the branches for power over arms control policy, particularly in its partisan implications, is extremely harmful. The country benefits when it can show a united face, especially to its potential adversaries.

Unified government is thus the ideal for these observers.

A contrary hypothesis—we call it the "divided government" hypothesis—was advanced by Thomas Schelling in his landmark study, *The Strategy of Conflict* (1960: 19), in which he argued, in effect, that divided government could actually *strengthen* the President's ability to negotiate effectively with foreign powers:

> The well-known principle that one should pick good negotiators to represent him and then give them complete flexibility and authority—a principle commonly voiced by negotiators themselves—is by no means as self-evident as its proponents suggest; the power of a negotiator often rests on a manifest inability to make concessions and meet demands.

Schelling (1960: 28) then observed that when the U.S. government negotiates with other governments,

> If the executive branch is free to negotiate the best arrangement it can, it may be unable to make any position stick and may end by conceding controversial points because its partners know, or believe obstinately, that the United States would rather concede than terminate the negotiations. But, if the executive branch negotiates under legislative authority, with its position constrained by law, and it is evident that Congress will not be reconvened to change the law within the necessary time period, then the executive branch has a firm position that is visible to its negotiating partners.

These two incompatible hypotheses about the costs and benefits of unified and divided government coexisted in the international relations literature for almost three decades without any significant effort having been made at a resolution. And of course, these two hypotheses also coexisted uneasily with the Realists' argument that domestic institutions—whether exhibiting unified government or divided government—were irrelevant to the most consequential decisions involving international relations.

Fifteen years ago, however, in an essay titled "Diplomacy and Domestic Politics: The Logic of Two-Level Games" (1988), Robert Putnam drew the attention of students of foreign policy making and diplomacy back to the study of the impact of domestic politics on international negotiations. His essay reviewed some of the literature on domestic politics and foreign policy, and then sketched out in simple diagrammatic terms some ways of thinking about how domestic politics might affect international negotiations. He also attempted to delineate how several different domestic factors—such as the nature of the domestic veto institutions, and the preferences of, and coalitions among, the domestic actors—might affect a President's ability to negotiate effectively with a foreign power.

Putnam recognized that his essay did not present a definitive model of two-level games but should primarily be seen as an effort to stimulate further study; as he put it (1988: 435),

> Formal analysis of any game requires well-defined rules, choices, payoffs, players, and information, and even then, many simple two-person, mixed-motive

games have no determinate solution. Deriving analytical solutions for two-level games will be a difficult challenge.

Putnam's essay stimulated considerable work on these two-level games (see e.g., Drezner 2003; Evans, Putnam, and Jacobson 1993; Milner 1997; Mitchell 2002; Trumbore 1998). And despite Putnam's pessimism here, his challenge did stimulate a substantial response by scholars skilled in the development of formal models; see Downs and Rocke (1995), Duchesne (1997), Iida (1993), Mayer (1992), Milner and Rosendorff (1996, 1997), Mo (1994, 1995), Trumbore and Boyer (2000), Tarar (2001a), and the contributors to a 1997 symposium on two-level games in the *Journal of Conflict Resolution*.

Almost all of these formal models (Pahre 1997, 2004a comprise the major exceptions) share a quartet of key assumptions. The first assumption is that the actors involved in policymaking have *divergent goals and interests*; that is, divided government is always assumed. The second assumption is that these actors are *uncertain* about each other's goals, bargaining strategies, aspiration levels, electoral viability, or other such variables. Putnam emphasized the importance of both sets of factors, and both are undoubtedly important in many particular cases. Unfortunately, however, since results from these models are normally influenced by both sets of factors, it often remains unclear to what degree each class of variables is responsible for the character of the results. That is, does some particular result reflect more the actors' divergent goals and interests—that is, divided government—or the uncertainty each actor has about the other actor or actors?

Some studies did treat uncertainty as a variable, and actually generated results for when there is no uncertainty. But the interpretability of these complete-information results was often undermined by the third and fourth assumptions. The third assumption involves the adoption of bargaining theories that make point predictions. The two most common bargaining theories adopted are the Stahl-Rubinstein noncooperative bargaining model (Rubinstein 1982; Stahl 1972), which has been used as a framework for several models of two-level games (see e.g., Duchesne 1997; Iida 1993; Mo 1994), and the Nash bargaining solution (Nash 1950), which has been used by other models (see e.g., Milner and Rosendorff 1996). One difficulty with these bargaining models is that they have not withstood empirical test especially well; as Alvin Roth (a leading experimental economist and expert on bargaining theories) has observed about the current generation of bargaining models, "Although some of their qualitative predictions have received some support, the existing models have performed poorly as point predictors" (Roth 2002). Another difficulty is that by focusing on point predictions, these models draw our attention away from the nature of the *constraints* that the preferences of the negotiators and the domestic veto institutions impose on the range of possible outcomes that could be reached, no matter what particular bargaining model is assumed. As we will see in this chapter the extent of the constraints, and their impact on the fortunes of the negotiators, can vary quite dramatically, but these findings are concealed by the bargaining theories that have been adopted.

The fourth assumption, which has generally been made implicitly rather than explicitly in previous studies, is that *the current status quo policy* or the *current state of affairs*, or else some kind of *reversion point*, is irrelevant to policymaking. The most common approach, it appears, is to simply assume away any impact that the status quo policy, the current state of affairs, or reversion point may have. For example, the diagrammatic model of two-level games in Putnam's original work completely ignores any role for the status quo, while the Stahl-Rubinstein bargaining model assumes that any agreement is always better than no agreement at all; therefore, the location of the status quo does not affect the actors' negotiations. However, Putnam's original model does not make any sense without the incorporation of a status quo point or reversion point, and this chapter shows that if the status quo point or reversion point is assumed not to be irrelevant, the result is that its particular location (i.e., its relative value to each actor) can have a tremendous impact on what agreement—if any—negotiators are able to reach.

In our view, then, a model of two-level games is needed in which international negotiators and their domestic veto institutions may have divergent preferences (i.e., there may be either divided government or unified government), in which there is a status quo policy or some current state of affairs, some reversion point, that holds if international agreement is not reached, in which each actor has complete information about each other's policy preferences and about the relative value each places on the status quo, and which assumes nothing about what particular policy the international negotiators select from among the politically feasible set of policies. We think that this kind of model should have been among the first developed after publication of Putnam's 1988 article. The purpose of our chapter is to present such a model.

Our chapter is constructed as follows. In the first section, we describe the basic assumptions for our model and then present some simple results about when the status quo policy will be in equilibrium. After this, we systematically analyze what happens when bargaining between the two nations' chief executives takes place in a single issue dimension. First, we show what happens when there are no veto institutions; we also suggest that there is an alternative interpretation of this version of our model, in which each country has a unified government (in the sense that each country's veto institution has preferences identical to those of its chief executive). Second, we show what happens when the first country has a veto institution (alternatively, it has a divided government) but the second has no veto institution (alternatively, it still has a unified government). Third, we show what happens when each country has a veto institution (alternatively, each country has a divided government).

In the section after that, we analyze what happens when bargaining between the two chief executives takes place in two issue dimensions. Finally, we integrate the one-dimensional results into a series of diagrams that summarize the overall relationships between the ideal points of the chief executives and the veto institutions, given all possible locations for the initial status quo policy. We then use these diagrams to construct our penultimate set of diagrams that show the conditions under which each chief executive is helped or hurt by unified and divided government.

Our results demonstrate that current understanding of the impact of domestic veto institutions on international negotiations is quite inadequate. In particular, our results do not provide substantial support either for the unified-government hypothesis or for Schelling's divided-government hypothesis or, for that matter, for the Realists' assertion that domestic institutions are irrelevant. Instead, each of these hypotheses turns out to be correct under some conditions but incorrect under many other conditions. In general, the impact of unified or divided government depends far more on the location of the status quo than anyone contributing to the current literature appears to have foreseen.

Basic Assumptions and Initial Results on When the Status Quo Policy Is in Equilibrium

Within the United States, many different institutions and actors can be expected to affect negotiations with other countries. Foremost among them are the President and the Senate, but the House of Representatives, the federal courts, various executive branch agencies, numerous interest groups, and the mass public might be expected to play a role as well. For this chapter we focus just on the negotiation of international treaties, and for treaties the controlling provision of the Constitution is Article II, Section 2, which specifies that the President "shall have power, by and with the advice and consent of the Senate, to make treaties, provided two-thirds of the Senators present concur." Thus, for our model we focus on just the first two domestic institutions: the President and the Senate.

Following constitutional provisions and long-standing practice, we assume that it is the President who conducts the negotiations with the

Leader of some other country. When these negotiations are concluded, the President then submits a draft treaty to the Senate for ratification. For our model, we thus treat the President as an agenda-setter for the Senate: the Senate cannot amend draft treaties submitted to it, and so is put in a take-it-or-leave-it position by the President.[1]

Our focus on just the President and Senate does not necessarily mean that we are ignoring the views of the other domestic political actors. The reason is that the views of these other actors can often be expected to affect the preferences and choices of the President and members of the Senate, and thereby affect, albeit indirectly, the outcomes of treaty negotiations and any draft treaty's prospects for ratification. Nonetheless, we are not in any sense explicitly modeling how the President and Senators respond to the views of these other actors.

We will assume that there is just one other nation with which the President conducts treaty negotiations, and we assume that, like the United States, this other nation has a single chief executive—we will simply call her its "Leader"—who has sole authority to negotiate treaties on behalf of her nation. That is, she is the agenda-setter for her domestic veto institution just as the President is for the U.S. Senate.

We will construct a trio of models. We initially assume that neither the President nor this Leader has any domestic veto institution. This allows us to characterize the nature of international bargaining that is unconstrained by any domestic considerations.

Our second model assumes that the President must seek the Senate's approval for a draft treaty but the Leader has no such veto institution: if the Leader reaches agreement on a draft treaty with the President, the draft treaty can go into effect if the Senate ratifies it, while if the Senate refuses to ratify the draft treaty, the draft treaty does not go into effect and the status quo remains in force.

Our third model assumes that the Leader also has a veto institution with authority to ratify or reject any draft treaty that she negotiates with the President. In this case, if the Leader approves a draft treaty that she has negotiated with the President, the draft treaty can go into effect only if her nation's veto institution ratifies it and if the Senate ratifies it as well; if either veto institution refuses to ratify the draft treaty, it cannot go into effect, and so the status quo would remain in force.

However, instead of distinguishing these three models on the basis of the *presence* or *absence* of domestic veto institutions, there is an alternative interpretation: that each chief executive always has a domestic veto institution and that in some cases the veto institution has preferences that are identical to those of its chief executive whereas in other cases the veto institution has preferences that diverge from those of the chief executive. From this perspective, the President in the first model has a Senate whose preferences are identical to his, and the Leader also has a domestic veto institution whose preferences are identical to hers; that is, each chief executive has a unified government. In the second model, the President has a divided government in that the Senate has preferences that are different from his, but the Leader still has a unified government. In the third model, both the President and Leader face divided governments: the President has a Senate with preferences that are different from his, and the Leader has a veto institution with preferences that are different from hers.

In the next section of this chapter, we assume that policymaking between the two nations takes place in a one-dimensional issue space. It can be plausibly argued, however, that a model requires at least a two-dimensional issue space to adequately represent international negotiations, and in the section after that we develop (albeit much more briefly) a version of our model in a two-dimensional issue space. As it turns out, our two-dimensional model seems to have implications rather similar to those of our one-dimensional model, hence we put our primary emphasis on developing the one-dimensional model.

To simplify our analysis (without excessive loss of generality) we assume that the Senate contains just one individual; hence, if this individual Senator votes in favor of a draft treaty, the constitutional two-thirds vote required for ratification by the Senate is (trivially) satisfied. We make a similar assumption about the Leader's veto institution: it will consist of just one individual, which means that whatever voting margin is required for treaty ratification, this requirement is also (trivially) satisfied.[2]

Each individual actor—the President, the Senator, the Leader, and the member of the Leader's domestic veto institution (if one exists)—is assumed to have a most-preferred policy in the issue space; this individual's most-preferred point is his or her ideal point. We will use P to indicate the President's ideal point, S to indicate the Senator's ideal point, L to indicate the Leader's ideal point, and V to indicate the ideal point of member of the Leader's domestic veto institution. These labels—P, S, L, and V—will also serve as labels for the institution of which the individual actor is a member.

Each individual's goal is to get a policy adopted that is as close as possible to his or her own ideal point. The farther away some policy is in any direction from an individual actor's ideal point, the less the actor likes the policy; a farther-away policy gives the actor less utility than a closer-in policy. We make no assumption about whether the decrease in an actor's utility is symmetric or asymmetric around his or her ideal point. However, to simplify the drawing of our illustrations, our diagrams all assume that the decrease in an individual actor's utility is symmetric around his or her ideal point. When there is just one dimension, this means that a policy that is some distance to the left of the actor's ideal point yields the same utility as a policy that is the same distance to the right of the actor's ideal point. When there are two dimensions, the symmetric-loss assumption means that each individual actor cares equally about the two issue dimensions. Thus, given some status quo policy, **SQ**, in a two-dimensional policy space, the set of policies that yield a utility equal to **SQ** for the actor is indicated by a circle through **SQ** and centered on the actor's ideal point; this circle is the actor's indifference curve through **SQ**. Of course, each individual actor has a large family of nested indifference curves around his or her ideal point, each particular indifference curve representing policies of equal utility to the individual.[3]

For any **SQ**, the set of policies that defeat it with the support of two or more of these institutional actors is the win-set of **SQ**, or $\mathbf{W}_{\ldots}(\mathbf{SQ})$. Thus, the set of policies that the President and Senate both prefer to **SQ** is $\mathbf{W}_{PS}(\mathbf{SQ})$; the set of policies that the President, Senate, and Leader all prefer to **SQ** is $\mathbf{W}_{PS/L}(\mathbf{SQ})$; and the set of policies that the President, Senate, Leader, and foreign veto institution, V, all prefer to **SQ** is $\mathbf{W}_{PS/LV}(\mathbf{SQ})$.

For any **SQ**, the set of policies that the President prefers to **SQ** is the President's preferred-to set of **SQ**; for consistency in notation, we abbreviate it as $\mathbf{W}_P(\mathbf{SQ})$—it is a "one person win-set." Similarly, the set of policies that the Senate prefers to **SQ** is the Senate's preferred-to set of **SQ**, or $\mathbf{W}_S(\mathbf{SQ})$; the set of policies that the other nation's Leader prefers to **SQ** is $\mathbf{W}_L(\mathbf{SQ})$; and the set of policies that the foreign veto institution prefers to **SQ** is $\mathbf{W}_V(\mathbf{SQ})$. Thus, the set of policies that the President and Senate both prefer to **SQ**—$\mathbf{W}_{PS}(\mathbf{SQ})$—is equivalent to $\mathbf{W}_P(\mathbf{SQ}) \cap \mathbf{W}_S(\mathbf{SQ})$. The set of policies that the President, Senate, and Leader all prefer to **SQ**—$\mathbf{W}_{PS/L}(\mathbf{SQ})$—is equivalent to $\mathbf{W}_P(\mathbf{SQ}) \cap \mathbf{W}_S(\mathbf{SQ}) \cap \mathbf{W}_L(\mathbf{SQ})$. And the set of policies that the President, Senate, Leader, and her veto institution, V, all prefer to **SQ**—$\mathbf{W}_{PS/LV}(\mathbf{SQ})$—is equivalent to $\mathbf{W}_P(\mathbf{SQ}) \cap \mathbf{W}_S(\mathbf{SQ}) \cap \mathbf{W}_L(\mathbf{SQ}) \cap \mathbf{W}_V(\mathbf{SQ})$.

A *core* is the set of options that cannot be upset by joint action of two or more of these institutions, given the preferences of the actors in these institutions. Thus, we can speak of a *Domestic Core*, which is the set of policies that cannot be upset by joint action of the President and Senate; we label it $\mathbf{CORE}_{PS}$ When the other nation has a veto institution, we can speak of a *Foreign Core*, or $\mathbf{CORE}_{LV}$; this is the set of policies that cannot be upset by joint action of the Leader and her veto institution, V.

We can also speak of an *International Core*, which is the set of policies that cannot be upset by joint action of institutions from both nations. When neither nation has a veto institution, the *International Core* is labeled $\mathbf{CORE}_{P/L}$; it is the set of policies that the President and Leader cannot jointly agree to replace by some other policy. When the United States alone has a domestic veto institution (the Senate), the *International Core* is indicated by $\textbf{CORE}_{PS/L}$; this is the set of policies that the President, Leader, and Senate cannot jointly agree to replace by some other policy. And when the other nation has a domestic veto institution as well, the *International Core* is indicated by $\textbf{CORE}_{PS/LV}$; this is the set of policies that cannot be upset by joint action of the President, Senate, the foreign Leader, and her veto institution.

It is useful to understand the relationships between any of these cores and the win-set of any status quo policy in the institutions generating the core. If $\textbf{SQ}$ lies in a core, this means (by definition) that there is no other option that can defeat $\textbf{SQ}$. Thus, if $\textbf{SQ}$ is in the core, $\textbf{W}_{...}(\textbf{SQ})$ must be empty; that is, $\textbf{W}_{...}(\textbf{SQ}) = \varnothing$. If $\textbf{SQ}$ is not in the core, then $\textbf{W}_{...}(\textbf{SQ})$ is nonempty: that is, $\textbf{W}_{...}(\textbf{SQ}) \neq \varnothing$. And if $\textbf{W}_{...}(\textbf{SQ})$ is empty, there exists a core and $\textbf{SQ}$ lies inside it.

Note that if $\textbf{SQ}$ is located at the ideal point of either the President, the Senate, the Leader, or her veto institution, then the actor at whose ideal point $\textbf{SQ}$ is located will not agree to any change in $\textbf{SQ}$: the reason is that any change in $\textbf{SQ}$ would leave that actor worse off. In effect, this means that when $\textbf{SQ}$ is identical to the President's or Senate's ideal point, $\textbf{SQ}$ is located in the *Domestic Core*, and that when $\textbf{SQ}$ is identical to the Leader's or V's ideal point, $\textbf{SQ}$ is located in the *Foreign Core*.

Given these definitions and discussion, we can summarize our key arguments in the following way. One set of equilibrium conditions occurs when $\textbf{SQ}$ lies in the *Domestic Core*:

Proposition 2.1 (Domestic Equilibria). $\textbf{SQ}$ is in equilibrium if $\textbf{SQ} \in \textbf{CORE}_{PS}$.
When this proposition holds, it means that $\textbf{W}_{PS}(\textbf{SQ}) = \varnothing$.

A second set of equilibrium conditions occurs when $\textbf{SQ}$ lies in the *Foreign Core*:

Proposition 2.2 (Foreign Equilibria). $\textbf{SQ}$ is in equilibrium if $\textbf{SQ} \in \textbf{CORE}_{LV}$.
When this proposition holds, it means that $\textbf{W}_{LV}(\textbf{SQ}) = \varnothing$.

A corollary of Propositions 2.1 and 2.2 immediately follows:

Proposition 2.3 (Individual Institutional Equilibria). $\textbf{SQ}$ is in equilibrium if:

(a) $P = \textbf{SQ}$, or
(b) $S = \textbf{SQ}$, or
(c) $L = \textbf{SQ}$, or
(d) $V = \textbf{SQ}$.

When this proposition holds, it means that either (a) $\textbf{W}_P(\textbf{SQ}) = \varnothing$, or (b) $\textbf{W}_S(\textbf{SQ}) = \varnothing$, or (c) $\textbf{W}_L(\textbf{SQ}) = \varnothing$, or (d) $\textbf{W}_V(\textbf{SQ}) = \varnothing$.

A fourth set of equilibrium conditions occurs when **SQ** lies in the *International Core*:

Proposition 2.4 (International Equilibria).   **SQ** is in equilibrium if:

(a) $\mathbf{SQ} \in \mathbf{CORE}_{P/L}$ (when there are no veto institutions);

(b) $\mathbf{SQ} \in \mathbf{CORE}_{PS/L}$ (when the United States has a veto institution);

(c) $\mathbf{SQ} \in \mathbf{CORE}_{PS/LV}$ (when both countries have veto institutions).

When this proposition holds, it means that (a) $\mathbf{W}_{P/L}(\mathbf{SQ}) = \varnothing$, or (b) $\mathbf{W}_{PS/L}(\mathbf{SQ}) = \varnothing$, or (c) $\mathbf{W}_{PS/LV}(\mathbf{SQ}) = \varnothing$.

Finally, note that the *Domestic Core*—$\mathbf{CORE}_{PS}$—is located within both the *International Cores*, $\mathbf{CORE}_{PS/L}$ and $\mathbf{CORE}_{PS/LV}$. The reason is that if the President and Senate cannot agree on a policy to upset **SQ**, then requiring in addition that any change in **SQ** be approved by the other nation's Leader as well (and perhaps by her veto institution too) does not somehow render it possible for the President and Senate to agree on some policy to upset **SQ**. That is, if **SQ** lies between P and L (on a one-dimensional line), then nothing can upset **SQ**, regardless of where the ideal points of the two nations' veto institutions are located. For the same reason, the *Foreign Core* of $\mathbf{CORE}_{LV}$ is located within the *International Core* of $\mathbf{CORE}_{PS/LV}$. And for similar reasons, the *International Core* of $\mathbf{CORE}_{P/L}$ is located in both the $\mathbf{CORE}_{PS/L}$ and $\mathbf{CORE}_{PS/LV}$ *International Cores*. Finally, we note that $\mathbf{CORE}_{P/L}$ combined with $\mathbf{CORE}_{PS}$ produces $\mathbf{CORE}_{PS/L}$, and that $\mathbf{CORE}_{P/L}$ combined with both $\mathbf{CORE}_{PS}$ and $\mathbf{CORE}_{LV}$ produces $\mathbf{CORE}_{PS/LV}$. We can summarize these relationships among cores as follows:

Proposition 2.5 (Core Relationships).   The following relationships among cores hold:

(a) $\mathbf{CORE}_{PS} \subset \mathbf{CORE}_{PS/L}$,

(b) $\mathbf{CORE}_{PS} \subset \mathbf{CORE}_{PS/LV}$,

(c) $\mathbf{CORE}_{LV} \subset \mathbf{CORE}_{PS/LV}$,

(d) $\mathbf{CORE}_{P/L} \subset \mathbf{CORE}_{PS/L}$,

(e) $\mathbf{CORE}_{P/L} \subset \mathbf{CORE}_{PS/LV}$,

(f) $\mathbf{CORE}_{PS} \cup \mathbf{CORE}_{P/L} = \mathbf{CORE}_{PS/L}$, and

(g) $\mathbf{CORE}_{PS} \cup \mathbf{CORE}_{LV} \cup \mathbf{CORE}_{P/L} = \mathbf{CORE}_{PS/LV}$.

Propositions 2.1–2.5 characterize the general nature of the relationships among *P, S, L, V*, and **SQ**.

Finally, we define the *Negotiation set*—the *N*-set, for short—as consisting of the point (or points) for which the President and Leader have no mutually preferable alternative, as constrained by the requirements of any domestic veto institutions. For each point outside the *N*-set, there exists a point (or points) inside the *N*-set that *both* the President and Leader find superior. However, if there is more than one point inside the *N*-set, they

will have conflicting interests over these points. For some conditions, the
N-set will be empty, which means that no agreement to upset **SQ** can be
reached.

The precise definition of the N-set will be tailored to the particular set of
institutions involved. We first define and characterize the N-set when there
are no veto institutions (i.e., just P and L). Then we define and characterize
the N-set when there is a Senate but no foreign veto institution (i.e., P, S,
and L). Finally, we define and characterize the N-set when there is both a
Senate and a foreign veto institution (i.e., P, S, L, and V).

We should emphasize that our purpose here is not to make specific predictions about what particular policy will be selected by the President and
Leader; only in a few situations will the N-set contain just one point.
Instead, we seek to clarify the nature of the *constraints* that domestic veto
institutions impose on the agreements that the chief executives might reach.
It is the *range of allowable agreements* in which we are interested, *not the particular agreement* that the chief executives might reach within this allowable
range. To make predictions about which particular agreement the chief
executives might reach (as constrained by any domestic veto institutions), a
further set of assumptions to characterize some kind of bargaining model
would be needed. But then the results would in part reflect the assumptions
of whichever bargaining model we happened to adopt, thereby rendering
less clear the impact of the domestic veto institutions and unified or divided
government.

International Negotiations
in One Issue Dimension

In this section we initially consider negotiations in just one issue dimension
between the President and Leader when there are no domestic veto institutions or at least no domestic veto institutions about which the President and
Leader must be concerned (e.g., there is unified government in both countries); so just one set of preference orderings for these two actors—P and
L—needs to be examined. Next we consider what happens to these negotiations in the presence of the Senate (the President has divided government
but the Leader has unified government); three sets of preference orderings
of these three actors—L, P, and S—need to be examined. We end the section by considering the negotiations in the presence of both the Senate and
the foreign veto institution (each chief executive has a divided government);
four sets of preference orderings for these four actors—L, P, S, and V—need
to be examined here.

Negotiations between the President and Leader (with No Veto Institutions)

When there are no domestic veto institutions (i.e., no S or V), or else each chief executive has a unified government, the President and Leader will bargain over the choice of points on the L-P segment of the issue dimension (that is, over points in $\mathbf{CORE}_{P/L}$); in other contexts, this L-P line— $\mathbf{CORE}_{P/L}$—is known as the *contract curve* for P and L. $\mathbf{CORE}_{P/L}$ has the property that, for every $\mathbf{SQ}$ not in $\mathbf{CORE}_{P/L}$, there exists at least one point in $\mathbf{CORE}_{P/L}$ that both the President and Leader prefer to $\mathbf{SQ}$. This means that, in the absence of constraints by any veto institutions (i.e., by S or V), the President and Leader have a mutual interest in selecting some point in $\mathbf{CORE}_{P/L}$ (though assuming $P \neq L$, they will disagree about what this point should be).

However, not all points in $\mathbf{CORE}_{P/L}$ will necessarily be available for consideration by the President and Leader. Instead, what points in $\mathbf{CORE}_{P/L}$ the President and Leader consider to be available for joint consideration will also be a function of $\mathbf{W}_P(\mathbf{SQ})$ and $\mathbf{W}_L(\mathbf{SQ})$. The reason is that neither chief executive will agree to a new policy that he or she considers to be worse than $\mathbf{SQ}$. For this particular context, then, we define the N-set as the set of points in $\mathbf{CORE}_{P/L}$ that (a) are better than $\mathbf{SQ}$ for both the President and Leader, and for which (b) the President and Leader can find no mutually preferred alternative. More technically, we define the N-set as follows:

Definition 2.1 (P and L).   The N-set is the set of points $\cup\mathbf{x}_i$ ($_i = 1, \ldots$, k) in $\mathbf{W}_{P/L}(\mathbf{SQ}) \cap \mathbf{CORE}_{P/L}$ such that $\mathbf{W}_{P/L}(\mathbf{x}_i) = \varnothing$.

With only the President and Leader, then, the N-set contains just those points in $\mathbf{CORE}_{P/L}$ that are better than $\mathbf{SQ}$ for both the President and Leader.

When the N-set here is not empty, it will always contain more than one point, and the President and Leader will have differing preferences over which of these points to select (assuming that $P \neq L$). In this case, the two chief executives will need to engage in some kind of bargaining if they are to achieve the mutual gains that the nonempty N-set makes possible. (As noted, though, we do not seek to model this bargaining process.)

While Definition 2.1 is the most general characterization of the N-set for just the President and Leader, in practice what policies in $\mathbf{CORE}_{P/L}$ are available for their consideration will be a function of either just $\mathbf{W}_P(\mathbf{SQ})$ or just $\mathbf{W}_L(\mathbf{SQ})$. The reason is that when $\mathbf{SQ}$ lies outside $\mathbf{CORE}_{P/L}$, one of these two actors will have an ideal point that is closer to $\mathbf{SQ}$ than the other actor (assuming $P \neq L$). The result is that the preferred-to set of the actor who is closer to **SQ** will constrain outcomes more than the other actor's preferred-to set. In fact, the preferred-to set of the actor whose ideal point is farther from **SQ** could be dropped from *Definition 2.1* without changing the resulting *N*-set in the slightest. But since which actor's ideal point is closer to **SQ** may vary from case to case, we cannot predict a priori which actor's preferred-to set should be included in the expressions characterizing the *N*-set. Hence, we have included both preferred-to sets in Definition 2.1, in the form of $\mathbf{W}_{P/L}(\mathbf{SQ})$, with the understanding that one of them—either $\mathbf{W}_P(\mathbf{SQ})$ or $\mathbf{W}_L(\mathbf{SQ})$—will turn out to be functionally irrelevant in any particular case.

When **SQ** lies in $\mathbf{CORE}_{P/L}$, this means that **SQ** cannot be upset. There are three general locations for such an **SQ**: **SQ** could be identical to the President's ideal point (see Proposition 2.3a), **SQ** could be identical to the Leader's ideal point (see Proposition 2.3c), or **SQ** could lie somewhere between *L* and *P* on the *L-P* line (see Proposition 2.4a). In each case, **SQ** will be in equilibrium. Thus, when $\mathbf{SQ} \in \mathbf{CORE}_{P/L}$, the N-set will be empty.

There are some locations for **SQ**—they are always "extreme" locations (i.e., far from the *P-L* line)—such that the *N*-set will necessarily consist of the entire $\mathbf{CORE}_{P/L}$. To determine how extreme **SQ** must be for the *N*-set to contain all of $\mathbf{CORE}_{P/L}$, consider the points in figure 2.1 that are closer to *P* than is *L*: this set of points is $\mathbf{W}_P(\mathbf{L})$, the set of points that *P* prefers to *L*. Now consider the points that are closer to L than is *P*: this set of points is $\mathbf{W}_L(\mathbf{P})$, the set of points that *L* prefers to *P*. It follows that the points that are *either* closer to P than is *L or* closer to *L* than is *P* (or equidistant between *P* and *L*) is the set-union of these two sets of points, or $\mathbf{W}_P(\mathbf{L}) \cup \mathbf{W}_L(\mathbf{P})$. If some **SQ** falls inside this set-union, it means that this **SQ** is either closer to *P* than to *L*, or closer to *L* than to *P*, or equidistant between them. In any case, the result is that $\mathbf{W}_P(\mathbf{SQ}) \cap \mathbf{W}_L(\mathbf{SQ})$ would not include all of $\mathbf{CORE}_{P/L}$. So if we want to identify the conditions under which all of $\mathbf{CORE}_{P/L}$ falls inside the *N*-set, the answer is that the following relationship must hold:

$$\mathbf{SQ} \notin \{\mathbf{W}_P(\mathbf{L}) \cup \mathbf{W}_L(\mathbf{P})\} \tag{2.1}$$

In other words, if **SQ** falls outside this region, then both $\mathbf{W}_P(\mathbf{SQ})$ and $\mathbf{W}_L(\mathbf{SQ})$ will contain all of $\mathbf{CORE}_{P/L}$, which means that bargaining by the President and Leader will be unconstrained, hence they could potentially select any point in $\mathbf{CORE}_{P/L}$.

We now explore in greater detail this baseline case in which the President and the Leader are bargaining with each other and do not have to worry about any veto institutions (either because there exist no veto institutions or because the veto institutions have ideal points at their respective chief

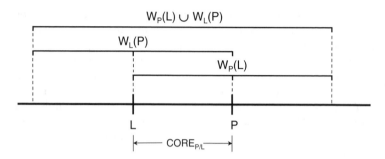

Figure 2.1 If SQ Lies Outside $W_P(L) \cup W_L(P)$, the N-set Includes All of $CORE_{P/L}$

executives' ideal points). Our general approach is to assume some left-right order for the ideal points of the two institutional actors, and then systematically vary the location of **SQ**, moving **SQ** from right to left, given this particular order. The two relevant ideal points, L and P, can occur in just two different orderings: L-P and P-L. Since the results for one ordering are a mirror image of the results for the other, we need consider only one ordering, which will be L-P.

Note that in the diagrams that accompany the one-dimensional analysis, the heavy solid line indicates either $CORE_{P/L}$, $CORE_{PS/L}$, or $CORE_{PS/LV}$ (depending on whether we have two, three, or four institutions), and the symbols "$+++$" indicate the range of points in the N-set. When the N-set contains just one point, which means that the President and the Leader will agree to select this point, this single mutually agreeable policy will be indicated by "$*$."

Case 1: The ideal points are in the order L-P

Within this general case, there are five different locations for SQ that are important to examine; see the diagrams in figure 2.2.

Case 1a (see figure 2.2a). Here **SQ** lies to the right of $W_P(L) \cup W_L(P)$ (i.e., the conditions in Equation 2.1 are met), which means that negotiations are not constrained to any particular segment of $CORE_{P/L}$; the entire $CORE_{P/L}$ is the N-set here. The President will thus argue for the choice of a policy at P, while the Leader will argue for the choice of a policy at L.

Case 1b (figure 2.2b). In this case **SQ** does not lie outside $W_P(L) \cup W_L(P)$, and so $W_P(SQ)$ does not include all of $CORE_{P/L}$. Since **SQ** is closer to P than to L, the N-set here is the set of points defined by $W_P(SQ) \cap CORE_{P/L}$. The President will argue for the choice of a policy at the right-hand boundary of the N-set (which is his own ideal point), while the Leader

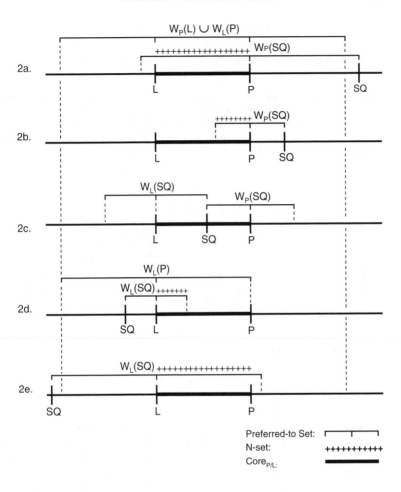

Figure 2.2 Case 1—For the L-P Ordering, there are Five Key Locations for SQ

will argue for the choice of a policy at the lefthand boundary of the *N*-set (which is the lefthand boundary of $\mathbf{W}_P(\mathbf{SQ})$ in $\mathbf{CORE}_{P/L}$).

Case 1c (figure 2.2c). Since **SQ** lies inside $\mathbf{CORE}_{P/L}$ here, **SQ** cannot be upset (see Proposition 2.4a). Hence, the *N*-set is empty: the President will want to move policy rightward from **SQ**, and the Leader will want to move policy leftward from **SQ**, so no mutual improvement is possible.

Case 1d (figure 2.2d). Since **SQ** lies to the left of *L* but falls inside $\mathbf{W}_L(\mathbf{P})$, $\mathbf{W}_L(\mathbf{SQ})$ will not include all of $\mathbf{CORE}_{P/L}$. The *N*-set here is thus the set of points defined by $\mathbf{W}_L(\mathbf{SQ}) \cap \mathbf{CORE}_{P/L}$. The Leader will argue for the choice of a policy at the lefthand boundary of the N-set (i.e., for a policy at her own ideal point of L), while the President will argue for the choice of a policy at the righthand boundary of the N-set (which is the righthand boundary of $\mathbf{W}_L(\mathbf{SQ})$ in $\mathbf{CORE}_{P/L}$).

Case 1e (figure 2.2e). Finally, $\mathbf{SQ}$ here lies to the left of $\mathbf{W}_P(\mathbf{L}) \cup \mathbf{W}_L(\mathbf{P})$ (i.e., the conditions in Equation 2.1 are met). Hence, the N-set includes all of $\mathbf{CORE}_{P/L}$. In this case, the Leader will argue for the choice of a policy at L, while the President will argue for the choice of a policy at P.

Negotiations between the President and Leader, with the Senate as a Veto Institution

We now consider what happens when the President faces a domestic veto institution, the Senate. Following the same logic as previously, we need to identify the N-set for the President and Leader, but the definition of the N-set must now take into account the constraints imposed by the Senate. The N-set here can be defined as follows:

Definition 2.2 (P, S, L). The N-set is the set of points $\cup \mathbf{x}_i$ ($i = 1, \ldots ,$k) in $\mathbf{W}_{PS/L}(\mathbf{SQ}) \cap \mathbf{CORE}_{PS/L}$ such that $\mathbf{W}_{P/L}(\mathbf{x}_i) = \varnothing$.

In effect, the N-set here is the set of points in $\mathbf{CORE}_{PS/L}$ that (a) are better than $\mathbf{SQ}$ for the President, Senate, and Leader, and for which (b) the President and Leader have no mutually preferred alternative.

When $\mathbf{SQ}$ lies in $\mathbf{CORE}_{PS/L}$, $\mathbf{SQ}$ cannot be upset. For example, $\mathbf{SQ}$ could lie somewhere in $\mathbf{CORE}_{P/L}$ (i.e., it could be equal to P, it could be equal to L, or it could lie between P and L); thus, $\mathbf{SQ}$ could not be upset because the President wants to move $\mathbf{SQ}$ in one direction while the Leader wants to move $\mathbf{SQ}$ in the opposite direction. Alternatively, $\mathbf{SQ}$ could lie somewhere in a $\mathbf{CORE}_{PS}$ that lies outside $\mathbf{CORE}_{P/L}$; thus, $\mathbf{SQ}$ could not be upset because the President wants to move $\mathbf{SQ}$ in one direction while the Senate wants to move $\mathbf{SQ}$ in the opposite direction.

As before, there are some locations for $\mathbf{SQ}$ such that the N-set will necessarily be the entire $\mathbf{CORE}_{P/L}$. For this to occur, $\mathbf{SQ}$ cannot be closer to P, L, or S than they are to each other. More systematically, this means that we must consider the following six preferred-to sets:

(1) $\mathbf{W}_P(\mathbf{L})$, the set of points that P prefers to L,
(2) $\mathbf{W}_P(\mathbf{S})$, the set of points that P prefers to S,
(3) $\mathbf{W}_L(\mathbf{P})$, the set of points that L prefers to P,

(4) $\mathbf{W}_L(\mathbf{S})$, the set of points that L prefers to S,
(5) $\mathbf{W}_S(\mathbf{P})$, the set of points that S prefers to P, and
(6) $\mathbf{W}_S(\mathbf{L})$, the set of points that S prefers to L.

It follows that the set of points that are closer to P than is L, *or* closer to P than is S, *or* closer to L than is P, *or* closer to L than is S, *or* closer to S than is P, *or* closer to S than is L is the set-union of these sets, or $\mathbf{W}_P(\mathbf{L}) \cup \mathbf{W}_P(\mathbf{S}) \cup \mathbf{W}_L(\mathbf{P}) \cup \mathbf{W}_L(\mathbf{S}) \cup \mathbf{W}_S(\mathbf{P}) \cup \mathbf{W}_S(\mathbf{L})$. If some **SQ** falls inside this set-union, it means that this **SQ** is either closer to P than to S or L, or closer to L than to S or P, or closer to P than to L or S. In any of these instances, the result is that $\mathbf{W}_P(\mathbf{SQ}) \cap \mathbf{W}_L(\mathbf{SQ}) \cap \mathbf{W}_S(\mathbf{SQ})$ would not include all of **CORE**$_{P/L}$. So for all of **CORE**$_{P/L}$ to be inside the N-set, the following relationship must hold:

$$\mathbf{SQ} \notin \{\mathbf{W}_P(\mathbf{L}) \cup \mathbf{W}_P(\mathbf{S}) \cup \mathbf{W}_L(\mathbf{P}) \cup \mathbf{W}_L(\mathbf{S}) \cup \mathbf{W}_S(\mathbf{P}) \cup \mathbf{W}_S(\mathbf{L})\} \quad (2.2)$$

In other words, if **SQ** is farther away from P, L, and S than P, L, and S are from each other, then $\mathbf{W}_P(\mathbf{SQ}) \cap \mathbf{W}_L(\mathbf{SQ}) \cap \mathbf{W}_S(\mathbf{SQ})$ will contain all of **CORE**$_{P/L}$, which means that bargaining between the President and Leader will be unconstrained and any point in **CORE**$_{P/L}$ could potentially be selected. Figure 2.3 provides an illustration. For this particular diagram, the complex expression in Equation 2.2 reduces to $\mathbf{W}_L(\mathbf{SQ}) \cup \mathbf{W}_S(\mathbf{SQ})$. This happens because L and S are the "outside" actors in this diagram, which means that the preferred-to sets of the "interior" actor—who is P, in this case—do not affect the result.

When the President, Leader, and Senate are all involved in treaty negotiations, six different orderings of the P, L, and S ideal points are possible: (1) L-P-S; (2) S-P-L; (3) L-S-P; (4) P-S-L; (5) S-L-P; and (6) P-L-S. However, the first pair—(1) and (2)—are mirror images of each other, so we need consider only the L-P-S ordering. The second pair—(3) and (4)—are also mirror images, so we need consider only the L-S-P ordering. And the third pair—(5) and (6)—are likewise mirror images, so we need consider only the S-L-P ordering. We now examine these three orderings.

Case 2: The ideal points are in the order L-P-S

Within this general case there are seven different locations for **SQ** that are useful to consider; see the diagrams in figure 2.4.

Case 2a (see figure 2.4a). In this case, **SQ** lies so far to the right of S that $\mathbf{W}_S(\mathbf{SQ})$ includes *all* of the L-P line (i.e., it includes all of **CORE**$_{P/L}$); that is, the conditions in Equation 2.2 are met. Hence, the N-set includes the entire L-P line. Of course, the Leader most prefers her own ideal point, and

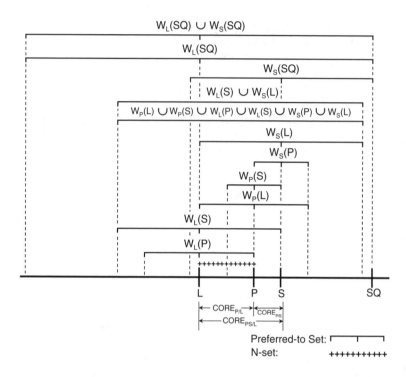

Figure 2.3   When SQ Lies Outside $W_L(SQ) \cup W_S(SQ)$, the N-set Includes All of $CORE_{P/L}$

the President most prefers his own ideal point, so their bargaining over the *N*-set will involve which point on the *L-P* line to select.

Case 2b (figure 2.4b). Here **SQ** lies somewhat closer to S, and the resulting $\mathbf{W}_S(\mathbf{SQ})$ is smaller and does not include all of the *L-P* line (i.e., it no longer includes all of $\mathbf{CORE}_{P/L}$). What is produced is an *N*-set that is the segment of $\mathbf{W}_S(\mathbf{SQ})$ falling inside the *L-P* line. The President most prefers the righthand end of this *N*-set (which is identical to his ideal point), while the Leader most prefers the lefthand end of the *N*-set (which is the lefthand end of $\mathbf{W}_S(\mathbf{SQ})$ in $\mathbf{CORE}_{P/L}$).

Case 2c (figure 2.4c). In this case **SQ** is now so close to S that $\mathbf{W}_S(\mathbf{SQ})$ no longer intersects $\mathbf{CORE}_{P/L}$. As a result, the President and the Leader both find that the point at the lefthand end of $\mathbf{W}_S(\mathbf{SQ})$, indicated by the "*," is the best either can do. This is a case in which there is no need for any bargaining between the President and Leader: they will agree on this single point in the *N*-set.

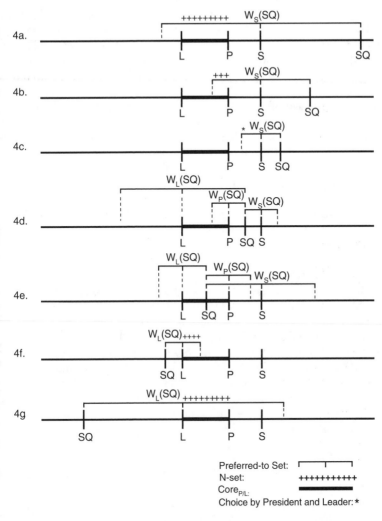

Figure 2.4 Case 2—For the L-P-S Ordering, there are Seven Key Locations for SQ

Case 2d (figure 2.4d). Here **SQ** lies between *S*, on the one hand, and *L* and *P*, on the other. While the Senate wants to move **SQ** rightward, the Leader and President want to move **SQ** leftward. In other words, **SQ** is in equilibrium because $\mathbf{SQ} \in \mathbf{CORE}_{PS/L}$; see Proposition 2.4b. Hence, no change in **SQ** will be possible.

Case 2e (figure 2.4e). In this case, **SQ** lies between L and P. While the Leader wants to move **SQ** leftward, the President and Senate both want to move **SQ** rightward. In other words, **SQ** is in equilibrium because $\textbf{SQ} \in \textbf{CORE}_{P/L}$; see Proposition 2.4a. Again, no change in **SQ** is possible.

Case 2f (figure 2.4f). Here **SQ** lies a short distance to the left of L. In this case, $\textbf{W}_L(\textbf{SQ})$ does not include all of $\textbf{CORE}_{P/L}$, thereby generating an *N*-set that is the segment of the *L-P* line lying inside $\textbf{W}_L(\textbf{SQ})$. The Leader will prefer the lefthand boundary of the *N*-set (which is located at her own ideal point), while the President will prefer the righthand boundary of the *N*-set (the righthand end of $\textbf{W}_L(\textbf{SQ})$ in $\textbf{CORE}_{P/L}$).

Case 2g (figure 2.4g). In this last case, **SQ** lies so far to the left of *L* that the resulting $\textbf{W}_L(\textbf{SQ})$ includes all of $\textbf{CORE}_{P/L}$, thereby generating an *N*-set that is the entire *L-P* line; that is, the conditions in Equation 2.2 are met. The President will prefer the righthand boundary of this *N*-set, which is his own ideal point, while the Leader will prefer the lefthand boundary of this *N*-set, which is her own ideal point.

Case 3: The ideal points are in the order L-S-P

Within this general case there are six different locations for **SQ** that are useful to distinguish; see the diagrams in figure 2.5. Note that since *S* lies between *L* and *P*, *S* is thereby included in $\textbf{CORE}_{P/L}$, which is the *L-P* line. (This also means that $\textbf{CORE}_{PS}$ is contained in $\textbf{CORE}_{P/L}$.)

Case 3a (figure 2.5a). In this case, **SQ** lies so far to the right of *P* that $\textbf{W}_P(\textbf{SQ})$ includes all of $\textbf{CORE}_{P/L}$; that is, the conditions in Equation 2.2 are met. Hence, $\textbf{W}_P(\textbf{SQ})$ does not constrain the bargaining between the President and the Leader. As a result, the *N*-set includes the entire *L-P* line, which is $\textbf{CORE}_{P/L}$. Of course, the Leader most prefers her own ideal point, and the President most prefers his own ideal point, so the bargaining between them will involve which point on the *L-P* line to select.

Case 3b (see figure 2.5b). Here **SQ** lies somewhat closer to *P*, and as a result $\textbf{W}_P(\textbf{SQ})$ does not include all of $\textbf{CORE}_{P/L}$. Thus, the *N*-set is the segment of $\textbf{W}_P(\textbf{SQ})$ that lies inside the *L-P* line. The President most prefers the righthand end of this *N*-set (which is identical to his ideal point), while the Leader most prefers the lefthand end of the *N*-set (i.e., the lefthand end of $\textbf{W}_P(\textbf{SQ})$ in $\textbf{CORE}_{P/L}$, a point that here falls just to the left of *S* here). The Senate will ratify anything the chief executives propose: their proposal will always be better for the Senate than **SQ**.

Case 3c (figure 2.5c). In this case, **SQ** lies between *S* and *P*, which means that it is inside $\textbf{CORE}_{PS/L}$ (i.e., the *L-P* line). Hence, **SQ** will be in equilibrium because $\textbf{SQ} \in \textbf{CORE}_{PS/L}$; see Proposition 2.4b.

Case 3d (figure 2.5d). In this case, **SQ** lies between *L* and *S*, which again means that it is inside $\textbf{CORE}_{P/L}$ (i.e., the *L-P* line). Hence, **SQ** is in equilibrium because $\textbf{SQ} \in \textbf{CORE}_{P/L}$; see Proposition 2.4a.

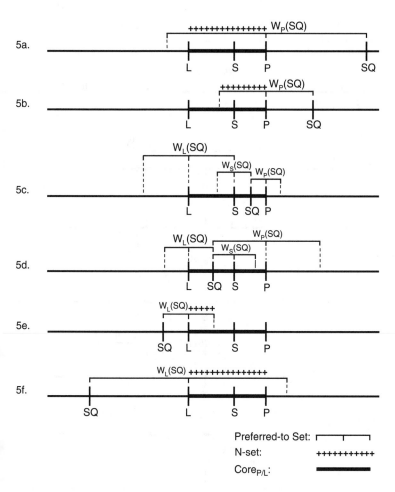

Figure 2.5 Case 3—For the L-P-S Ordering, there are Six key Locations for SQ

Case 3e (figure 2.5e). Here **SQ** lies a short distance to the left of *L*. In this case, $\mathbf{W}_L(\mathbf{SQ})$ intersects $\mathbf{CORE}_{P/L}$, thereby generating an *N*-set that is the segment of $\mathbf{W}_L(\mathbf{SQ})$ that lies inside the *L-S-P* line. The Leader will prefer the lefthand boundary of the *N*-set (located at her own ideal point), while the President will prefer the righthand boundary of the *N*-set (i.e., the righthand end of $\mathbf{W}_L(\mathbf{SQ})$ in $\mathbf{CORE}_{P/L}$).

Case 3f (figure 2.5f). In this last case, **SQ** lies so far to the left of *L* that the resulting $\mathbf{W}_L(\mathbf{SQ})$ includes all of $\mathbf{CORE}_{P/L}$, thereby generating an *N*-set that is the entire *L-P* line; that is, the conditions in Equation 2.2 are met. The Leader will prefer the lefthand boundary of the *N*-set (which is her own

ideal point), while the President will prefer the righthand boundary of this
N-set (which is his own ideal point).

Case 4: The ideal points are in the order S-L-P

Within this general case there are six different locations for **SQ** that are
useful to distinguish; see the diagrams in figure 2.6.

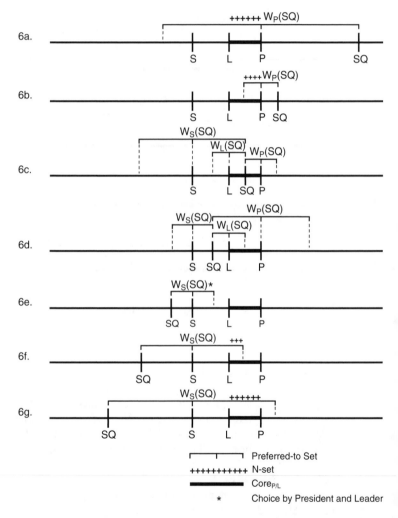

Figure 2.6 Case 4—For the S-L-P Ordering, there are Seven Key Locations for SQ

Case 4a (see figure 2.6a). In this case, **SQ** lies so far to the right of *P* that $\mathbf{W}_P(\mathbf{SQ})$ includes all of the *L-P* line segment; that is, the conditions in Equation 2.2 are met, so the *N*-set here is the entire *L-P* line. Of course, the Leader most prefers her own ideal point in this *N*-set, and the President most prefers his own ideal point.

Case 4b (figure 2.6b). Here **SQ** lies so close to *P* that $\mathbf{W}_P(\mathbf{SQ})$ does not include all of the *L-P* line (i.e., it no longer includes all of $\mathbf{CORE}_{P/L}$). This produces an *N*-set that is the segment of $\mathbf{W}_P(\mathbf{SQ})$ lying inside the *L-P* line. The President most prefers the righthand end of the *N*-set (which is at his ideal point), while the Leader most prefers the lefthand end of this *N*-set (i.e., the lefthand end of $\mathbf{W}_P(\mathbf{SQ})$ in $\mathbf{CORE}_{P/L}$).

Case 4c (figure 2.6c). In this case, **SQ** lies between *L* and *P*, which means that it is inside $\mathbf{CORE}_{P/L}$ (i.e., the *L-P* line). Thus, $\mathbf{SQ} \in \mathbf{CORE}_{P/L}$ and so **SQ** is in equilibrium; see Proposition 2.4a. This means that the Leader and President will be unable to agree on any policy to replace **SQ**.

Case 4d (figure 2.6d). Here **SQ** lies between S, on the one hand, and *L* and *P*, on the other. Thus, $\mathbf{SQ} \in \mathbf{CORE}_{PS/L}$ and so **SQ** is in equilibrium; see Proposition 2.4b. While the Leader and President want to move **SQ** rightward, the Senate wants to move **SQ** leftward.

Case 4e (figure 2.6e). In this case, **SQ** lies to the left of S but close to it. The resulting $\mathbf{W}_S(\mathbf{SQ})$ does not intersect $\mathbf{CORE}_{P/L}$ but it does intersect the *S-L* line segment. As a result, the *N*-set contains just one point, labeled "*", at the right end of $\mathbf{W}_S(\mathbf{SQ})$, which both *L* and *P* find is the best they can do. Hence, they will select this point.

Case 4f (figure 2.6f). Here **SQ** lies somewhat farther to the left of *S*, and the resulting $\mathbf{W}_S(\mathbf{SQ})$ includes a portion of the *L-P* line. This produces an *N*-set that is the segment of $\mathbf{W}_S(\mathbf{SQ})$ that lies inside the *L-P* line. The Leader most prefers the lefthand end of the *N*-set (which is at her ideal point), while the President most prefers the righthand end of the *N*-set (which is the righthand end of $\mathbf{W}_S(\mathbf{SQ})$ in $\mathbf{CORE}_{P/L}$).

Case 4g (figure 2.6g). Finally, **SQ** now lies so far to the left of *L* here that $\mathbf{W}_S(\mathbf{SQ})$ includes all of the *L-P* line segment; that is, the conditions in Equation 2.2 are met. Hence, the *N*-set includes the entire *L-P* line. Of course, the Leader most prefers her own ideal point in this *N*-set and the President most prefers his own ideal point.

Negotiations between the President and the Leader, with the Senate and a Foreign Veto Institution

Finally, we must consider what happens when there are two domestic veto institutions, one for the President and one for the Leader; that is, each chief executive has a divided government. Following the same logic as previously, we need to determine the N-set for the President and Leader, when their choices are constrained by both the Senate and its foreign counterpart. With all four of our institutional actors, the N-set is defined as follows:

Definition 3 (P, S, L, V).   The N-set is the set of points $\cup \mathbf{x}_i$ ($i = 1, \ldots, k$) in $\mathbf{W}_{PS/LV}(\mathbf{SQ}) \cap \mathbf{CORE}_{PS/LV}$ such that $\mathbf{W}_{P/L}(\mathbf{x}_i) = \varnothing$.

In effect, the N-set here is the set of points in $\mathbf{CORE}_{PS/LV}$ that (a) are better than $\mathbf{SQ}$ for the President, Senate, Leader, and foreign veto institution, and for which (b) the President and Leader can find no mutually preferred alternatives.

As before, we first need to identify the locations for $\mathbf{SQ}$ such that the N-set will necessarily be the entire $\mathbf{CORE}_{P/L}$. For this to hold, $\mathbf{SQ}$ cannot be closer to P, L, S, or V than they are to each other. This means (unfortunately) that we must consider the following 12 preferred-to sets:

  (1) $\mathbf{W}_P(\mathbf{L})$, the set of points that P prefers to L,
  (2) $\mathbf{W}_P(\mathbf{S})$, the set of points that P prefers to S,
  (3) $\mathbf{W}_P(\mathbf{V})$, the set of points that P prefers to V,
  (4) $\mathbf{W}_L(\mathbf{P})$, the set of points that L prefers to P,
  (5) $\mathbf{W}_L(\mathbf{S})$, the set of points that L prefers to S,
  (6) $\mathbf{W}_L(\mathbf{V})$, the set of points that L prefers to V,
  (7) $\mathbf{W}_S(\mathbf{P})$, the set of points that S prefers to P,
  (8) $\mathbf{W}_S(\mathbf{L})$, the set of points that S prefers to L,
  (9) $\mathbf{W}_S(\mathbf{V})$, the set of points that S prefers to V,
(10) $\mathbf{W}_V(\mathbf{P})$, the set of points that V prefers to P,
(11) $\mathbf{W}_V(\mathbf{L})$, the set of points that V prefers to L, and
(12) $\mathbf{W}_V(\mathbf{S})$, the set of points that V prefers to S.

It follows that the set of points that are closer to P than is L or S or V, *or* closer to L than is P or S or V, *or* closer to S than is P or L or V, *or* closer to V than is P or L or S is the set-union of these points, or

$$\mathbf{W}_P(\mathbf{L}) \cup \mathbf{W}_P(\mathbf{S}) \cup \mathbf{W}_P(\mathbf{V}) \cup \mathbf{W}_L(\mathbf{P}) \cup \mathbf{W}_L(\mathbf{S}) \cup \mathbf{W}_L(\mathbf{V}) \cup \mathbf{W}_S(\mathbf{P})$$
$$\cup \ \mathbf{W}_S(\mathbf{L}) \cup \mathbf{W}_S(\mathbf{V}) \cup \mathbf{W}_V(\mathbf{P}) \cup \mathbf{W}_V(\mathbf{L}) \cup \mathbf{W}_V(\mathbf{S}).$$

If some $\mathbf{SQ}$ falls inside this set-union, it means that this $\mathbf{SQ}$ is either closer to P than to S or L or V, or closer to L than to S or P or V, or closer to P than to L or S or V, or closer to S than to P or L or V. So, for all of

CORE$_{P/L}$ to fall inside the *N*-set, the following relationship must hold:

$$SQ \notin \{W_P(L) \cup W_P(S) \cup W_P(V) \cup W_L(P) \cup W_L(S) \cup W_L(V) \cup W_S(P)$$
$$\cup\ W_S(L) \cup W_S(V) \cup W_V(P) \cup W_V(L) \cup W_V(S)\} \qquad (2.3)$$

In other words, if **SQ** is farther away from *P, L, S*, and *V* than *P, L, S*, and *V* are from each other, then $W_P(SQ) \cap W_L(SQ) \cap W_S(SQ) \cap W_V(SQ)$ will contain all of **CORE**$_{P/L}$. Since the resulting *N*-set thus contains all of **CORE**$_{P/L}$, the President and the Leader could potentially select any point in **CORE**$_{P/L}$. Figure 2.7 provides an illustration. Notice that for the *V-L-P-S* ordering in this diagram, the complex expression in Equation 2.3 reduces to $W_V(S) \cup W_S(V)$. since *V* and *S* are the "outside" actors in this particular diagram, the preferred-to sets of the "interior" actors do not affect the overall result. So if **SQ** lies outside $W_V(S) \cup W_S(V)$ here, the *N*-set will include the entire *L-P* line.

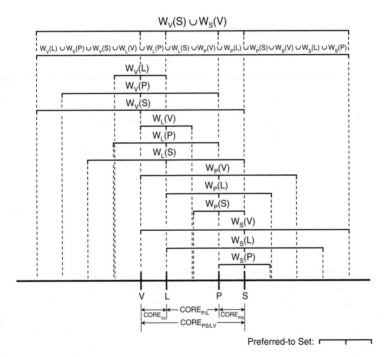

Figure 2.7 When SQ Lies Outside $W_v(S) \cup W_S(V)$, the N-set Includes All of CORE$_{P/L}$

As before, it will be important to consider the different orderings of the P, L, S, and V ideal points that are possible. There are 24 possible orderings:

(1) L-P-S-V	(5) V-S-P-L	(9) L-V-S-P	(13) P-S-V-L	(17) P-V-L-S	(21) S-L-V-P
(2) L-P-V-S	(6) S-V-P-L	(10) L-V-P-S	(14) S-P-V-L	(18) P-V-S-L	(22) L-S-V-P
(3) L-S-P-V	(7) V-P-S-L	(11) P-L-V-S	(15) S-V-L-P	(19) P-S-L-V	(23) V-L-S-P
(4) L-S-V-P	(8) P-V-S-L	(12) P-L-S-V	(16) V-S-L-P	(20) V-P-L-S	(24) S-L-P-V

Note that the second column is a mirror image of the first, the fourth column is a mirror image of the third, and the sixth column is a mirror image of the fifth. Hence, even with these mirror images taken into consideration, there are still 12 possible orderings that we should consider.

However, we can further simplify here by considering just the relationships between two generic chief executives and two generic veto institutions, without attaching country-specific labels to any of them. The reason we can simplify in this manner, and do so without any loss of generality, is that our general results are not affected by the identity of any particular Leader or any particular veto institution in an ordering: all that matters is the four preferred-to sets (whatever their particular identifying labels) and their intersection with the *International Core* of the two chief executives. It follows that there are just *four* orderings to consider (using P as the label of the generic chief executive and V as the label of the generic veto institution). (1) P-P-V-V; (2) P-V-P-V; (3) P-V-V-P; and (4) V-P-P-V.

We now examine these four orderings in turn. Because the general logic should be clear by now, only an abbreviated discussion will be provided for each particular case. In the accompanying diagrams, the chief executives and veto institutions will have more specific labels (i.e., either P_1 or P_2, and either V_1 or V_2) to make clear which particular ideal point is being referenced, but it should be understood for each case that P_1 and P_2 could be interchanged, as could V_1 and V_2, without any change in the general results. Note that the *International Core* without any veto institutions will be labeled $\mathbf{CORE}_{P/P}$, and the *International Core* with two veto institutions will be labeled $\mathbf{CORE}_{PV/PV}$.

Case 5: The ideal points are in the order P_1-P_2-V_1-V_2

There are six different locations for $\mathbf{SQ}$ that are useful to examine; see the diagrams in figure 2.8.

Case 5a (see figure 2.8a). $\mathbf{SQ}$ lies so far to the right of its nearest actor, V_2, that the conditions in Equation 2.3 are met. Hence, all of $\mathbf{CORE}_{P/P}$—which is the P_1-P_2 line in the diagram—is included in $\mathbf{W}_{V2}(\mathbf{SQ})$, and is thus in the N-set.

Case 5b (figure 2.8b). This $\mathbf{SQ}$ lies closer to V_2, with the result that $\mathbf{W}_{V_2}(\mathbf{SQ})$ here includes only the righthand segment of $\mathbf{CORE}_{P/P}$. This

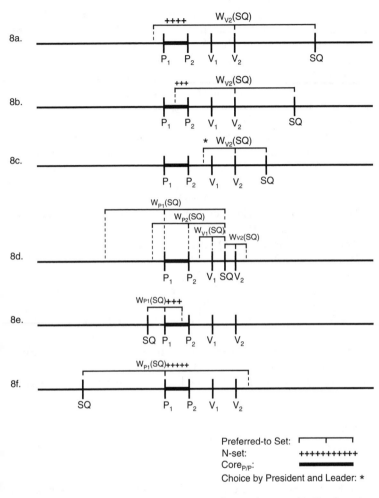

Figure 2.8 Case 5—For the P_1-P_2-V_1-V_2 Ordering, there are Six Key Locations for SQ

means that the *N*-set includes only the segment of $\mathbf{W}_{V2}(\mathbf{SQ})$ that lies inside the P_1-P_2 line.

Case 5c (figure 2.8c). **SQ** here is still to the right of V_2 but so close to it that $\mathbf{W}_{V_2}(\mathbf{SQ})$ does not intersect $\mathbf{CORE}_{P/P}$ at all. Hence, the two chief executives will agree on the policy at the lefthand end of $\mathbf{W}_{V_2}(\mathbf{SQ})$, as shown by the "*" in the diagram.

Case 5d (figure 2.8d). When **SQ** lies anywhere on or between V_2 on the right and P_1 on the left (such as the **SQ** between V_1 and V_2 shown in the diagram), such an **SQ** cannot be upset. In effect, **SQ** lies in **CORE**$_{PV/PV}$, and so will be in equilibrium, as described by Proposition 2.4c.

Case 5e (figure 2.8e). This **SQ** lies somewhat to the left of P_1, with the result that $\mathbf{W}_{P_1}(\mathbf{SQ})$ intersects only the lefthand segment of **CORE**$_{P/P}$. This means that the N-set includes only the segment of $\mathbf{W}_{P_1}(\mathbf{SQ})$ that which lies inside the P_1-P_2 line.

Case 5f (figure 2.8f). This **SQ** lies so far to the left of P_1 that the conditions in Equation 2.3 are met, with the result that $\mathbf{W}_{P_1}(\mathbf{SQ})$ includes all of **CORE**$_{P/P}$. This means that the N-set includes the entire P_1-P_2 line.

Case 6: The ideal points are in the order P_1-V_1-P_2-V_2

There are six different locations for **SQ** that are useful to examine; see the diagrams in figure 2.9.

Case 6a (see figure 2.9a). **SQ** lies so far to the right of the nearest actor, V_2, that all of **CORE**$_{P/P}$—which is the P_1-P_2 line—is included in $\mathbf{W}_{V_2}(\mathbf{SQ})$, and is thus in the N-set.

Case 6b (figure 2.9b). This **SQ** lies closer to V_2, with the result that $\mathbf{W}_{V_2}(\mathbf{SQ})$ includes only the righthand segment of **CORE**$_{P/P}$. This means that the N-set includes only this segment of $\mathbf{W}_{V_2}(\mathbf{SQ})$ that lies inside the P_1-P_2 line.

Case 6c (figure 2.9c). **SQ** here is still to the right of V_2 but so close to it that $\mathbf{W}_{V_2}(\mathbf{SQ})$ does not intersect **CORE**$_{P/P}$ at all. Hence, the two chief executives will agree on the policy at the lefthand boundary of $\mathbf{W}_{V_2}(\mathbf{SQ})$, as shown by the "*" in the diagram.

Case 6d (figure 2.9d). When **SQ** lies anywhere on or between V_2 on the right and P_1 on the left, it cannot be upset. In effect, it lies in **CORE**$_{PV/PV}$, and so will be in equilibrium, as described by Proposition 2.4c. See the **SQ** between V_1 and V_2, for example.

Case 6e (figure 2.9e). This **SQ** lies somewhat to the left of P_1, with the result that $\mathbf{W}_{P_1}(\mathbf{SQ})$ intersects only the lefthand segment of **CORE**$_{P/P}$. This means that the N-set includes only the segment of $\mathbf{W}_{P_1}(\mathbf{SQ})$ that lies inside the P_1-P_2 line.

Case 6f (figure 2.9f). This **SQ** lies so far to the left of P_1 that $\mathbf{W}_{P_1}(\mathbf{SQ})$ includes all of **CORE**$_{P/P}$. This means that the N-set includes all of **CORE**$_{P/P}$.

Case 7: The ideal points are in the order P_1-V_1-V_2-P_2

There are five different locations for **SQ** that are useful to examine; see the diagrams in figure 2.10.

Case 7a (see figure 2.10a). **SQ** lies so far to the right of the nearest actor, P_2, that all of **CORE**$_{P/P}$—which is the P_1-P_2 line—is included in the N-set.

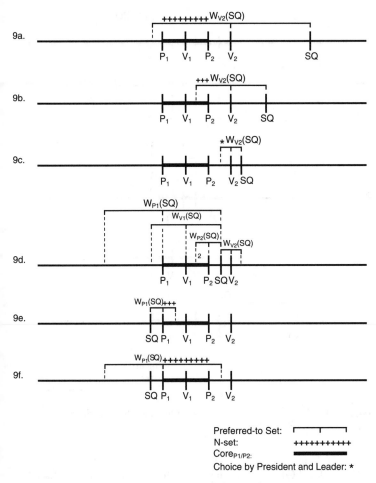

Figure 2.9   Case 6—For the P_1-V_1-V_2-P_2 Ordering, there are Six Key Locations for SQ

Case 7b (figure 2.10b). This **SQ** lies closer to P_2, with the result that $\mathbf{W}_{P_2}$(**SQ**) includes only the righthand segment of **CORE**$_{P/P}$. This means that the N-set includes only the segment of $\mathbf{W}_{P_2}$ (**SQ**) that lies inside the P_1-P_2 line.

Case 7c (figure 2.10c). When **SQ** lies anywhere on or between P_2 on the right and P_1 on the left, it cannot be upset. In effect, it lies in **CORE**$_{PV/PV}$, and so, by Proposition 2.4c, it will be in equilibrium. See the **SQ** between V_1 and V_2, for example.

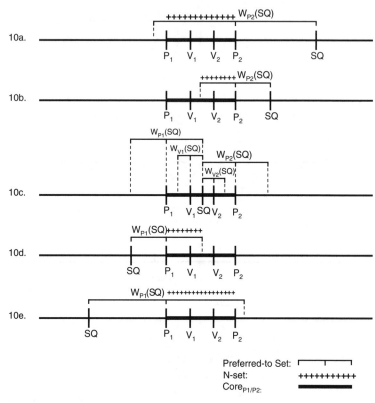

Figure 2.10   Case 7—For the P_1-V_1-V_2-P_2 Ordering, there are Six Key Locations for SQ

Case 7d (figure 2.10d). This **SQ** lies somewhat to the left of P_1, with the result that $\mathbf{W}_{P_1}(\mathbf{SQ})$ intersects only the lefthand segment of $\mathbf{CORE}_{P/P}$. This means that the N-set includes only the segment of $\mathbf{W}_{P_1}(\mathbf{SQ})$ that lies inside the P_1-P_2 line.

Case 7e (figure 2.10e). This **SQ** lies so far to the left of P_1 that $\mathbf{W}_{P_1}(\mathbf{SQ})$ includes all of $\mathbf{CORE}_{P/P}$. This means that the N-set includes all of $\mathbf{CORE}_{P/P}$.

Case 8: The ideal points are in the order V_1-P_1-P_2-V_2

There are seven different locations for **SQ** that are useful to examine; see the diagrams in figure 2.11.

Case 8a (see figure 2.11a). **SQ** lies so far to the right of V_2 that all of $\mathbf{CORE}_{P/P}$—which is the P_1-P_2 line—is included in the N-set.

Case 8b (figure 2.11b). This **SQ** lies closer to V_2, with the result that $\mathbf{W}_{V_2}(\mathbf{SQ})$ includes only the righthand segment of $\mathbf{CORE}_{P/P}$. This means

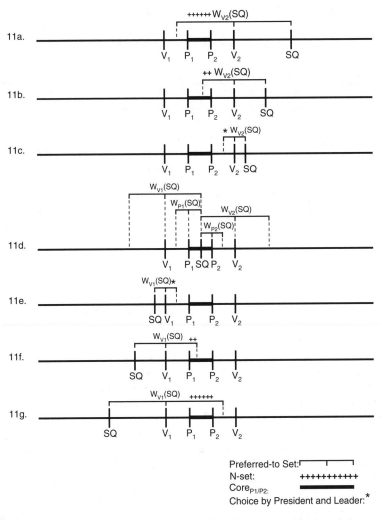

Figure 2.11 Case 8—For the V_1-P_2-P_1-V_2 Ordering, there are Six Key Locations for SQ

that the *N*-set includes only the segment of $\mathbf{W}_{V_2}(\mathbf{SQ})$ that lies inside the P_1-P_2 line.

Case 8c (figure 2.11c). The **SQ** here is still to the right of V_2 but so close to it that $\mathbf{W}_{V_2}(\mathbf{SQ})$ does not intersect $\mathbf{CORE}_{P/P}$ at all. Hence, the two chief executives will agree on the policy at the lefthand end of $\mathbf{W}_{V_2}(\mathbf{SQ})$, shown by the "*" in the diagram.

Case 8d (figure 2.11d). When **SQ** lies anywhere on or between V_2 on the right and V_1 on the left, it cannot be upset. In effect, it lies in **CORE**$_{PV/PV}$, and so, by Proposition 2.4c, will be in equilibrium. See the **SQ** between P_1 and P_2, for example.

Case 8e (figure 2.11e). The **SQ** here is to the left of V_1 but so close to it that $\mathbf{W}_{V_1}(\mathbf{SQ})$ does not intersect **CORE**$_{P/P}$ at all. Hence, the two chief executives will agree on the policy at the righthand boundary of $\mathbf{W}_{V_1}(\mathbf{SQ})$, as shown by the "*" in the diagram.

Case 8f (figure 2.11f). This **SQ** lies somewhat farther to the left of V_1, with the result that $\mathbf{W}_{V_1}(\mathbf{SQ})$ intersects the lefthand segment of **CORE**$_{P/P}$. This means that the *N*-set includes the segment of $\mathbf{W}_{V_1}(\mathbf{SQ})$ that lies inside the P_1-P_2 line.

Case 8g (figure 2.11g). This **SQ** lies so far to the left of V_1 that $\mathbf{W}_{V_1}(\mathbf{SQ})$ includes all of **CORE**$_{P/P}$. This means that the *N*-set includes all of **CORE**$_{P/P}$.

International Negotiations in Two Issue Dimensions

The preceding analysis of treaty negotiation in one dimension spells out the logic of these two-level, complete-information games in substantial detail. The same basic logic applies to treaty negotiation in two dimensions as well. The major difference is that, precisely because of the presence of two dimensions, there are more degrees of freedom, and so it is not nearly as clear what particular kinds of cases need to be examined for a thorough and systematic analysis. Hence, in this section we merely provide a number of examples to convey the flavor of how domestic institutions may constrain international negotiations in two dimensions.

Nonetheless, our examples here do show that the general range of outcomes that can emerge in one-dimensional games can also arise in these two-dimensional games as well. The major qualitative difference we observe is that while in one dimension, whenever the *N*-set lies outside **CORE**$_{P/L}$, the *N*-set will consist of just a single point (see figures 2.4c, 2.6e, 2.8c, 2.9c, 2.11c, and 2.11e), in two dimensions an *N*-set lying outside **CORE**$_{P/L}$ will usually consist of a line (i.e., it will consist of more than a single point).

Negotiations between the President and Leader, with No Veto Institutions

We first examine some examples of negotiations between the President and Leader when there are no veto institutions (or both chief executives have

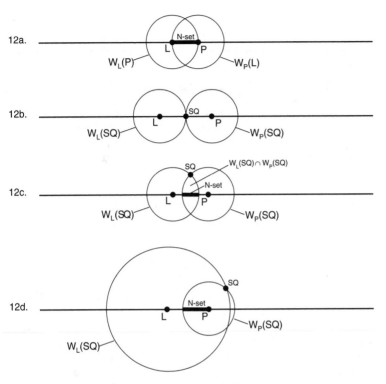

Figure 2.12   Case 9—The N-set with L and P in Two Dimensions

unified governments). As was the case for one dimension, the line connecting L and P is $\mathbf{CORE}_{P/L}$, and unconstrained bargaining between the President and the Leader will lead to outcomes on the L-P line. When there are no veto institutions, Definition 2.1 for the N-set holds, and the N-set will always be part or all of the P-L contract curve (just as is the case with one dimension), and the N-set will be indicated by the heavy solid line. For illustrations consider the following diagrams in figure 2.12.

Case 9a (see figure 2.12a). Recall that the N-set will include all of $\mathbf{CORE}_{P/L}$—that is, all of the L-P line—when $\mathbf{SQ} \notin \{\mathbf{W}_L(\mathbf{P}) \cup \mathbf{W}_L(\mathbf{P})\}$; see Equation. In the diagram here, $\mathbf{SQ}$ lies outside $\{\mathbf{W}_L(\mathbf{P}) \cup \mathbf{W}_L(\mathbf{P})\}$, hence, the N-set includes all of $\mathbf{CORE}_{P/L}$.

Case 9b (see figure 2.12b). If $\mathbf{SQ}$ lies anywhere on the line connecting L and P, which is $\mathbf{CORE}_{P/L}$, it will be in equilibrium: the President will want to move $\mathbf{SQ}$ rightward, while the Leader will want to move $\mathbf{SQ}$ leftward. In the diagram here, the N-set is thus empty.

Case 9c (figure 2.12c). In this case, **SQ** lies between L and P (on the horizontal dimension) but above L and P (on the vertical dimension). The lens-shaped region below **SQ** is the set of points that both P and L prefer to **SQ**; that is, this region is $\mathbf{W}_L(\mathbf{SQ}) \cap \mathbf{W}_P(\mathbf{SQ})$. The *N*-set will thus be the segment of the *L-P* line (i.e., of $\mathbf{CORE}_{P/L}$) that lies inside this lens-shaped region of $\mathbf{W}_L(\mathbf{SQ}) \cap \mathbf{W}_P(\mathbf{SQ})$.

Case 9d (figure 2.12d). **SQ** here is somewhat more extreme on the horizontal dimension. Because **SQ** is closer to P than to L, the President is the more constraining institution. The *N*-set that results is the segment of $\mathbf{CORE}_{P/L}$—that is, of the *L-P* line—which lies inside $\mathbf{W}_P(\mathbf{SQ})$.

Negotiations between the President and Leader, with the Senate as a Veto Institution

When the Senate is the veto institution, Definition 2 for the *N*-set holds. See the illustrative diagrams in figure 2.13. In these diagrams, if P, L, and S all lie in a straight line, then the resulting $\mathbf{CORE}_{PS/L}$ will be a straight line. When P, L, and S do not lie in a straight line, then the resulting $\mathbf{CORE}_{PS/L}$ will be the triangle formed by the P, L, and S ideal points. When $\mathbf{CORE}_{PS/L}$ is a triangle in the following diagrams, we lightly shade the triangle.

Case 10a (figure 2.13a). In this case, **SQ** is in a location such that the conditions in Equation 2.2 are met: **SQ** lies outside $\mathbf{W}_L(P) \cup \mathbf{W}_L(S)$ $\mathbf{W}_P(L) \cup \mathbf{W}_P(S) \cup \mathbf{W}_S(L) \cup \mathbf{W}_S(P)$, hence, all of $\mathbf{CORE}_{PS/L}$ will be in the *N*-set. The Senate here does not constrain bargaining between the President and Leader.

Case 10b (see figure 2.13b). The *L-P-S* triangle here is $\mathbf{CORE}_{PS/L}$, and any **SQ** inside this triangle will be in equilibrium. While there could be as many as two institutions that want to move such an **SQ** in some particular direction, there will never be three institutions that want to do so; at least one of the institutions will always veto a proposal to upset **SQ**. Hence, the *N*-set will be empty in this case.

Case 10c (figure 2.13c). In this case, $\mathbf{W}_L(\mathbf{SQ}) \cap \mathbf{W}_P(\mathbf{SQ})$ intersects a middle segment of $\mathbf{CORE}_{P/L}$, and the Senate does not constrain bargaining between the President and Leader. The resulting *N*-set lies in the middle of the *L-P* line, that is, in the middle of the $\mathbf{CORE}_{P/L}$ line.

Case 10d (figure 2.13d). With a Senate and an **SQ** that both lie to the right of P, $\mathbf{W}_S(\mathbf{SQ})$ constrains the *N*-set to the righthand end of $\mathbf{CORE}_{P/L}$.

Case 10e (figure 2.13e). This case illustrates an *N*-set that does not include any part of $\mathbf{CORE}_{P/L}$, which is the *L-P* line. The reason is that $\mathbf{W}_S(\mathbf{SQ})$ constrains bargaining to the small circle around S, and this circle

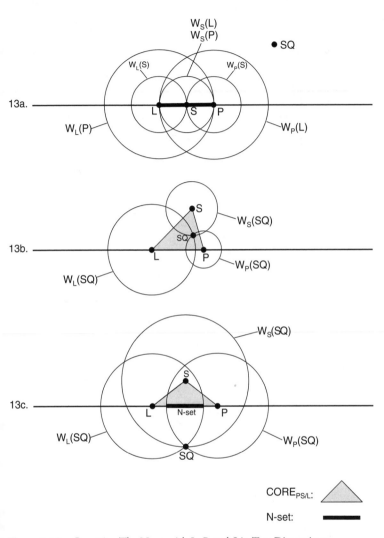

Figure 2.13 Case 10—The N-set with L, P, and S in Two Dimensions

does not include any part of the *L-P* line. The Leader's best point in this circle—that is, in $\mathbf{W}_S(\mathbf{SQ})$—is the point labled *l*, while the President's best point in this same circle is labeled *p*. The *N*-set is the heavy curved line connecting the *l* and *p* points: it is the part of the boundary of the $\mathbf{W}_S(\mathbf{SQ})$ circle that lies inside the triangular $\mathbf{CORE}_{PS/L}$. This is the *N*-set because for

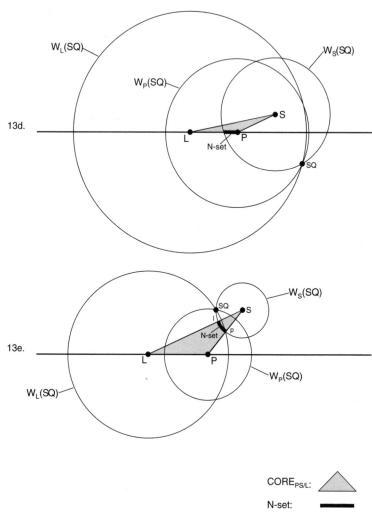

Figure 2.13 Continued

every other point inside $\mathbf{W}_S(\mathbf{SQ}) \cap \mathbf{CORE}_{PS/L}$, there is some point on this line connecting l and p that both the Leader and President prefer and, for every point on this $l-P$ line, there is no other point that the Leader and President both prefer.

Case 10f (figure 2.13f). This case illustrates another *N*-set that does not include any part of $\mathbf{CORE}_{P/L}$. $\mathbf{W}_S(\mathbf{SQ})$ again constrains bargaining to the

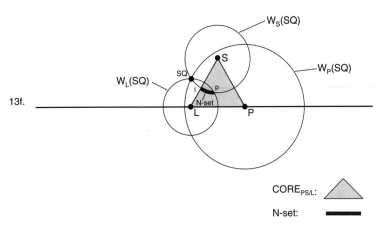

Figure 2.13   Continued

circle around *S*. The Leader's best point in this circle—that is, in $\mathbf{W}_S(\mathbf{SQ})$— is point *l*, while the President's best point in this circle is point *p*. The *N*-set is the part of the boundary of the $\mathbf{W}_S(\mathbf{SQ})$ circle that lies inside both $\mathbf{W}_L(\mathbf{SQ})$ and $\mathbf{CORE}_{PS/L}$, as shown by the heavy curved line that connects the *l* and *p* points. This is the *N*-set because for every other point inside $\mathbf{W}_S(\mathbf{SQ}) \cap \mathbf{W}_L(\mathbf{SQ}) \cap \mathbf{CORE}_{PS/L}$, there is some point on this *l-P* line that both the Leader and President prefer and, for every point on this *l-P* line, there is no other point that both the Leader and President prefer.

Negotiations between the President and Leader, with a Veto Institution for Each Country

When there are two veto institutions, *Definition 2.3* for the *N*-set holds; see figure 2.14 for two illustrative diagrams. In each case, the lightly shaded *L-P-S-V* quadrilateral is $\mathbf{CORE}_{PS/LV}$.

Case 11a (see figure 2.14a). **SQ** here is located inside the shaded quadrilateral, $\mathbf{CORE}_{PS/LV}$. Any **SQ** located inside this quadrangle will be in equilibrium: as many as three of these institutions could prefer some other point to **SQ**, but there is no location for **SQ** such that all four of these institutions will prefer some other point to **SQ**. Hence, the *N*-set is empty for any location of **SQ** inside the shaded area.

Case 11b (figure 2.14b). In this example, $\mathbf{CORE}_{PS/LV}$ is again a shaded quadrilateral, but **SQ** now lies outside the quadrilateral. The small lens sloping southeastward from **SQ** is the set of points that *P*, *L*, *S*, and *V* all prefer

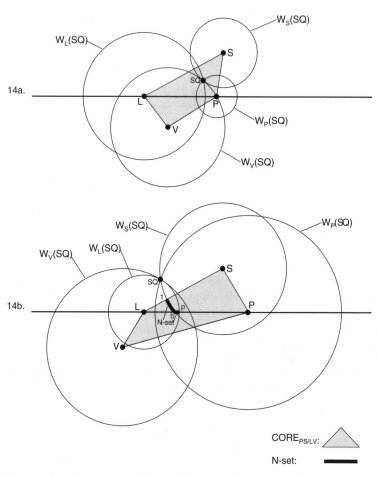

Figure 2.14 Case 11—The N-set with L, P, S, and V in Two Dimensions

to **SQ**; it is $\mathbf{W}_P(\mathbf{SQ}) \cap \mathbf{W}_L(\mathbf{SQ}) \cap \mathbf{W}_S(\mathbf{SQ}) \cap \mathbf{W}_V(\mathbf{SQ})$. The N-set must lie inside $\mathbf{W}_P(\mathbf{SQ}) \cap \mathbf{W}_L(\mathbf{SQ}) \cap \mathbf{W}_S(\mathbf{SQ}) \cap \mathbf{W}_V(\mathbf{SQ}) \cap \mathbf{CORE}_{PS/LV}$. Note that the Leader's best point in this area is point l on the L-S boundary, and note also that the President's best point in this area is point p on the L-P line. Interestingly, the N-set here is a kinked line. One segment extends from point l to the point labeled b on the L-P line (i.e., on $\mathbf{CORE}_{P/L}$); it follows the boundary of $\mathbf{W}_S(\mathbf{SQ})$ from l to b. The other segment extends from point b to point p; it follows the L-P line ($\mathbf{CORE}_{P/L}$) from b to p. This kinked line is the N-set because for every other point inside $\mathbf{W}_S(\mathbf{SQ}) \cap \mathbf{W}_L(\mathbf{SQ})$, there is some point on this kinked *l-b-p* line that both the Leader and President prefer and, for every point on this *l-b-p* line, there is no other point that the Leader and President both prefer.

Generalizing the Results

The conceptual foundations for analyzing two-level games with complete information have now been established. We have determined when the status quo policy will be in equilibrium if there are no veto institutions (or there is unified government in each country), if there is one veto institution (or there is divided government for the President and unified government for the Leader), and if there are two veto institutions (or there is divided government for both the President and Leader). And when the status quo policy is not in equilibrium, we have characterized the set of policies—the *N*-set— over which the President and Leader should be expected to negotiate.

We can now use these results to address the central issues regarding the impact of divided and unified government, and of domestic veto institutions more generally, on international negotiations in one dimension. In particular, we address the following questions: (1) under what conditions will a national Leader's negotiating position be strengthened by divided government?; (2) under what conditions will the national Leader's negotiating position be weakened by divided government?; (3) under what conditions will divided government make an international agreement impossible?; and (4) under what conditions will divided government have no effect at all on the outcome of international negotiations? We focus on just the one-dimensional cases since knowing how to conduct a systematic analysis is much clearer.

The General Impact of the Status Quo

Our analysis in the preceding sections highlights how changes in the location of the status quo will affect outcomes. The impact of the status quo is most clearly seen in the one-dimensional cases described in part III. For each case in that section, we held the actors' ideal points constant while systematically changing the location of the status quo. In general, the impact of these changes in the status quo policy is quite variable:

- some locations for **SQ** lead to an *N*-set that consists of the entire **CORE**$_{P/L}$ (e.g., figures 2.2a, 2.4a, 2.5a, 2.6a, 2.8a, 2.9a, 2.10a, and 2.11a);

- some locations for **SQ** lead to an N-set that is a small segment of **CORE**$_{P/L}$ favoring the President but not the foreign Leader (e.g., figures 2.2b, 2.4b, 2.5b, 2.6b, 2.8b, 2.9b, 2.10b, and 2.11b);
- some locations for **SQ** lead to an N-set that is a small segment of **CORE**$_{P/L}$ favoring the foreign Leader but not the President (e.g., figures 2.2d, 2.4f, 2.5e, 2.6f, 2.8e, 2.9e, 2.10d, and 2.11f);
- some locations for **SQ** lead the chief executives to agree on some policy outside **CORE**$_{P/L}$ that favors the President (e.g., figures 2.4c, 2.8c, 2.9c, and 2.11c);
- some locations for **SQ** lead the chief executives to agree on some policy outside **CORE**$_{P/L}$ that favors the foreign Leader (e.g., figures 2.6e and 2.11e); and,
- some locations for **SQ** lead to no change in policy at all because the chief executives cannot agree on some policy that they both prefer to **SQ** *and* that the veto institutions (if any) would also prefer to **SQ** (e.g., figures 2.1c, 2.4d, 2.4e, 2.5c, 2.5d, 2.6c, 2.6d, 2.8d, 2.9d, 2.10c, and 2.11d).

We may summarize the meaning of these results in the following manner:

Observation 2.1. If the two chief executives do not have identical ideal points, there exist locations for **SQ** (see Propositions 1–4) for which no mutually beneficial agreement is possible (i.e., for which the N-set is empty).

Observation 2.2. Holding institutional ideal points constant, changes in the location of **SQ** can have a dramatic impact on the existence, size, and location of the N-set, and thus on which chief executive, if either, benefits from the final outcome.

The Impact of the Status Quo on a Chief Executive's Negotiating Position

While these first two observations summarize the general impact of changes in the size and location of the N-set, they do not tell us much about how changes in the location of **SQ** can affect the fortunes of any particular chief executive. To clarify this matter we graph the relationships between the location of **SQ** and the location of the N-set with respect to the ideal points of P, L, S, and V. This produces figure 2.15 (which graphs the **SQ**/N-set relationships for Case 1, in which there are no veto institutions), figures 2.16, 2.17, and 2.18 (which graph the **SQ**/N-set relationships for Cases 2, 3, and 4, in which there is one veto institution), and figures 2.19–2.22 (which graph the **SQ**/N-set relationships for Cases 5, 6, 7, and 8, in which there are two veto institutions). In these diagrams, the location of **SQ** is depicted on the horizontal axis, relative to the locations of the ideal points

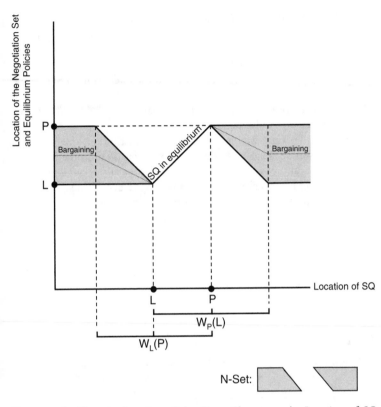

Figure 2.15 How the Location of the N-set Changes as the Location of SQ Changes—Case 1

of the chief executives and any veto institutions, while the location of the resulting N-set and other outcomes (for each horizontal-axis **SQ**) are graphed on the vertical axis.

To illustrate, consider Case 1 (involving just L and P), which is analyzed in figure 2.15; it integrates the five diagrams in figure 2.2. With **SQ** starting out on the far right on the horizontal axis, the N-set on the vertical axis initially spans the entire L-P line (that is, it includes all of **CORE**$_{P/L}$). Neither chief executive is advantaged here. As **SQ** moves leftward toward P (on the horizontal axis), the N-set begins to shrink upward toward P (on the vertical axis) when **SQ** passes the righthand boundary of $\mathbf{W}_P(\mathbf{L})$, and as **SQ** approaches P, the remaining points in the N-set are closer and closer to P. In this region, then, the President gains an increasing advantage over the foreign Leader as **SQ** approaches P. When **SQ** reaches P, however, the N-set is empty and no agreement can be reached, and as **SQ** continues to move leftward past P and toward L, **SQ** continues to be in equilibrium until it reaches L, which means that the President is increasingly disadvantaged, and the Leader increasingly advantaged, simply due to the increasingly leftward locations of **SQ**. When **SQ** moves leftward beyond L, the N-set begins to expand upward (increasingly benefiting the President) until **SQ** reaches the lefthand boundary of $\mathbf{W}_L(\mathbf{P})$, whereupon the N-set again includes all of **CORE**$_{P/L}$. When **SQ** moves beyond the lefthand boundary of $\mathbf{W}_L(\mathbf{P})$, neither chief executive is advantaged.

Next consider Case 2 (which has one veto institution, the Senate) in figure 2.16. With **SQ** again starting out on the far right on the horizontal axis, the N-set on the vertical axis initially spans the entire L-P line (that is, **CORE**$_{P/L}$). Neither chief executive is advantaged here. When **SQ** moves leftward past the righthand boundary of $\mathbf{W}_S(\mathbf{L})$, the N-set begins to shrink

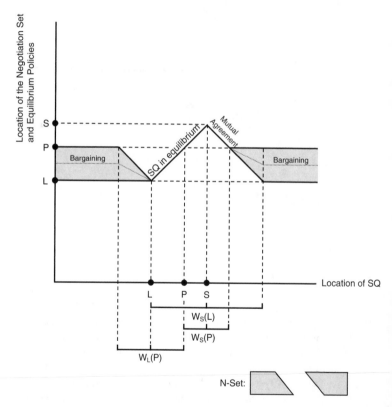

Figure 2.16 How the Location of the N-set Changes as the Location of SQ Changes—Case 2

upward until it reaches a point, at the lefthand boundary of $\mathbf{W}_S(\mathbf{P})$, at which the Leader would agree to a choice at the President's ideal point; thus, the President is increasingly advantaged. As **SQ** continues to move leftward toward S, the N-set (now just one point) continues upward toward the Senate's ideal point, and *both* the President and Leader are increasingly disadvantaged. Next, as **SQ** moves from S leftward to L, it is in equilibrium this entire distance: in this range, the President is first advantaged (until **SQ** reaches P) and then disadvantaged (as **SQ** moves from P toward L). As **SQ** moves leftward past L, the N-set begins to expand upward toward P, and once S reaches the lefthand boundary of $\mathbf{W}_L(\mathbf{P})$, the N-set again includes the entire L-P range (i.e., includes all of $\mathbf{CORE}_{P/L}$). In this final region, neither chief executive is advantaged. Figures 2.17–2.22 similarly graph Cases 3 through 8 involving one and two veto institutions.

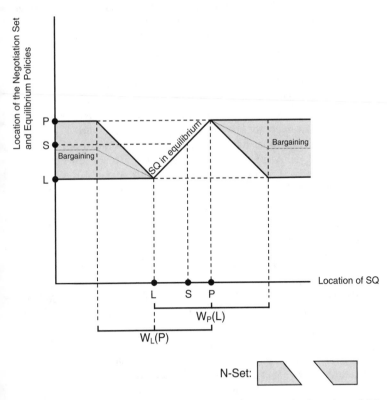

Figure 2.17 How the Location of the N-set Changes as the Location of SQ Changes—Case 3

Inspection of figures 2.15–2.22 reveals that changes in the location of **SQ** have a complex pattern of impacts on outcomes. In particular, it is important to note the following:

Observation 2.3. Holding institutional ideal points constant, as **SQ** moves leftward (or rightward), there is not a monotonic relationship between changes in the location of **SQ** and changes in the location of the *N*-set and other outcomes.

That is, as **SQ** moves leftward, the resulting *N*-sets and equilibrium outcomes (i.e., an **SQ** that cannot be upset) move *both* upward and downward.

If we narrow our perspective and focus just on the relationship between changes in the location of **SQ** and the closeness of the *N*-set or equilibrium outcomes (i.e., an **SQ** that cannot be upset) to the ideal point of any single actor, we similarly note that as **SQ** moves away from any actor's ideal point in either direction, the impact of **SQ**'s changing location on the *N*-set again lacks monotonicity. To show this, let us assume (only for the purposes of this example) that when the *N*-set contains multiple points (i.e., the shaded regions in figures 2.15–2.22), the President and Leader adopt a "split-the-difference" negotiating strategy, thereby selecting a point in the middle of the *N*-set; in figures 2.15–2.22, this particular outcome is shown by the dashed lines that bisect the shaded regions labeled "bargaining."

For example, consider figure 2.15. Begin with an initial **SQ** at *P*, and first move **SQ** rightward from *P*. The resulting outcome (on the vertical axis) declines toward the middle of the *N*-set (due to the split-the-difference assumption) and then remains there. Moving **SQ** leftward from *P*, the outcome (on the vertical axis) declines steadily downward to *L*, and then moves back upward to the middle of the *N*-set and remains there as **SQ** moves indefinitely leftward.

Similarly, in figure 2.16, an **SQ** starting at *P* and moving rightward first produces outcomes that move upward away from *P* toward *S*, then back downward toward *P*, and then farther downward to the middle of the N-set (in the shaded region), and then remaining there as **SQ** moves indefinitely rightward. Starting at *P* but moving leftward, the outcome declines from *P* to *L*, then increases upward to the middle of the *N*-set, where it remains as **SQ** moves leftward indefinitely.

Figures 2.17 and 2.18 show similar patterns (for the remaining cases for one veto institution), as do figures 2.19–2.22 (for the cases with two veto institutions). Figure 2.22 shows the most complex pattern of all: it graphs the **SQ**/*N*-set relationship when there are two veto institutions, each located outside **CORE**$_{P/L}$.

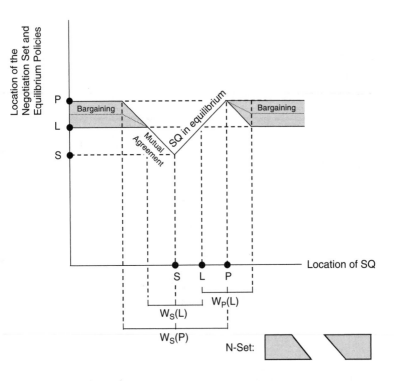

Figure 2.18 How the Location of the N-set Changes as the Location of SQ Changes—Case 4

In fact, this nonmonotonic impact of changes in the location of **SQ** appears whether we focus on the fortunes of either chief executive or on any veto institution. Of course, each institutional actor is guaranteed to do best—see the vertical axis in each diagram—when **SQ** is located at his or her ideal point: since each such actor has a veto over changes in **SQ**, each actor could simply veto any proposals to move **SQ** away from his or her ideal point. But with locations of **SQ** that are farther and farther away from any actor's ideal point, the decrease in utility which that actor suffers (or at least is likely to suffer, given the indeterminacies of bargaining over points in the N-set) is not monotonic: utility will decrease but in some cases it can go back up again as well. We can summarize our overall results here as follows:

Observation 2.4. Holding institutional ideal points constant, there is not a monotonic relationship between changes in the location of **SQ** and how

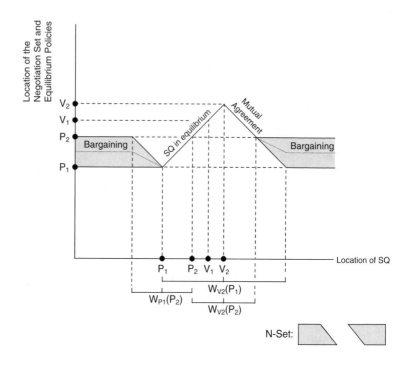

Figure 2.19 How the Location of the N-set Changes as the Location of SQ Changes—Case 5

close the *N*-set outcomes, and any other equilibrium outcomes, are to the ideal point of any one actor.

The Impact of Divided or Unified Government

It is important to note that there are conditions under which adding or subtracting veto institutions—which is equivalent to transitioning from unified to divided government—will have *no* impact on the pattern of outcomes. Consider what happens when we add a veto institution *inside* **CORE**$_{P/L}$: for instance, compare figure 2.15, which has no veto institutions, to figure 2.17, with one "internal" veto institution, and to figure 2.21, with two "internal" veto institutions. This is as if the President went from a unified government (figure 2.15) to a divided government (figure 2.17), but with the Senate now located *between* the President and the foreign Leader,

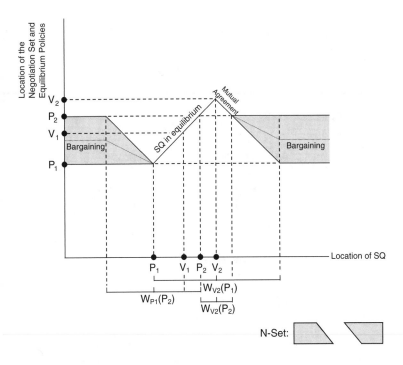

Figure 2.20 How the Location of the N-set Changes as the Location of SQ Changes—Case 6

and then a foreign veto institution is added between the President and Leader (figure 2.21). But note that the possibilities of mutual agreement between the President and leader are not changed. In general, then, adding "internal" veto institutions—inside **CORE**$_{P/L}$—never affects the **SQ**/N-set relationships at all. Hence, we conclude:

Observation 2.5. Adding veto institutions "inside" **CORE**$_{P/L}$ has no impact on outcomes (as defined by the N-sets and by the regions in which **SQ** is in equilibrium).

In contrast, however, adding veto institutions *outside* **CORE**$_{P/L}$ will generally change the relationships between **SQ** and the N-set. For instance, note in figure 2.15 that there are no areas of mutual agreement: either **SQ** is in equilibrium (in the L-P range), so no negotiated agreement is possible at all, or else the N-set contains multiple points over which the two chief executives

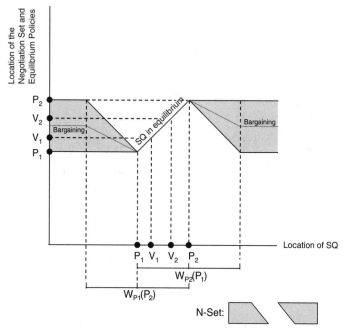

Figure 2.21 How the Location of the N-set Changes as the Location of SQ Changes—Case 7

will disagree. Adding one "external" veto institution outside **CORE**$_{P/L}$ adds a region in which mutual agreement is sometimes possible; see, for example, figure 2.16 on Case 2 and figure 2.18 on Case 4. Adding two "external" veto institutions (see figure 2.19 on Case 5 and figure 2.20 on Case 6) creates an expanded region in which mutual agreement will be reached, given the figure 2.15 baseline. In figure 2.22 (on Case 8), adding the two veto institutions, one on either side of **CORE**$_{P/P}$, adds two separate regions, one on either side of **CORE**$_{P/P}$, in which mutual agreement will be reached. Hence we have:

Observation 2.6. There exist conditions under which adding veto institutions "outside" **CORE**$_{P/L}$ (i.e., to the left and/or to the right of the *L-P* line) creates some possibilities of mutual (nonconflictual) agreement between the President and Leader.

Interpreting this in terms of unified and divided government, it means that some possibilities of mutual (nonconflictual) agreement can be created if

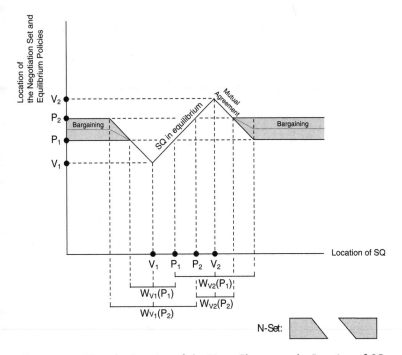

Figure 2.22 How the Location of the N-set Changes as the Location of SQ Changes—Case 8

the government transitions from unified to divided, *as long as the veto institutions move to the "outside" of the L-P contract curve.*

Next, recall that the unified-government hypothesis and Schelling divided-government hypothesis are both claims that adding domestic veto institutions will affect the national Leaders' success in international bargaining. The unified-government hypothesis is that adding a domestic veto institution will weaken a President, while the divided-government hypothesis is that adding a domestic veto institution will strengthen a President. A more refined combination of these two hypotheses might be that adding a domestic veto institution *between* the President and Leader will weaken the President, while adding a domestic veto institution *outside* the President (away from the foreign Leader's position) will help the President. Let us consider these claims in light of our model.

Figure 2.23 presents a series of seven paired examples in which we show what happens when we begin with a case with no veto institutions (so we have just *L* and *P*, i.e., a unified government) in the top diagram, and then

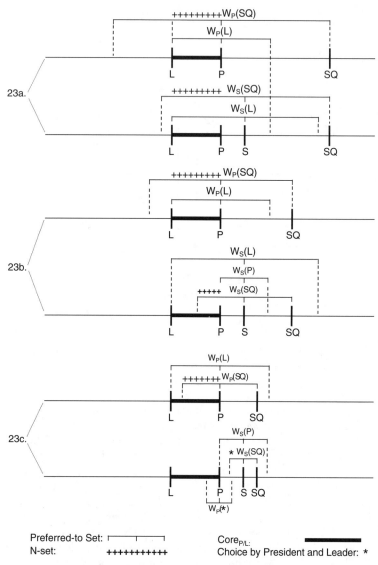

Figure 2.23   Changes in the N-set When S is Added Outside the L-P Line

we add a Senate in the bottom diagram (alternatively, the Senate moves from a location at P to a location to the right of P, thereby creating a divided government). For each pair of examples, we assume a fixed set of locations for the President and Leader; what differs across the pairs of examples

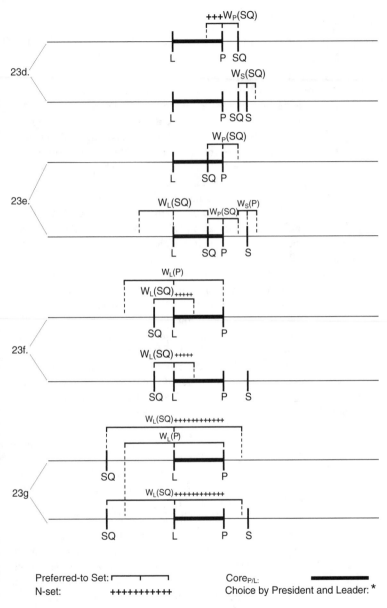

Figure 2.23 Continued

is that we assume a status quo policy at different locations (moving **SQ** from right to left).

We find that there are seven regions characterized by different kinds of outcomes:

- In Figure 2.23a, **SQ** in the top diagram is located outside $\mathbf{W}_P(\mathbf{L})$, so the N-set is the entire L-P line. In the bottom diagram, S is added to the right of the L-P line. But because the same **SQ** from the top diagram is located outside $\mathbf{W}_S(\mathbf{L})$ in the bottom diagram, the N-set is still the entire L-P line. Hence, the N-sets in both the top and bottom diagrams include the entire L-P line (i.e., all of **CORE**$_{P/L}$). As a result, the addition of the Senate—that is, this move from unified to divided government—does not make any difference to either the President or Leader. (Recall that while adding veto institutions *inside* **CORE**$_{P/L}$ does not affect outcomes at all, as noted by Observation 5, figure 2.23a here is an instance in which the veto institution is added *outside* **CORE**$_{P/L}$ and yet the outcome remains unaffected.)

- In figure 2.23b, **SQ** in the top diagram still falls outside $\mathbf{W}_P(\mathbf{L})$, so the N-set is the entire L-P line. In the bottom diagram, however, the same **SQ** falls inside $\mathbf{W}_S(\mathbf{L})$ but outside $\mathbf{W}_S(\mathbf{P})$. Hence, the N-set in the bottom diagram is constrained toward P. This means that, with this **SQ**, the addition of the Senate helps the President and hurts the Leader because less of the resulting N-set is located close to L.

- In figure 2.23c, **SQ** in the top diagram falls inside $\mathbf{W}_P(\mathbf{L})$, so the N-set is the segment of the L-P line inside $\mathbf{W}_P(\mathbf{SQ})$. In the bottom diagram, **SQ** falls to the right of S but inside $\mathbf{W}_S(\mathbf{P})$. Hence, the N-set in the bottom diagram consists of the single point labeled "*" at the lefthand end of the $\mathbf{W}_S(\mathbf{SQ})$ preferred-to set. The Leader is clearly hurt by this change to divided government: the N-set has moved from the entire region between L and P (top diagram) to the single point to the right of P (bottom diagram). However, the impact on the President is indeterminate: on the one hand, the portion of the L-P line that lies to the left of the lefthand boundary of $\mathbf{W}_P(*)$ is no longer feasible (which benefits the President), but the far-righthand segment of that now-infeasible N-set (in particular, the points on the L-P line that are inside $\mathbf{W}_P(*)$) is better for the President than the point at "*." Without knowing precisely what agreement the President and Leader would have reached in the top diagram, it is impossible to judge whether the outcomes in the bottom diagram are better or worse for the President.

- In Figure 2.23d, with **SQ** in the top diagram, the N-set is the portion of the L-P line that lies inside $\mathbf{W}_P(\mathbf{SQ})$. In the bottom diagram (with S added), **SQ** is in equilibrium: the Senate wants to move policy rightward from **SQ** while the President and Leader want to move it leftward. The addition of the Senate thus eliminates the top diagram's N-set from consideration by the President and Leader. Both the President and leader are hurt by the addition of the Senate here (i.e., by the Senate's creation of divided government by its move from P to the location at S in the bottom diagram). The Leader is hurt because the N-set stretching leftward from P (top diagram) is replaced by an equilibrium **SQ** to the right of P (bottom diagram). And the President is hurt because the N-set in the top diagram yields several points that are better for the President than **SQ**, while the bottom diagram contains only **SQ**.

- In figure 2.23e, **SQ** is located between L and P, and so cannot be upset. This means that adding the Senate (i.e., moving the Senate from P to its location at S in the bottom diagram) will make no difference to the President or Leader.
- In figure 2.23f, **SQ** is located to the left of L but within $\mathbf{W}_L(\mathbf{P})$. Since the constraining actor in both the top diagram (without S) and bottom diagram (with $_S$) is the Leader, adding the Senate (i.e., moving the Senate from P to its location at S in the bottom diagram) makes no difference to either the President or Leader.
- In figure 2.23g, in both the top and bottom diagrams **SQ** is located to the left of L and outside the $\mathbf{W}_L(\mathbf{P})$ preferred-to set. Since $\mathbf{W}_L(\mathbf{P})$ contains the entire L-P line ($\mathbf{CORE}_{P/L}$) in either case, adding the Senate makes no difference to either the President or Leader.

Figure 2.24 condenses these various outcomes from Figure 2.23 into one summary diagram. Figure 2.24 indicates that five regions are relevant to the issue of whether the presence of the Senate at the indicated location (i.e., the movement of the Senate from P to the indicated location, as in a change from unified government to some kind of divided government) makes any difference to the President and Leader. For any **SQ** in what we have labeled region I, adding the Senate at the indicated location (moving the Senate to here from P) makes no difference to either the President or the leader. For any **SQ** in region II, adding the Senate at the indicated location helps the President and hurts the Leader. For any **SQ** in region III, adding the Senate at the indicated location has an indeterminate impact on the President but hurts the Leader. For any **SQ** in region IV, adding the Senate at the indicated location hurts both the President and Leader. For any **SQ** in region V, from P leftward indefinitely, adding the Senate at the indicated location makes no difference to the President or the Leader.

Figure 2.25 is the summary diagram of what happens when we begin with no veto institutions and then add (move) two veto institutions, one (S) to the right of the President, P, and one (V) to the left of the Leader, L.[4]

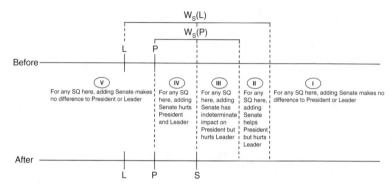

Figure 2.24   Summary of Outcomes When S is Added to the Right of L and P

There are nine significant regions in figure 2.25:

- for any **SQ** in region I, adding S and V makes no difference to either the President or the Leader;
- for any **SQ** in region II, adding S and V helps the President and hurts the Leader;
- for any **SQ** in region III, adding S and V has an indeterminate impact on the President but hurts the Leader;
- for any **SQ** in region IV, adding S and V hurts both the President and the Leader;
- for any **SQ** in region V, adding S and V makes no difference to either the President or the Leader (because **SQ** remains in equilibrium);
- for any **SQ** in region VI, adding S and V hurts both the President and the Leader;
- for any **SQ** in region VII, adding S and V hurts the President and has an indeterminate impact on the Leader;
- for any **SQ** in region VIII, adding S and V hurts the President and helps the Leader; and
- for any **SQ** in region IX, adding S and V makes no difference to the President or the Leader.[5]

In figure 2.26, involving the addition (movement) of a veto institution, V, to the left of the Leader, given the presence of a Senate, S, to the right of the President, P, there are five significant regions:

- for any **SQ** in region I, adding V makes no difference to either the President or the Leader;
- for any **SQ** in region II, adding V hurts both the President and the Leader;

77

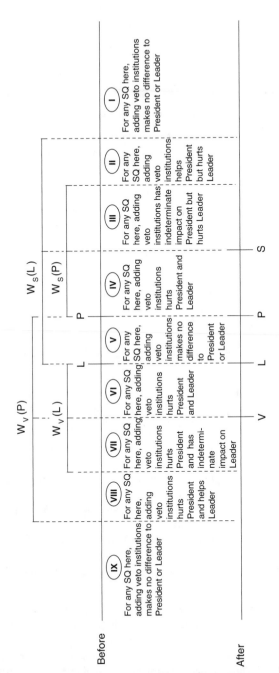

Figure 2.25 Summary of Outcomes When V is Added to the Left of L and S is Added to the Right of P

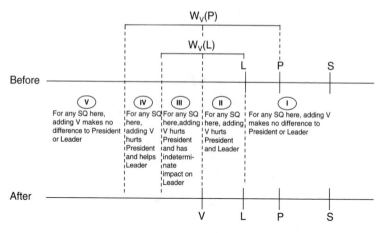

Figure 2.26   Summary of Outcomes When V is Added to the Left of L, P, and S

- for any **SQ** in region III, adding *V* hurts the President and has an indeterminate impact on the Leader;
- for any **SQ** in region IV, adding *V* hurts the President and helps the Leader; and
- for any **SQ** in region V, adding *V* makes no difference to the President or the Leader.

In Figure 2.27, involving the addition (movement) of a Senate, *S*, to the right of the President, *P*, given the presence of a veto institution, *V*, to the left of the Leader, *L*, there are also five significant regions:

- for any **SQ** in region I, adding *S* makes no difference to either the President or the Leader;
- for any **SQ** in region II, adding *S* helps the President and hurts the Leader;
- for any **SQ** in region III, adding *S* has an indeterminate impact on the President but hurts the Leader;
- for any **SQ** in region IV, adding *S* hurts both the President and the Leader;
- for any **SQ** in region V, adding *S* makes no difference to the President or the Leader.

Finally, we note that since adding veto institutions *between* the President and Leader will not change outcomes at all (see figure 2.21), we do not present a diagram of the (non)impact of these additions.

These results should provide a final resolution of the debate over the impact of divided and unified government, and of domestic veto institutions

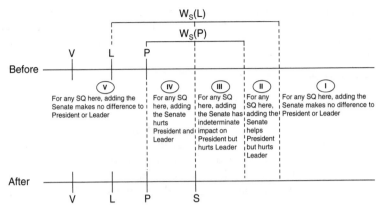

Figure 2.27 Summary of Outcomes When S is Added to the Right of V, L, and P

on international negotiations more generally, given complete information and one issue dimension. In our view, these results demonstrate that neither the national-unity hypothesis nor Schelling's divided-government hypothesis even begins to comprehend the complexity of the outcomes that can emerge. We would summarize these results as follows:

Observation 2.7. Depending on the location of the status quo, creating divided government by adding (or moving) either one or two veto institutions can be expected to yield almost every possible combination of outcomes, including helping the President and hurting the Leader, helping the Leader and hurting the President, hurting both the President and Leader, helping both the President and Leader, helping the President but having an indeterminate impact on the Leader, and helping the Leader but having an indeterminate impact on the President.

Note that we have been discussing the impact of *adding* veto institutions, that is, of transitioning from unified government to divided government. But in fact, the same results hold when moving in the other direction, from divided to unified government:

Observation 2.8. Depending on the location of the status quo, creating unified government by subtracting (or moving) either one or two veto institutions can be expected to have almost every possible combination of outcomes, including helping the President and hurting the Leader, helping the Leader and hurting the President, hurting both the President and Leader, helping both the President and Leader, helping the President but having an indeterminate impact on the Leader, and helping the Leader but having an indeterminate impact on the President.

In general, it appears that adding or subtracting veto institutions never has an indeterminate impact on *both* the President and Leader. That is, this indeterminate impact on both the President and Leader seems to be the only impact that does *not* occur.

The Impact of Changing Institutional Ideal Points

Thus far, we have considered what happens when the location of the status quo changes and what happens when we add or subtract veto institutions—that is, a move from unified to divided government, or vice versa—at varying locations inside and outside **CORE**$_{P/L}$. Next we consider the following question: what happens when we change the location of the ideal points of the various institutional actors?

Figures 2.15–2.22 can be used to address this question as well, and they provide a simple answer:

Observation 2.9. Changes in locations of particular institutional ideal points do not change the *qualitative* patterns in the outcomes, as long as the overall left-right *order* of institutional ideal points is retained.

This means, for example, that as long as Case 2 retains the overall *L-P-S* ordering (for figure 2.16), Case 3 retains the overall *L-P-S* ordering (for figure 2.17), and so forth, the overall appearance of each diagram will not change. Some parts of each diagram may get "stretched" and other parts may get "squeezed" or "condensed" as the institutional ideal points change, but the diagram will have the same basic elements. That is, each diagram will have some combination of a region in which **SQ** is in equilibrium, a region in which the chief executives will have to engage in some negotiation to select an outcome (and perhaps a region in which mutual agreement is possible), and the sizes of these regions will get bigger or smaller as ideal points change, but the basic structure of each diagram will stay the same. [6]

The Irrelevance of Which Veto Institution Is Attached to Which Chief Executive

Our final observation is one that is suggested by the manner in which we handled the original cases (Cases 5 through 8) involving two veto institutions. We argued that nothing was lost by erasing the distinctions between chief executives as well as the distinctions between veto institutions. Instead of having to analyze 24 different orderings, only four orderings needed to be examined.

However, this does lead to an interesting—and, in some ways, unexpected—result that bears some emphasis. The key point is that, within the confines of our model, *it does not matter which nation's veto institution is located where*, in the particular sense that reversing the labels of the two veto institutions does not affect outcomes at all. For example, if it is the Senate that is located to the U.S. President's right and the foreign veto institution that is located to the Leader's left, our general results and observations would not change at all if it were the foreign veto institution that is located to the President's right and the Senate that is located to the Leader's left. Both the foreign veto institution and the Senate have veto powers, and both must approve treaties, so which veto institution is located where is irrelevant (as long as the required margin of approval—as with the two-thirds margin for the U.S. Senate—is the same in both veto institutions). The same holds for the interchangeability of the chief executives' ideal points: the general pattern of outcomes remains the same. Hence we have:

Observation 2.10.   The ideal points of each country's chief executives are interchangeable, as are the ideal points of each country's veto institutions: as long as the required margin of approval is the same in the two veto institutions, such switches will have no impact on the equilibrium conditions for **SQ**, or on the size or location of the *N*-set.

Conclusion

The unified-government hypothesis and Schelling's divided-government hypothesis are both correct, under some conditions, but both are incorrect under many other conditions. As far as we can determine, no one (certainly including ourselves) foresaw the wide variety of outcomes that should be expected from the addition of one or two veto institutions (i.e., of changing from unified to divided government). Nor did anyone foresee the alternating mixture of outcomes that result as the status quo moves across the issue dimension: the unified-government hypothesis holds for a couple of *disconnected* regions, as does the divided-government hypothesis. Nor did anyone foresee the possibility that the addition of domestic veto institutions (i.e., changing from unified to divided government) would sometimes *help both chief executives* and would sometimes *hurt both chief executives*. As it turns out, there is not one simple generalization that can be made about the impact of domestic veto institutions, or of divided or unified government, on a chief executive. Instead, a remarkably wide range of impacts can be expected, and the impacts are all critically mediated by the location of the status quo policy (or the current state of affairs) relative to the locations of the ideal points of the chief executives and the veto institutions.

In our view, these results have some rather significant implications for those scholars who are attempting to determine *empirically* what impact, if any, domestic veto institutions and divided government actually have on international negotiations. Our results demonstrate that—to exaggerate only slightly—almost anything can happen, even in just one dimension. Thus, if an empirical study discovers that domestic veto institutions and divided government have had some particular kind of impact on, say, international trade negotiations, this is only to be expected: since we have demonstrated that a very wide range of things can be expected to happen, an empirical demonstration that one of these things has actually happened cannot be judged to be much of an advance in our knowledge.

It follows that if we wish to determine whether domestic veto institutions and divided government are actually having the impact that they should be predicted to have, empirical studies will have to take into account two key sets of variables. First, we have demonstrated that different orderings of the main actors' ideal points can affect whether or not the status quo policy is in equilibrium, and if the status quo policy is not in equilibrium, what set of policies the President and Leader might consider in trying to replace the status quo. This suggests that, in conducting a statistical study that tests whether domestic veto institutions and divided government actually have an impact on outcomes, the analyst should use a control for the preference orderings that are empirically observed; the reason is that our model's predictions about whether the Senate or foreign veto institution will influence outcomes critically depends on these orderings. Failure to control for these orderings may lead to meaningless results.

Second, we have demonstrated that the location of the status quo policy (or current state of affairs) also plays a crucial role in affecting outcomes. This means that, in statistically testing whether the presence of a domestic veto institution such as the Senate has an impact on outcomes, the analyst should also control for the location of the status quo. Failure to do so may also lead to meaningless results.

In sum, while our analysis here has been entirely theoretical, it may be our model's potential role in improving the quality of empirical studies that it will find its greatest usefulness.

Chapter 3

Do Democracies Trade More Freely?

B. Peter Rosendorff

Do democracies trade more freely? If so, what are the characteristics of the democratic polity that are relevant to trade policy? This chapter surveys the empirical evidence to address the first question, and presents a simple model of trade and politics to address the second.

Democracies are, in general, characterized by divided polities. Two specific forms of this divided polity—separation of powers across decision makers and electoral accountability of leaders—are key to the trade-liberalizing tendencies of these regimes. The presence of a divided polity alters the reversion points—which in turn shifts the agendas for trade liberalization. The effect is to make democracies both more willing to cooperate in Preferential Trading Agreement (PTA) formation, to liberalize unilaterally, as well as better able to extract concessions from nondemocracies. Divided polities affect both unilateral and bilateral strategies and outcomes in the trade liberalizing arena.

Within economics, the political origins of trade barriers have been thoroughly investigated. The approach usually follows a similar pattern: take a simplified Heckscher-Ohlin or Ricardo-Viner specific factors model to describe the economic environment, and overlay some political structure to explore the formation of barriers to free trade: direct democracy by Mayer (1984), political support from competing groups as in Hillman (1982) or Grossman and Helpman (1994), lobbying by Bhagwati (1982), Findlay and Wellisz (1982), Magee Brock and Young (1989). In so doing, the economic approach has been to focus on the pressures brought to bear on vote- or support-maximizing politicians to supply policy. Hence the political economy of trade literature focuses on the choice over the level of tariff (and occasionally on the choice of instrument) based on underlying redistributional incentives of policymakers or on the ability of interest groups to influence the policymakers.

These modifications of the policymakers' objective function (policymakers are modelled as politically responsive) and the trade barrier formation processes modelled in this literature are at best "reduced forms" of the political process. Institutional features of the polity are usually missing, and certainly cross-country variations in these institutions have not been considered. Rodrik (1995) observes the paucity of work on the cross-country variation in the levels of protection, and identifies that institutions matter in this context (1484).

Scholars in international relations and comparative politics have, on the other hand, stressed the notion that international arrangements (regarding collective security, for example) operate within a system that is both anarchic (in the sense of no authority to enforce contracts), and characterized by a complex system of self-enforcing agreements that limit unilateral improvements in domestic conditions or a state's power at the expense of another's. This system, itself the outcome of bargaining and negotiation between countries, relies on the willingness of states to "cooperate" with each other. These scholars have noted the willingness of democracies to cooperate along a variety of dimensions: they fight fewer wars with each other, or with autocracies than do autocracies with each other (Russett 1993), or to recognize and enforce one another's laws[1]. Explanations have hinged on institutional features (Bueno de Mesquita et al. 1999), such as electoral competition.

Here we investigate whether the regime type of a state operating in an anarchic global trading environment affects its willingness to abstain from beggar-thy-neighbor (or rent-shifting) policies that improve domestic conditions at the expense of its trading partners. If democracies fight fewer wars with each other, do they fight fewer trade wars with each other? The evidence suggests that the institutions of democracy work to enhance cooperation over trade policies.

This chapter presents a single, coherent model structure that explores these questions and then summarizes some of the recent empirical results. Where democracies are characterized by divided polities, the central conclusions of this chapter are that democracies

1. have a greater tendency to *unilateral* liberalization;
2. are more cooperative with respect to their willingness to join tariff-reducing PTAs, and

3. are better able to extract concessions (in the form of reduced tariffs) from their trading partners than are non-democracies.

Legislatures and Elections

Two characteristics of the structure of democratic states are examined here: the responsiveness of the policymakers to the interests of the broad electorate (the role of elections and consent), and the role of domestic legislatures in democracies (the effect of divided government or separation of powers). Both institutions (elections and separated authority) can be viewed as characteristic of a "divided polity."

Following Pahre (this volume, chapter 1), we define a divided polity as the institutional structure in which there are two or more actors whose choices affect the outcome of the policy game. This is a characteristic of the "rules of the game"—the structure of the polity—and is not a consequence of the preferences of the actors.[2] This definition of "divided polity" is very broad. It captures the direct effect of two branches of government (an executive and a legislature) that must agree on policy before it is implemented, as in the ratification games of this volume (Pahre, this volume chapter 4), and elsewhere (e.g., Iida 1993; Mansfield et al. 2000; Martin 2000; Milner and Rosendorff 1996, 1997; Mo 1995; Pahre 1997). It also captures the indirect effect—where a policymaker attempts to balance the conflicting claims of competing constituents in order to maximize the probability of reelection (or political support, more generally). For instance, the executive tries to address the protectionist desires of special interests and those of the societal in the aggregate, for whom less protection or even free trade may be preferred. At election time, voters choose whether or not to vote for the incumbent and lobbying interests choose whether or not to contribute to the campaign funds of the incumbent or an opponent. These decisions will undoubtedly affect the policy chosen by the incumbent, and hence the outcome of the policy game.

In a broader sense, both elections and divided authority are institutional mechanisms to induce governments to behave in a "representative manner." Persson, Roland, and Tabellini (1997) show that separation of powers (when appropriately designed) induces the revelation of the information necessary for voters to make informed decisions. If voters behave retrospectively, government behavior is constrained to be more representative. Ferejohn (1986) shows that elections can act to limit the extractive behavior of executives in the presence of moral hazard. Milner and Kubota (2005) share our interest in the effect of political institutions on trade policy. They suggest that with democracy comes an expansion of the support base for a policymaker (the "winning coalition" "selectorate," following Bueno de Mesquita 1999, increases in size). A tariff raises the price, lowering the support consumers might have for the policymaker. A policymaker can maintain consumer support by providing a transfer to those consumers who are members of the winning coalition. As the selectorate (and the winning coalition) increases in size, more transfers are required that become too expensive; alternatively, the policymaker can lower the tariff, effectively improving the welfare of consumers at large. As the selectorate gets large, the optimal policy switches from a tariff to freer trade. While Kubota and Milner focus on the extension of the franchise, the institutions of interest here are legislatures (and the separation of powers) and elections (the accountability of the executive), both of which are characteristic of democracies.

Democracy and Divided Polity

A state is identified as "democratic" if elections act to keep leaders to some degree accountable to the voters at large. The absence of regular, free, and fair elections identifies a state as nondemocratic (Mansfield et al. 2002; Powell 2000; Schumpeter [1942] 1976). But to win elections, politicians must satisfy competing interests. The voters at large, responding to the income effects of protection, may prefer zero or moderate tariffs, while import competing firms are likely to demand high levels of protection; export interests lobby for zero tariffs or even subsidies for exports. A vote-maximizing policymaker must balance these demands, and will do so at the margin. We permit the degree of democracy to be proxied by the degree to which the preferences of the voters at large are represented in the policymaking process of the executive.

The first claim is that *when the voters' control over political leaders via competitive elections increases, the willingness to liberalize increases and the desire to protect special interests at the expense of the broad electorate reduces.*

The view that elections keep incumbents accountable is deeply ingrained in democratic culture (Manin, Przeworski, and Stokes 1999). An election can sanction a poorly behaved incumbent with eviction from office. The prospect of not being reelected leads incumbents to shirk less in representing the electorate (the retrospective voting approach (Barro 1973; Ferejohn 1986)). Second, we show that *as the voters' electoral control rises, the willingness of the executive to cooperate rises.* Democracies are more likely to strike trade barrier reducing agreements.

The third claim concerns the nature of the international bargain. Electoral accountability increases the bargaining power of the international negotiator. If international negotiators choose a tariff pair that is Pareto efficient, *a more democratic state extracts more concessions from (and offers fewer concessions to)* its trading partners in international trade negotiations.

A country will also be identified as (more) democratic when there is divided authority over policymaking. The presence of multiple veto players in the policymaking process is not in itself a measure of democracy (Tsebelis 2002), but the presence of a domestic legislature that must ratify/enact/implement a trade policy reflects a polity that is more democratic than one that invests almost complete authority in a chief executive.

The fourth claim is that *if a country is endowed with a more protectionist legislature, the bargaining powers of the international trade negotiators will increase at the international bargaining table.* The negotiators will, under democracy, extract greater concessions from other countries than under alternative regime specifications.

In the electoral case, we defined two groups (voters and special interests) who differ largely in their preferences over outcomes. Similarly, in the separation of powers case, the executive and the legislature are likely to have differing preferences. Clearly, preferences matter—but preferences alone do not determine outcomes. The desires of constituents affect policymaking, but the nature of the effect of preferences depends on the institutions through which these preferences are expressed. Institutions mediate conflicting desires, and differing institutions will generate differences in outcomes even under the same preference orderings. In what follows we specify a rather straightforward preference ordering, and investigate solely the impact of changes in the institutional details on trade policy outcomes.

The Underlying Economy

Trade policy is fundamentally redistributive—tariffs raise some relative prices and hence raise some incomes relative to others. Different groups experience trade policy differently, and these differences lead to differences in preferences over policy. In what follows we present the bare essentials of a three good, two country world economy—in order to derive the effects of trade policy on economic actors' well-being and hence their interest in proposing or opposing a tariff. In the next section we bring in the institutional structure in order to understand how these groups with divergent preferences interact to generate a trade policy outcome.

Consider two countries that are identical, except for their regime type and their endowments. Each country produces and consumes three goods labelled x and m and z. On the demand side, utility is assumed to be additively separable, $U(x, m) = u(x) + u(m) + z$, where z is the numeraire good, and the units are chosen such that the price of a unit of z is 1. On the supply side, home's endowment of x is given as $\beta > \frac{1}{2}$, while foreign's endowment of x is $1 - \beta$. World output is therefore fixed at unity. Similarly, home's endowment of m is $1 - \beta$ while foreign's endowment is β. Since preferences are identical, home will export good x and will import good m.

Home can apply the specific tariff t on the imports of good m. If the price abroad of good m is p_m, then the local price is $p_m + t$, in which t is home's (nonprohibitive) tariff. Similarly, if the price of x at home is p_x, then the price of x abroad is $p_x + \tau$ where τ is the (nonprohibitive) tariff applied by foreign.

Utility maximization and market clearing yields equilibrium prices, consumption, imports, and exports. See the appendix for details. Social welfare is expressed as the sum of consumer surplus, profits (of the export and import-competing firms) and tariff revenue: $W(t, \tau) = C(x(\tau), m(t)) + \Pi^x(\tau) + \Pi^m(t) + T(t)$. Similarly, for foreign, $W^*(t, \tau) = C^*(x(\tau), m(t)) + \Pi^{x*}(\tau) + \Pi^{m*}(t) + T^*(\tau)$.

The Welfare Optimizing Tariff

Assume for now that each government has only social welfare in mind (this assumption will be relaxed in the next section). The governments choose their tariffs simultaneously, and we investigate the Nash equilibrium in tariff levels. The separability of the payoffs leads to a reaction function for each player that is independent of the other player's tariffs—the Nash equilibrium is one of dominant strategies. Home government solves for arg max$_t W(t, \tau)$ that we label t^W; similarly, foreign solves for arg max$_\tau W^*(t, \tau)$ that we label τ^{W*}. It is well established that the optimal tariffs are positive as a small tariff generates a reduction in consumer surplus that is more than compensated for by an improvement in the terms of trade. This is the Johnsonian beggar-thy-neighbor tariff: in a two country world, both countries are "large," and implement the optimal tariff. By symmetry, $t^W = \tau^{W*}$. Notice too that home has a preferred foreign tariff τ^W: $W_\tau < 0$; this implies that home's (and foreign's) preferred foreign (home) tariff is $\tau^W = 0 (= t^{W*})$.

Representation

Any policymaker (in any regime) is assumed to experience benefits from two sources: in addition to the benefit associated with increasing social welfare, governments obtain a fraction of the rents that accrue to the import-competing sector (Bhagwati's (1998) "takings," government's "grasping hand" of Olsen (1993)). These rents could take the form of political contributions to the government (as in democracies in which lobbies organize and collectively contribute to a political candidate's electoral campaign fund) or they can take the form of extraction or appropriation as might be the case in an autocratic society in which individual property rights are not perfectly secure. This political support function is therefore rising both in the profits of the firms and in social welfare.

$$G(t, \tau, \Psi) = c\Pi^m(t) + \Psi W(t, \tau)$$

in which c is a positive and exogenous constant, $c \in (0, 1)$ and $\Psi > 0$ measures the responsiveness of the representative to the concerns of the voters at large.[3] Variation across representatives and regimes will be captured by Ψ, an institutional parameter that measures the importance to the policymaker of the interests of the broad society. The larger is Ψ, the more responsive is the policymaker to the interests of the electorate at large and the better is the "quality of democracy" (Bhagwati 1998). The smaller is Ψ, the more the policymaker is captured by the special interests represented by the firms, and the less representative of broad societal interests the policymaker is.

We will denote foreign's regime type as Ψ^*, and foreign's policymaker maximizes

$$G^*(t, \tau, \Psi^*) = c\Pi^{x*}(\tau) + \Psi^* W^*(t, \tau)$$

Once again, the two governments set their tariff policies simultaneously, and the Nash equilibrium in tariffs are dominant strategies. Each policymaker of type Ψ (at home) solves for arg max$_t$ $G(t, \tau, \Psi)$. Similarly in foreign and the pair of Nash strategies are functions of each country's regime type: $(t^G(\Psi), \tau^G(\Psi^*))$.

Notice that $t^G(\Psi) > t^W$; when the interests of the protectionist sector are taken into account by the policymaker—for electoral reasons—the tariff is larger than the purely social welfare maximizing tariff.

Democracy and Liberalization

Our first result establishes that any representative that is more responsive to the interests of the electorate at large will adopt a lower domestic tariff unilaterally. Since the optimal strategy is a dominant strategy, the policymaker will always adopt a lower tariff as s/he becomes more responsive to social welfare relative to the special interests of the import-competing sector.

Proposition 1 $\quad \dfrac{\partial t^G}{\partial \Psi} < 0 \ and \ \dfrac{\partial t^G}{\partial c} > 0.$

The proofs are in the appendix. This implies that the more responsive a policymaker is to broader societal concerns, the lower is the noncooperative Nash tariff. Democracy provides an incentive to unilaterally liberalize.[4]

Trade policy however is the outcome of negotiations between countries. Our interest is the effect of regime type on the prospects for international cooperation; in particular, when will the politically motivated policymakers agree to forgo beggar-thy-neighbor tariffs and cooperate within a liberalized trading regime?

Elections and Cooperation

Does the policymaker have more or less to gain from cooperating at free trade as his/her responsiveness to the electorate rises? Consider the tariff game played an infinite number of times, and let us examine the properties of a cooperative equilibrium, in which cooperation is supported by the threat of an infinite reversion to the Nash equilibrium—the grim trigger punishment.

There are two important components to a cooperative solution. What are the gains from cooperation? And, can cooperation be sustained? Fearon (1998) addresses this issue of bargaining and enforcement, and suggests that sometimes they are at odds: the stronger are the enforcement provisions of any agreement, the tougher will be the bargaining to get to an agreement in the first place, given that the players will have to stick to it for a long time. Alternatively, the looser is the enforcement criterion, the more willing players may be to reach an agreement sooner.

Consider the prisoners' dilemma structure outlined in the game with a single policymaker in each country. The noncooperative tariff is t^G, and define some cooperative tariff $t^C < t^G(\Psi)$ and $\tau^C < \tau^G(\Psi^*)$ for all (Ψ, Ψ^*). The optimal defection here is also t^G (this follows from the separability of utility/ the equilibrium in dominant strategies). Consider the equilibrium in which countries cooperate unless or until a defection is observed, in which case the grim trigger is pulled. The first result is that the gains from cooperation rise with the level of democracy at home. The intertemporal gains from cooperation are

$$g_C (\Psi,\Psi^*) = \frac{1}{1-\delta}\left[G\left(t^C,\tau^C,\Psi\right) - G(t^G(\Psi),\tau^G(\Psi^*),\Psi)\right]$$

in which δ is the discount rate.

Proposition 2   As a country becomes more democratic, ceteris paribus, its gains from cooperation increase. That is $(\frac{\partial}{\partial \Psi})g_C(\Psi,\Psi^*)>0$.

The proof is in the appendix; the intuition here is straightforward. As home becomes more democratic, the policymaker has more to gain from enhancing social welfare. Social welfare is always enhanced by cooperation, and hence the policymaker does relatively better (at the margin).

What about the incentive to defect? The gains from defection are $g_D(\Psi) = G\left(t^G(\Psi), \tau^C,\Psi\right) - G\left(t^C, \tau^C, \Psi\right)$. Define $g\left(\Psi, \Psi^*\right) = g_C\left(\Psi, \Psi^*\right) - g_D(\Psi)$, the difference between sticking to the cooperative regime and defecting once, and being punished thereafter.

Proposition 3   For any pair of cooperative tariffs, the difference between the gains (for the home executive) from cooperating and the gains from defecting grow with the degree of democracy at home; that is, $(\frac{\partial}{\partial \Psi})g(\Psi,\Psi^*)>0$.

As the measure of democracy rises—in this instance, accountability to the will of the society at large—governments have more to gain from acceding to free trade agreements. There is an increased, unilateral willingness to be more cooperative in the international environment.[5]

We have focussed here on the accountability of the executive to the will of the electorate at large, and found a unilateral incentive to liberalize and a more accommodating position in the international negotiating environment.

Electoral Accountability and the Nature of the Agreement

Consider now how the cooperative tariff pair (t^C, τ^C) might be found. Any number of bargaining structures can be considered. Our only restriction here will be that the pair chosen must be *efficient* in the sense that the pair maximizes joint political support. That is, we now require that $(t^C, \tau^C) =$ arg max $G(t, \tau, \Psi) + G^*(t, \tau, \Psi^*)$. Notice that efficiency here is measured not in terms of social welfare, but rather is determined by a pair of tariffs that maximize the sum of both governments' political support.

Separability of the political support functions yields $t^C(\Psi, \Psi^*)$ and τ^C (Ψ, Ψ^*). Clearly $t^C(\Psi, \Psi^*) < t^G(\Psi)$ and $\tau^C(\Psi, \Psi^*) < \tau^G(\Psi^*)$; joint maximization requires that each country adopt a lower tariff than they would under the Nash, noncooperative environment.

How does increased electoral accountability affect the efficient tariff pair? Does more democracy at home increase or decrease the country's bargaining power when negotiations begin? The next proposition establishes that as a country becomes more democratic, it can extract greater concessions from its trading partners, in the form of lower tariffs abroad. Further, depending on parameter values (in particular, the slope of the demand functions), the home tariff could rise or fall as home becomes more democratic. That is, the home tariff could rise, and the foreign tariff always falls as home becomes more democratic—a more democratic state may be able to offer fewer concessions in addition to being able to extract greater concessions from its trading partners. In a sense, the "bargaining power" shifts in favor of the democratic state.

Proposition 4   As a country becomes more democratic, its partner's efficient tariff falls, that is, $(\frac{\partial}{\partial \Psi})\tau^C(\Psi, \Psi^*) < 0$. *Moreover, if* $p_m' > \pi$, *then a country's own efficient tariff rises as it becomes more democratic, that is,* $(\frac{\partial}{\partial \Psi})t^C(\Psi, \Psi^*) > 0$.

As the electorate becomes stronger in having social welfare reflected in the government's objective function, they demand more access to foreign markets—hence the fall in the foreign tariff. Domestically, if the efficient tariff drives the domestic tariff below the social welfare maximizing level, increased voice of the electorate will force the efficient tariff up, raising the domestic tariff. If, on the other hand, the efficient tariff is higher than the social welfare maximizing level, increased electoral accountability will force it downward.

In summary, increased electoral accountability at home increases its bargaining power with respect to the level of the foreign tariff—it will fall. Further under appropriate conditions, the domestic tariff may rise with increased democracy. Freedom at home can pry open markets abroad.

Do we find a similar sort of result when we shift our attention from the role of elections in a democracy to the effect of separating powers over policy to multiple branches of government? We find that democracies are more willing to provide concessions to other democracies when bargaining over mutual tariff reductions. This is the focus of the next section.

Institutions: Separation of Powers

An important aspect of democracy is the division of authority (or authority is jointly held) across branches of government. In the trade policy realm, the legislature usually delegates authority to the executive (a prime minister or president) to negotiate with other states over trade issues. This of course gives the executive some authority or discretion to negotiate over trade policy at the international bargaining table. Two possible roles for the legislature emerge. A legislature may be required to *ratify* any proposal before it can be implemented. Such a ratification process is characteristic of democracies (Mansfield et al. 2000; Milner 1997; Milner and Rosendorff 1997) and occurs in both presidential and parliamentary systems. Ratification is often prior to the negotiation of the agreement in parliamentary systems—the prime minister may have to cobble together an acceptable policy with the legislative majority before taking office, and any incentive to defect from such an agreement is circumscribed by the parliament's ability to pass a no-confidence motion in the government. In other instances, a trade agreement may require implementing legislation before it can be adopted; in others, a referendum or plebiscite may be necessary. In presidential systems, formal ratification procedures are required. Such a structure balances authority across institutions of government, and has an effect on the degree of liberalization that is feasible (see Pahre 1997 as an example).

The second role for the legislature is that it takes responsibility for implementation of trade policy when international negotiations have *broken down*. In the United States, the legislature is ultimately responsible for international agreements under the Constitution; in parliamentary systems, an act of parliament can determine the level of trade barriers if necessary. The effects of varying this assumption, and investing authority over the outcome when negotiations break down (sometimes called the "status quo" outcome) in a variety of agents, is studied in chapter 4 of this volume (Pahre, chapter 4). In this chapter we focus on the effect of ultimate responsibility lying with a relatively protectionist legislature.

We establish in this section that democracies offer fewer concessions and can extract greater concessions than can autocracies when bargaining over trade barriers. That is, democracies can force lower tariffs abroad than can autocracies in the same negotiations; furthermore, democracies lower their tariffs less than do autocracies in the same negotiations.

For the purposes of our model, consider now a second player in any democracy, which we call the legislature, L, in addition to the executive, labelled E. We assume, following Rogowski (1987) that since members of the legislature represent smaller constituencies than the executive (who is responsive to a national constituency), it is easier for special interests to influence preferences of their representatives. Representatives from smaller districts are unable to be insulated from the protectionist interests of groups well represented in their districts. The effect is that for members of the legislature generally, and for the median member particularly, $\Psi^E > \Psi^L$. The effect of this assumption is to make the legislature more protectionist than the executive.

For the purposes of the analysis, countries are symmetric, with $\Psi^A = \Psi^{A^*}$.

In an autocracy, there is no division of power. We do make a restriction about the nature of representation under autocracy: autocrats do not usually weigh the interests of social welfare very highly—they are not very responsive to the interests of the average member of society since they are not reined in by elections or any other form of citizen control.[6] To bias the model against our intended result (that democrats concede more when negotiating with other democrats), we prove the most difficult case in which autocrats have preferences that are just as liberal as democratic executives. This way, the political institutions are shown to affect policies, and that the results are not driven by preferences. That is, we examine the case in which $\Psi^E = \Psi^{A^*}$

We adopt a bargaining approach. Consider first the two autocrats. The pair of autocratic executives A and A^* must bargain to an agreement. Should A and A^* fail to agree, the Nash equilibrium pair of tariffs to the noncooperative tariff setting game played by the two autocrats is implemented. That is, failure by the executives to negotiate successfully leads to the pair (t^A, τ^{A^*}) being implemented, yielding threat point payoffs of

$$g^{AA^*} = (G^A(t^G(\Psi^A), \tau^G(\Psi^{A^*}), \Psi^A), G^{A^*}(t^G(\Psi^A), \tau^G(\Psi^{A^*}), \Psi^{A^*})).$$

We are faced with a standard bargaining problem. Given the symmetry of the two countries, we apply the egalitarian solution (Mas-Colell et al. 1995: 841), and require that the gains from cooperation be split equally among the agents[7]. In figure 3.1, in which the utility possibility frontier is indicated, the bargaining solution lies on the 45° line at AA^*.

Consider now a mixed pair (one autocrat, abroad, and one democrat, at home). Both are aware that any failure to successfully negotiate a deal will mean that the democratic legislature and the autocrat set tariffs

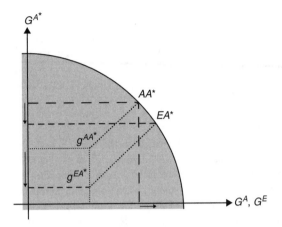

Figure 3.1   The Autocratic Pair and the Mixed Pair

noncooperatively. If negotiations breakdown, the foreign negotiator A^* will implement its dominant strategy τ^{A^*}, in the noncooperative game, while the home legislature behaves similarly, and adopts t^L. The international negotiators negotiate to an agreement; with respect to their domestic polities, the international negotiators are the agenda-setters—they set the cooperative tariffs. The legislature can reject the agreement and implement its best, noncooperative domestic tariff—the legislature controls the reversion point. The threat point payoffs then would be $g^{EA^*} = (G^E(t^G(\Psi^L), \tau^G(\Psi^{A^*}), \Psi^E), G^{A^*}(t^G(\Psi^L), \tau^G(\Psi^{A^*}), \Psi^{A^*}))$.

Our strategy here is to compare the location of g^{EA^*} and g^{AA^*} in payoff space. Suppose we start from the situation in which $\Psi^L = \Psi^E$, that is the legislature and the executive share the same weight on social welfare. Then we will let Ψ^L fall incrementally (i.e., the legislature becomes more protectionist relative to the executive).

Consider the payoff to the foreign autocrat, $G^{A^*}(t^L, \tau^{A^*}, \Psi^{A^*})$; as the foreign legislature begins to separate from the executive, the home breakdown tariff begins to rise. Higher (home) tariffs means that foreign's welfare unambiguously falls—foreign's exports start to shrink, reducing foreign's welfare. So g^{EA^*} must lie south of g^{AA^*}.

At home, the executive has now ceded control to the legislature if negotiations break down. But the tariff that the legislature would set if negotiations were to break down would be exactly the same as that the executive would set because $\Psi^L = \Psi^E$. That is, $t^G(\Psi^L) = t^G(\Psi^E)$. Hence the home executive, at the margin, sees no reduction in its welfare. Putting these two effects together, we see that g^{EA^*} lies directly below g^{AA^*}, as indicated in figure 3.1.

Let us now compare the two cases. Notice in figure 3.1 that, relative to the jointly autocratic case (at AA^*), the payoff to the democratic state (at EA^*) is higher and the payoff to the foreign state is lower. Either the democracy's tariffs have risen, the autocrat's have fallen, or both. In either case, we can describe the democracy as becoming less willing to offer concessions during bargaining, and more able to extract greater concessions out of its (nondemocratic) bargaining partners.

The result here is consistent with a conjecture of Schelling's: a hard-line legislature can be used by the executive branch to extract an international agreement more in the home executive's interest[8] (Schelling 1960: 28–29). The foreign autocrat, in comparison, has no hard-line legislature to point to in order to extract more concessions. The paradoxical effect of bringing a protectionist legislature into the analysis is to extract greater concessions (perhaps via lower tariffs) abroad, and to offer fewer concessions (and obtain high tariffs) at home.

Summarizing the finding of this section, we have

Proposition 5   A democracy (relative to an autocracy) offers fewer concessions to and extracts greater concessions from an autocracy in trade barrier negotiations.

Stylized facts / Empirical Evidence

In the previous sections the more democratic is the polity, the better is that state in extracting concessions in trade barrier negotiations. Democracies were shown to be more likely to unilaterally liberalize and were more cooperative internationally. The institutional features of interest were the presence of a protectionist legislature and the accountability of the executive to the electorate. Clearly, the institutional structure of government decision making has an influence over the trade barrier levels chosen, and the willingness to engage in cooperative trade policy.

In this section I report some empirical results drawn from Bliss and Russett (1998), Mansfield et al. (2000, 2002), and Remmer (1998), with the purpose of providing some evidence in support of the hypotheses ventured earlier.

The general empirical approach is to investigate the role of regime type after the standard explanatory variables for the volume of trade are controlled for. In this approach, a standard gravity model of trade is adopted to capture the effects of the "economic" variables. GDPs, populations, and distance are usually included in the regressions: higher GDPs, smaller populations, and smaller distances are all expected to lead to higher trade volumes.[9] Crucial to these analyses is that an appropriate measure of regime is used. In particular, it is crucial that the measures used capture to some degree at least the role of elections and separation of powers. The Polity III data do a relatively good job.

Polity III

The Polity III dataset of Jaggers and Gurr (1995) on regime type combines data on five dimensions that address the institutional differences between democracies and autocracies. These five categories can be divided into two sets, one highlighting accountability to the electorate, and the other, institutions:

1. Accountability to the Electorate: Consent
   • the competitiveness of the process for selecting a country's chief executive
   • the openness of the process
   • the competitiveness of political participation within a country
2. Institutions and Restraint
   • the extent to which institutional constraints limit the chief executive's decision-making authority
   • the degree to which binding rules govern participation in the political process.

Jaggers and Gurr score each country–year pair along each of these dimensions, and generate two aggregate scores—one estimates the level of democracy, the other, autocracy, each on a 0–10 point scale. Usually the difference between the democratic score and the autocratic score is taken to establish a continuous regime score on a 21 point scale, running from −10 to 10. While it is clear that these measures do capture, to some degree, the institutional features of interest, they are far from being a complete measure of the complex condition known as "democracy." For instance, they omit the "freedoms" we usually associate with democracy—press, association, speech etc. They also omit what might be a crucial determinant of commercial relations, the role of the rule of law, independent judiciary, protection of private property, freedom from arbitrary expropriation, etc. Nevertheless, the theoretical approach is to focus not on legal protections, but rather on institutional features of government in order to investigate their effects on trade policy. No doubt these other aspects of democracy may act to strengthen the willingness of policymakers to reduce trade barriers—this is a matter for better data and future research.

Bliss and Russett (1998): Democracy Matters

Bliss and Russet (BR) (1998) consider 882 pairs of states for each year between 1962 and 1989. For each pair the (log of the) sum of exports and imports between them were regressed on a measure of the regime score of the least democratic state in the pair, among other variables. BR consider only the score of the least democratic of the pair, on the belief that it is the least democratic state that acts as the "weak link"—the least democratic partner would most influence relations between the states.

The other variables BR include are a measure of language differences, the existence of preexisting militarized disputes, whether the countries were militarily allied and whether the country had an open trade stance, in addition to the gravity variables. In pooled time series estimations, BR find that democracy is significantly and positively related to trade volume.

Mansfield et al. (2000): Joint Democracy Matters

These results are confirmed by a similar set of regressions undertaken by Mansfield et al. (2000), in which the volume of trade, once again controlled for by the gravity variables, is significantly affected by the regime characteristics of both countries in the pair. Using the same measure of democracy for each state as BR, a country was labelled a democracy if its score was above 6, and autocracy if its score was below -6. The volume of trade was regressed against two dummy variables (the first would take the value of 1 when the pair was mixed—one democracy and one autocracy, and the second would take on a value of 1 if the pair were jointly autocratic). The omitted category was then the democratic pair, and the coefficients for the two dummies would then be interpreted relative to the omitted category. The sample is all pairs of states listed as members of the interstate system by the Correlates of War Project (Singer and Small 1994) for 1960, 1965, 1970, 1975, 1980, 1985, and 1990. Again pooled time series regressions were estimated.

The coefficient on the mixed case was negative and significant—mixed pairs are likely to have significantly less trade between them than are joint democracies. Mixed dyads were predicted to engage roughly in 15–20 percent less trade than those that composed two democracies. The results for pairs of autocracies were not significant, however.

This result is shown to be robust to alternative specifications of the thresholds for democracy and autocracy.

Remmer (1998): Economic Cooperation

Instead of trade flows on the left-hand side, consider the effects of regime type on the likelihood of a state signing an economic agreement with a trading partner. Such an agreement may be a tariff reduction agreement, or any other deal that facilitates freer trade. This sidesteps the problems of endogeneity in the regressions mentioned: trade volumes are affected by GDP, and GDP is affected by the gains from trade. In order to avoid this simultaneity problem, consider instead the willingness of a state to sign an international trade agreement, or more precisely to join a preferential trading area (PTA). In order to be consistent with the general agreement on trade and tariffs (GATT) these PTAs pledge to substantially eliminate barriers to trade between the signatories.

Remmer investigates the countries of the Mercosur and finds that democracy did lead to more economic agreements, even before the Mercosur was founded. She runs logistic regressions, running the number of economic agreements signed between a pair of Mercosur countries in a given year, against measures of democracy. Her dichotomous regime variable is different from, but highly correlated with the Polity dataset used in the rest of the studies cited here. She finds some support from the proposition that democracy promotes cooperation—democratic pairs are several times more likely to enter into economic agreements with one another than other pairs of states.

Mansfield et al. (2002): Democracy and PTAs

In a similar investigation, Mansfield et al. (2002) study the effect of regime type on the willingness of a broad set of states to enter into common PTA.[10] The unit of analysis is the dyad, and the dependent variable is a dummy that takes the value 1 when both members of the dyad are signatories to a common PTA. Again, the Jaggers and Gurr (1995) regime scores are used, and as before the 21 point scale generated by the difference between the democracy score and the autocracy score for each state is used. The sum of the regime scores for each country in the dyad is then computed.

This variable runs from −20 to 20, with larger scores indicating that the pair of countries is more democratic. Again, we focus on post–World War II data, and all pairs of countries for which data is available for each five-year period between 1960 and 1990 are examined. The data is pooled across time and country-pairs and a logistic regression is conducted, and the significance tests are based on Huber standard errors (appropriate for time-series cross section models with binary dependent variables). The estimate of the democratic score is positive and significant at the 0.1 percent level.

Mansfield et al. (2002) also establish that the result is robust to alternative specifications: in one case they replace the sum of the two regime scores with the individual regime scores, and the estimates are positive and significant; they also use an alternative dataset with fewer countries, but annual data, and once again, democratic dyads are more likely to establish PTAs than mixed pairs, or pairs of autocracies.

Using the estimates of the regression, the authors predict the probability of a PTA forming in any year across the possible dyads. Two democracies are more than double as likely to sign a PTA as are a mixed pair, which in turn are more than double as likely to cooperate in a PTA as two autocracies.

Alternative Explanations

We have argued that divided polity leads to greater trade liberalization—lower tariffs and an increased willingness to cooperate internationally on trade issues. This increased willingness to cooperate internationally among democracies has been noted by other scholars, particularly among political scientists. Democracies share similar values and norms that lead to nonviolent solutions to conflict (Dixon 1994); they have a rule of law that protects property and does not permit rent seeking or expropriation (Olson 1993).

In slightly different formulation, a number of scholars have suggested that trade liberalization seems to be coincident with democratization (e.g., Haggard and Webb 1994). However Rodrik (1994) suggests that trade policy reforms are usually preceded by changes in the political regime, in any direction, democracy, or otherwise. Geddes (1992) and Przeworski (1991) have suggested that fledgling democracies are susceptible to challenge, and are the least likely to reform. Verdier (1998) suggests that increased democracy means that similar sectors in each country are empowered politically, and the effect is likely to be more protection at least while trade is powered by comparative advantage.

These works provide little insight into the effect of the institutional structure of democracies on policy; democracy empowers and restrains the use of that power to make policy. It delegates and separates power and authority across branches and agents. It is exactly these structural differences that are the focus of this chapter.

The link between trade and regime type is somewhat bound up with the question of the link between democracy and peace. If democracy supports trade, and trade supports peace, then there is another urgent reason to encourage democratization in unstable regions of the globe. These ideas are founded in Kant and Cobden: peace and democracy are closely tied via the desire to maintain good trading relations. Bliss and Russett (1998) quote President Clinton's 1994 State of the Union address:

> Ultimately, the best strategy to ensure our security and build a durable peace is to support the advance of democracy elsewhere. Democracies don't attack each other. They make better trading partners and partners in diplomacy.

Polacheck (1997) investigates closely the linkage between democracy, trade, and peace, and provides support for the liberal view that democracy leads to more trade; more trade implies greater gains from economic interaction that would be put in jeopardy by conflict. Hence war is less likely when there are large gains from trade that would be lost in the event of hostilities. Trade creates security externalities and Mansfield (1994) shows that war is negatively related to trade.

Conclusion

Regime type affects the volume of trade between countries, and their willingness to enter into free(r) trading arrangements with its trading partners. There is also evidence to suggest that democracies cooperate more generally in the international economic arena. This increased willingness to cooperate suggests that increased democratization will lead to more cooperation and less conflict in the world (trading) system.

The particular aspects of democracy that appear to be important are two: the effect of dividing authority over trade policy across different arms of government, each with slightly different sources of electoral power and influence; the second is the role of elections in maintaining accountability of policymakers to the society at large. Divided polity actually increases the bargaining power of the executives at the international bargaining table; accountability lessens the policymaker's incentive to divert wealth to special interests and to lower the deadweight costs of such redistribution.

Other aspects of democracy are no doubt important: the contestably of elections, the degree of divided government, the free flow of information, the freedom to associate and to lobby etc. These no doubt influence policymaking at some level. Similarly, aspects of autocracies are missing here—the role of the military and political oppression, for example. Moreover, there are some aspects of democracy that may appear to be undesirable with respect to well-functioning markets: too much lobbying by interest groups can lead to much wasted, unproductive resources that are merely dissipated by the lobbying effort, and have almost no effect on the policymakers—demosclerosis (Bhagwati 1982, Lohmann 1996). Similarly, there may be benefits from autocracy: a benevolent dictator may be insulated from pressures to protect or redistribute.

Comparative advantage and factor specificity are important in determining the pattern of trade and protection. But institutions matter too. Comparative advantage, factor endowments, and their specificity combine to determine who gains and loses from trade and barriers to trade. It is the nature of the political process that determines which of the affected sectors (the gainers or losers) are successful in the policymaking arena.[11]

This work is not intended to be a complete description of the effect of democracy on trade; rather it represents the first steps in theorizing the connections between regime type and redistributional policy; the first steps in understanding the economic benefits of democracy.

Appendix

Utility maximization yields the demand functions: $x = u'^{-1}(p_x)$ and $x^* = u'^{-1}(p_x + \tau)$, $m = u'^{-1}(p_m + t)$ and $m^* = u'^{-1}(p_m)$, and market clearing implies that local and foreign demand must sum to unity for each good: $u'^{-1}(p_x) + u'^{-1}(p_x + \tau) = 1$ and $u'^{-1}(p_m + t) + u'^{-1}(p_m) = 1$. Solving for the equilibrium prices yields $p_x(\tau)$ and $p_m(t)$. It is evident that

$$\frac{\partial p_x(\tau)}{\partial \tau} < 0 \text{ and } \frac{\partial p_m(t)}{\partial t} < 0 \text{ while } \frac{\partial (p_x(\tau) + \tau)}{\partial \tau} > 0$$

$$\text{and } \frac{\partial (p_m(t) + t)}{\partial t} > 0. \tag{1}$$

Home's equilibrium consumption of good x and m can be expressed as $x(\tau) = u'^{-1}(p_x(\tau))$ and $m(t) = u'^{-1}(p_m(t) + t)$, with

$$x' > 0 \text{ and } m' < 0. \tag{2}$$

To derive an expression for social welfare, notice that the indirect utility for this economy with income y is given by $y + C(x(\tau), m(t))$ where $C(x(\tau), m(t)) = u(x(\tau)) - p_x(\tau)x(\tau) + u(m(t)) - (p_m(t) + t)m(t)$ is the consumer surplus associated with the consumption of x and m. National income y is, of course, equal to the sum of profits and tariff revenue. Hence the social welfare is expressed as the sum of consumer surplus, profits, and tariff revenue: $W(t, \tau) = C(x(\tau), m(t)) + \Pi^x(\tau) + \Pi^m(t) + T(t)$ where $\Pi^x(\tau) = \beta p_x(\tau)$, $\Pi^m(t) = (p_m(t) + t)(1 - \beta)$ and tariff revenue is given by $T(t) = t(m(t) - (1 - \beta))$. Similarly, for foreign, $W^*(t, \tau) = C^*(x^*(\tau), m^*(t)) + \Pi^{x*}(\tau) + \Pi^{m*}(t) + T^*(\tau)$ where $C^*(x^*(\tau), m^*(t)) = u(x^*(\tau)) - (p_x(\tau) + \tau)x^*(\tau) + u(m^*(t)) - p_m(t)m^*(t)$, $\Pi^{x*}(\tau) = (p_x(\tau) + \tau)(1 - \beta)$ and $\Pi^{m*}(t) = p_m(t)\beta$. Tariff revenue is given by $T^*(\tau) = \tau(x^*(\tau) - (1 - \beta))$.

Setting $W_t = 0$ yields $t^W = (m(t) - (1 - \beta))(p'_m(t))/(m'(t)) > 0$ since imports are positive and both $p'_m(t)$ and $m'(t)$ are negative (from equations 1 and 2). Similarly, $\tau^{W*} = (x^*(\tau) - (1 - \beta))(p'_x(\tau))/(x^{*'}(\tau)) > 0$. Also $W_\tau = u'(x(\tau))x' - p'_x(\tau)x(\tau) - p_x(\tau)x'(\tau) + \beta p'_x(\tau) = -p'_x(\tau)x(\tau) + \beta p'_x(\tau) = p'_x(\tau)(\beta - x(\tau)) < 0$ since exports are positive. Recalling that $G(t, \tau, \Psi) = c\Pi^m(t) + \Psi W(t, \tau)$, and setting $G_t = 0$ yields $t^G = (-c(1 - \beta)(p'_m(t) + 1))/(\Psi m'(t)) + (p'_m(t))/(m'(t))(m(t) - (1 - \beta))$.

Proofs

Proofs of Proposition 1. Totally differentiating the first order condition, $0 = (\partial/\partial t)G_t dt + (\partial/\partial \Psi)G_t d\Psi$ or $(\partial t^G/\partial \Psi) = -G_{t\Psi}/G_{tt}$. Now $G_{tt} < 0$ (the second order condition) and $G_{t\Psi} = W_t$. The Nash tariff to this game is larger than that which maximizes W (that is, $t^G > t^W$); hence $W_t < 0$ when evaluated at (t^G, τ^G). Then $(\partial t^G/\partial \Psi) < 0$. The proof is similar for $(\partial t^G/\partial c) > 0$. ∎

Proof of Proposition 2. $(\partial/\partial \Psi)g_C(\Psi,\Psi^*) = (\partial/\partial \Psi)[G(t^C,\tau^C,\Psi) - G(t^G(\Psi), \tau^G(\Psi^*), \Psi)] = W(t^C,\tau^C) - (G_t(\partial/\partial \Psi)t^G(\Psi) + W(t^G(\Psi), \tau^G(\Psi^*)))$. Now $G_t = 0$ when evaluated at $(t^G (\Psi), \tau^G (\Psi^*))$. Hence $(\partial/\partial \Psi)g(\Psi,\Psi^*) = W(t^C,\tau^C) - W(t^G (\Psi), \tau^G(\Psi^*))$. Now $W(t^C, \tau^C) - W(t^W, \tau^W) > 0$ since cooperation dominates the Nash equilibrium to the optimal tariff setting game (in this symmetric world). Now $t^W < t^G$ (Ψ) and $\tau^W < T^G(\Psi^*)$ for all values of Ψ, Ψ^*; then home welfare declines as home tariff rises above the optimal tariff ($W_\tau < 0$ for all $t > t^W$) and home welfare declines as the foreign tariff rises ($W_\tau = p'_x (\tau) (\beta - x (\tau)) < 0$ for all $\tau > 0$). Hence $W(t^C, \tau^C) - W(t^G (\Psi),\tau^G(\Psi^*)) > W(t^C, \tau^C) - W(t^W, \tau^W) > 0$. ∎

Proof of Proposition 3. $(\partial/\partial \Psi) g (\Psi,\Psi^*) = (\partial/\partial \Psi) g_C(\Psi,\Psi^*) - (\partial/\partial \Psi)g_D(\Psi)$. $(\partial/\partial \Psi)g_C(\Psi,\Psi^*) > 0$ from proposition 2 and $(\partial/\partial \Psi) g_D(\Psi) = (\partial/\partial \Psi)G(t^G(\Psi),\tau^C,\Psi) = W(t^G(\Psi),\tau^C) - W(t^C,\tau^C)$ from the proof of Lemma 1. Now $W(t^G (\Psi), \tau^C) - W(t^C, \tau^C) < 0$, since welfare is reduced by a rise in tariffs from the cooperative level. Hence $(\partial/\partial \Psi) g (\Psi,\Psi^*) > 0$. ∎

Proof of Proposition 4. Let $\Gamma(t^C, \tau^C; \Psi, \Psi^*) = G(t, \tau, \Psi) + G^*(t, \tau, \Psi^*)$. Totally differentiating the first order condition on t, we have $0 = (\partial/\partial t)\Gamma_t dt + (\partial/\partial \Psi)\Gamma_t d\Psi + (\partial/\partial \Psi^*)\Gamma_t d\Psi^*$. Now $(\partial t^C/\partial \Psi^*) = -(\Gamma_{t\Psi^*}/\Gamma_{tt})$ and $\Gamma_{t\Psi^*} = W_t^* < 0$, while $\Gamma_{tt} < 0$ (the second order condition). So $(\partial t^C/\partial \Psi^*) < 0$ and by symmetry, $(\partial \tau^C/\partial \Psi) < 0$. Recall that $\Gamma_{t\Psi} = W_t$; if $t^W > t^C$, then $W_t > 0$ when evaluated at (t^C, τ^C). Then $(\partial \tau^C/\partial \Psi) > 0$. The condition for $t^W > t^C$ is easily shown to be $-p'_m < (c (1-\beta))/(\Psi^*(\beta - m^*) + c(1-\beta)) \equiv -\pi$. ∎

Proof of Proposition 5. Consider two autocracies, A and A^*. When negotiations break down, each implements the Nash tariff $(t^G(\Psi^A), \tau^G(\Psi^{A^*}))$, yielding payoffs $G^A(t^G(\Psi^A), \tau^G(\Psi^{A^*}), \Psi^A)$ and $G^{A^*}(t^G(\Psi^A), \tau^G(\Psi^{A^*}), \Psi^{A^*})$. Now allow home to become a democracy, initially with $\Psi^A = \Psi^E = \Psi^L$. Then $G^A(t^G(\Psi^A), \tau^G(\Psi^{A^*}), \Psi^A) = G^E(t^G(\Psi^L), \tau^G(\Psi^{A^*}), \Psi^E)$ and let Ψ^L fall slightly. Then $(d/d\Psi^L) G^E(t^G(\Psi^L),\tau^G(\Psi^{A^*}),\Psi^E)|_{\Psi^E=\Psi^L} = (\partial G^E/\partial t) (dt^G(\Psi^L)/d\Psi^L)|_{\Psi^E=\Psi^L}$, while $(d/d\Psi^L)G^{A^*}(t^G(\Psi^L),\tau^G(\Psi^{A^*}),\Psi^{A^*})|_{\Psi^E=\Psi^L} = (dG^{A^*}/dt) (dt^G(\Psi^L)/d\Psi^L)|_{\Psi^E=\Psi^L}$.

Now $(\partial G^E/\partial t)|_{\Psi^E=\Psi^L} = 0$ since $t^G(\Psi^E) = \arg \max G^E$. So $(d/d\Psi^L) G^E (t^G(\Psi^L)$, $\tau^G(\Psi^{A^*}),\Psi^E)|_{\Psi^E=\Psi^L} = 0$. $(dG^{A^*}/dt) < 0$ for all t and $(dt^G(\Psi^L)/d\Psi^L) < 0$ by Proposition 1. Hence $(d/d \Psi^L) G^{A^*}(t^G(\Psi^L), \tau^G (\Psi^{A^*}),\Psi^{A^*})| > 0$. So as Ψ^L falls, so does $G^{A^*}(t^G(\Psi^L), \tau^G(\Psi^{A^*}), \Psi^{A^*})$. Hence the reversion point g^{EA^*} lies directly below g^{AA^*} in figure 3.1. The bargaining outcome EA^* will lie to the southeast of AA^* for any utility possibility frontier. That is home's utility rises and foreign's falls. ∎

Chapter 4

Divided Government and International Cooperation in the Nineteenth Century

Robert Pahre

The literature on divided government initially examined preferences and institutions, in which the combination of ratification institutions and executive-legislative disagreement makes international cooperation more difficult (Friman 1993; Hammond and Prins 1999; Iida 1993; but Karol 2000; Milner 1997; Milner and Rosendorff 1997; Mo 1995; O'Halloran 1994; but Pahre 2001a). With complete information, the executives negotiate an agreement if the legislature allows, or do not negotiate at all if the legislature would not approve any agreement. Incomplete information about the legislature's preferences may lead executives to negotiate an agreement that the legislature (unexpectedly) rejects.

Scholars have not yet evaluated the power of hypotheses about co-operation based on different combinations of these assumptions. Like Hug and König in chapter 5, this chapter helps fill this gap. Unlike many existing studies, I seek to explain variation between cooperation and noncooperation, explicitly looking at cases when cooperation does not occur. To capture cases of noncooperation, I use a database of all trade treaties in a single issue area over the span of a century (1815–1913). The database also includes treaties that were negotiated but not ratified, allowing for systematic evaluation of the claim that incomplete information inhibits cooperation.

The first part of this chapter examines the ratification problem. I find that ratification was rarely a problem for nineteenth-century polities. Those nonratifications that we observe are highly concentrated in a few countries. This implies that incomplete information about the ratifier's preferences mattered for some countries but not for most members of the international system. Interestingly these countries tended to be democracies, which raises the possibility that the lack of information about the ratifier in a divided polity was responsible for those nonratifications that occurred. This incomplete information seems to vary crossnationally but not intertemporally. In other words, incomplete information might explain México's noncooperation compared to other Latin American countries but it does not explain variation in French cooperation over time. Though ratification may prevent agreement under complete information, the rarity of nonratifications even for countries that apparently had information problems suggests that ratification obstacles do not account for much variation between cooperation and noncooperation in this century. Many other democracies, for example, regularly ratified treaties.

Though the literature has studied the effects of divided government at the ratification stage, it has not considered how divided government may shape potential cooperation even before negotiations begin. To do this, this chapter also analyzes the effect of divided government on the reversion point, the outcome if cooperation breaks down. If divided government makes this reversion point more unattractive than the reversion point under unified government, it may make cooperation more likely. Whether divided government makes this point sufficiently unattractive depends on the preferences of the executive and the legislature as well as the institutions within which they choose this reversion point.

Because of the highly conditional nature of the hypotheses, a large-n quantitative test is not practical, and comparative case studies are a more appropriate choice of method (Pahre 2005). To show the importance of divided government and reversion points when explaining cooperation, I test the second set of claims against the cases of Austria-Hungary, Sweden-Norway, and the German *Zollverein*. Though not all of these countries shared the unlimited suffrage and responsible government that we associate with contemporary democracy, all were at least semidemocratic. In addition, all shared the structural features of polyarchy that characterize modern democracy and modern democratic theory. The theory and evidence here account for both cross-national and intertemporal variation, suggesting that divided government shapes cooperation through its effect on reversion points. The chapter also presents a historical perspective on the questions of democracy and foreign policy, one that may be useful for analyzing countries in a transition to democracy today.

The Ratification Stage

Ratification and Divided Government

In the last decade, scholars have increasingly explored the ways that domestic politics affects international cooperation. The most notable recent advances in domestic-level theory have built on Robert Putnam's (1988) theory of "two-level games." In this framework, chiefs of government negotiate an agreement internationally, subject to approval by one or more domestic actors. One of the strongest claims from this literature maintains that divided government makes international cooperation more difficult (Friman 1993; Iida 1993; Milner 1997; Milner and Rosendorff 1997; Mo 1995; O'Halloran 1994; but Pahre 2001a; Tarar 2001).[1] This literature has focused almost entirely on studies of the contemporary United States (Hug and König 2001; König and Hug 2000; Pahre 1997, 2001a), unjustifiably treating American patterns of agenda setting as general.

Following this literature, I use a spatial model to analyze the tariff question. Spatial theories model policy as a point in space on axes such as protectionism or free trade. In such a model, actors must decide whether to change policy away from the status quo (or reversion point). Each actor has an ideal policy, or bliss point, and evaluates policies in terms of their distance from this bliss point: the nearer, the better. For simplicity, I assume that utility is a negative function of the distance from the outcome of the game to this ideal point, so that indifference curves are circles around each player's ideal point.[2]

Figure 4.1 shows the basic logic of domestic political constraints within such a model. For simplicity, I begin with a single policy dimension along the x-axis (see Hammond and Prins, chapter 2, for full treatment). Three actors interact: Foreigners (F), the home Executive (E) and home

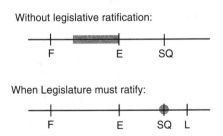

Figure 4.1   Adding a Ratification Constraint

Legislature (L).[3] These actors can negotiate to change policy away from the status quo (SQ).

The conventional way of modeling domestic politics simply adds a domestic ratification constraint to a model to see how this affects negotiations. To capture this line of reasoning, I show in the top of figure 4.1 the case when an executive (E) and foreigners (F) negotiate an agreement without a legislative constraint. They may choose any point in the win-set shown, which consists of those points that are at least as close to E as the status quo SQ. The hashed parts of the line show those points.

Adding a domestic legislature may make international agreement impossible. In the bottom of figure 4.1, the legislature (L) will veto any leftward change in the policy, while E and F will never negotiate any rightward shift. With this configuration of preferences, no agreement will occur when the negotiators need the legislature's approval. In other words, the win-set is the status quo (SQ), marked as a hashed circle in figure 4.1. The reasoning captured in this figure lies behind the veto player hypothesis examined throughout this volume.

This analysis clearly does a good job explaining why some countries face problems in cooperating with others. In Switzerland, for example, the Federal Assembly must approve all treaties and alliances. Even if the Federal Assembly ratifies a treaty, under many circumstances the people may subject the treaty to a referendum (Codding 1961: Chapter 5). These bodies can become stumbling blocks to Swiss participation in international cooperation, including the European Economic Area (associated with the European Union) today.

The Netherlands, with a strong two-house Estates General, may provide another example in which the legislature inhibits trade cooperation. The 1815 constitution gave the king limited power over foreign relations. Though weaker than other monarchs in Europe, the king's position was stronger than in the previous Batavian Republic, where "the foreign relations power was so weak that the Republic had made itself infamous for unbelievable dilatoriness in its relations with other states" (Vandenbosch 1944: 430). However, the King's power over foreign relations was reduced by constitutional revisions in 1848. He had to submit for parliamentary approval any treaty whose stipulations affected legal rights. After additional revisions in 1887, any treaty imposing financial obligations on the kingdom also required such approval (Vandenbosch 1944). The Estates General's veto power in such cases may have made trade cooperation less likely.

Examining some simple data yields results consistent with this interpretation of Switzerland and the Netherlands. Figure 4.2 shows the annual number of treaties in effect for four comparable small countries, Belgium, the Netherlands, Sweden, and Switzerland. The evidence shows that Belgium

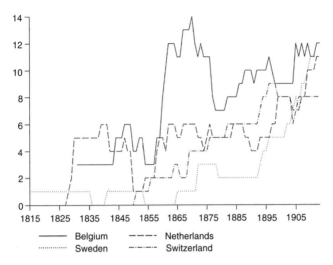

Figure 4.2   Trade Treaties in Effect: Four Smaller European Countries, 1815–1913

is almost always the most active cooperator among the three small states, a fact that is consistent with our analysis of Switzerland and the Netherlands. (I discuss Sweden Shortly) Dutch treaties fall especially far behind Belgium after 1848, with a strengthening of the Estates General. This pattern suggests that problems of treaty ratification may account for some of the cross-national variation between these three. However, intertemporal differences in the strength of Dutch (1848, 1887) or Swiss (1848) central institutions do not have any evident effects.

Though the conventional wisdom provides a useful account of such countries, these results may differ substantially if we model the reversion point explicitly. Figure 4.3 illustrates two possibilities, with agenda setting lodged in the executive or legislature, respectively. The top diagram illustrates a dictatorial system in which the executive both chooses policy and negotiates international agreements, while the bottom figure shows a "separation of powers" situation in which the legislature chooses policy but the executive negotiates international agreements. In the dictatorship, the executive chooses the status quo policy, and naturally chooses her ideal point E. International negotiations are impossible, because E will not agree with F on any change in this policy. In the separation of powers, the legislature chooses the status quo policy L. In this case, divided government creates a status quo that both E and F dislike. If they can negotiate an agreement that does not require legislative assent, E and F will jointly choose some

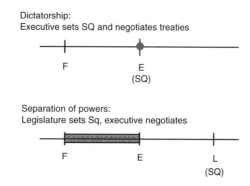

Figure 4.3 Reversion Points and International Cooperation

point in their win-set. Here, divided government combined with legislative control over the status quo makes cooperation possible.

We can see the logic of figure 4.3 at work in the 1860s, when France led an important wave of trade cooperation. This wave appears as a large increase in French treaties in effect, visible in figure 4.4; the apparent decline at the end of the wave reflects the nominal expiration of many treaties with Latin America, although most continued to be observed by both sides. Under the Restoration (1815–1830) and Orléans (1830–1848) monarchies, the legislature had made the tariff, though the executive could modify tariff lines temporarily pending ratification. As a result, commercial negotiations often proved elusive. The most notable series of failed talks occurred with the United Kingdom before 1860 (Ratcliffe 1978).

A change in institutions weakened the legislature's veto powers, though it maintained control of the tariff reversion point. Louis Napoléon's 1852 constitution gave the emperor the power to sign commercial treaties without the assent of the Chambers. Any such treaty would have the force of law and would supersede any previous provisions of tariff law (Dunham 1930; Thompson 1954). Both executive and legislative preferences changed between the mid- and late 1850s, so divided government increased. Louis Napoléon became convinced of the advantages of tariff liberalization, and he certainly favored a commercial treaty with England by 1859. In contrast, the legislature remained protectionist and slowly gained some independence from the executive. While Napoléon had hand-picked the legislature of 1852, he faced an increasingly strong minority in opposition after the elections of 1857 and 1860.

This combination of institutions and preferences closely matches the lower diagram in figure 4.3, which shows the result when the executive

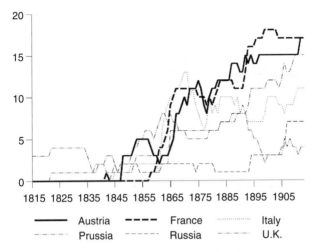

Figure 4.4   International Cooperation by Major Trading States

negotiates treaties but the legislature sets the reversion point. As I would predict, this increasingly divided government made international cooperation more likely. France reached the famous Cobden-Chevalier treaty in 1860, followed by a flurry of treaties with other European states. Figure 4.4 shows a marked upswing in France's treaties with Europe in this period. As Michel Chevalier had suggested to him, Napoléon used treaties to evade the legislature's authority over trade policy. It is noteworthy that the change in policy did not occur after the removal of the legislative veto, but only as the legislature's preferences diverged from the executive's preferences within the new institutional environment. Preferences and institutions interact to produce outcomes.

After Louis Napoléon's abdication, the Third Republic (1871–1945) again required legislative ratification of trade treaties. Treaties with Europe stagnated until the 1890s, when the Third Republic renewed most of the Second Empire's treaties as they expired.

We have seen, then, that divided government may have varying effects on cooperation. In Switzerland and the Netherlands, indirect evidence suggests that strong legislatures inhibited cooperation, as did the French legislature before 1848. In the 1860s, a peculiar combination of legislative tariff-making and executive treaty-making opened space for international cooperation in France. While figures 4.1 and 4.3 present obviously stylized examples, they illustrate an important general point: domestic politics affects not only ratification of agreements but also the status quo. Divided government, too, can affect both the status quo and the ratification of international agreements.

Ratification Failures

The theoretical analysis in the preceding section suggests two different effects of divided government. First, ratification problems may make cooperation less likely. The legislature may reject treaties outright, or the executive may not negotiate treaties in the first place so as to avoid rejection. This latter effect may be difficult to observe, while the first is easy. Second, divided government may shape the reversion point and thus make cooperation either more or less likely.

This section examines outright treaty rejections, that is, the easiest of these effects to observe. I argue that nonratifications do not seem to provide much variation in most countries' abilities to cooperate. However, the underlying conditions that bring about nonratification, especially incomplete information about legislative preferences, are highly concentrated in a few countries and do account for some cross-national variation between these countries and others.

When we look at the evidence we see first that nonratification is an uncommon event. Though over one thousand trade treaties were signed in the nineteenth century, only 43 were not ratified—a failure rate of only about four percent. Of course, the threat of nonratification may exert a powerful influence on the substance of any agreements reached. As I suggested in the previous section, this may have been true of Switzerland and the Netherlands.

Because the spatial theory of two-level games maintains that incomplete information is a necessary (but not sufficient) condition for nonratification, even this low rate of nonratification suggests that information is sometimes incomplete. The executive's uncertainty about legislative preferences, perhaps because of multiple and rapidly changing cleavages in the legislature, seems a likely suspect (Kahler 1993; Milner 1997). We should think, then, about possible causes of this uncertainty.

If executive uncertainty about certain types of legislatures causes nonratifications, then we would expect nonratifications to be highly concentrated by country. Some countries would have the requisite uncertainty, while others presumably would not. The data are consistent with this claim. Table 4.1 lists the number of nonratifications by country. Because of a lack of information for many cases, each nonratification is counted twice, regardless of which legislature rejected the treaty first.[4]

Table 4.1 Nonratified Trade Treaties by
Country, 1815–1913

Country	Nonratifications
México	14
France	9
Uruguay	7
Argentina	6
United States	6
Belgium	4
Guatemala	4
Italy	4
Netherlands	4
Austria	3
Prussia	4
Switzerland	3
Bolivia	2
Chile	2
Costa Rica	2
El Salvador	2
Nicaragua	2
Portugal	2
United Kingdom	2
Dominican Republic	1
Ecuador	1
Haiti	1
Honduras	1
Iran	1
Paraguay	1
Peru	1
Spain	1

Note: Each nonratified treaty is counted twice,
once for each signatory

More than half of all countries in the database (31 of 58) were never involved in a treaty rejection over the course of this century. At the other extreme, México was involved in one-third of all nonratified treaties (14 of 43), which I list in table 4.2. Argentina, France, the United States, and Uruguay round out the rogues' gallery, with one of these five states being involved in three-fourths of all nonratifications (32 of 43). Guatemala, Italy, the Netherlands, and Nicaragua were minor nonratifiers, whose addition encompasses 42 of the 43 nonratifications; only the 1869 El Salvador-Peru nonratification does not involve one of these nine states. Again, these nine

Table 4.2   Mexican Nonratifications, 1815–1913

States Parties	Treaty Date
México-United Kingdom	1825
México-Prussia	1826
México-United States	1826
France-México	1831
México-Prussia	1832
México-Prussia	1832
México-France	1832
México-Switzerland	1832
Ecuador-México	1838
Belgium-México	1839
Belgium-México	1854
El Salvador-México	1858
México-United States	1859
Guatemala-México	1888

are only a small fraction of all 58 countries in the database. Nonratification is highly concentrated in a few countries, and it is worth noting that these countries tend to be republics. None is a pure monarchy such as Russia.

Some countries make the list only because they signed several treaties with serial nonratifiers such as México, the United States, France, or Uruguay. Prussia's four nonratifications include three treaties rejected by México, and one by the United States. Both of Portugal's nonratifications were actually rejected by Uruguay. The Netherlands represent a more ambiguous case. Two of the Netherlands' four nonratifications were French treaties, though both were rejected by the Dutch Estates General (in 1881 and 1882). The discussion in the previous section suggests that both countries had significant legislatures.

It is striking that most of the century's trade treaties were negotiated between European countries, while most of the regular nonratifiers are to be found in the New World. This evidence suggests that treaty nonratification occurs more often in the presidential systems of the Americas than the parliamentary or quasidemocratic systems of the Old World. These New World countries were also relatively new, with developing party systems and political norms. This less settled institutional environment would presumably increase uncertainty about the legislature's preferences, making it more difficult to negotiate an acceptable treaty.[5] This too is consistent with the standard theory.

An example from two leading serial nonratifiers illustrates some of the dynamics at work. When the U.S. Senate rejected the 1859 agreement with

México, it hoped that withholding concessions would induce President Benito Juárez to cede territory to the United States in exchange for trade or financial incentives. Because President Juárez was besieged in Vera Cruz against domestic foes during these negotiations, uncertainty about Mexican preferences seems a reasonable inference. When the Mexican government refused to negotiate on the basis of territorial concessions, the United States eventually relinquished all territorial demands and successfully concluded a ratifiable commercial treaty (Lauck 1904). In this case, uncertainty about *foreign* preferences brought about a treaty's rejection.

This kind of domestic uncertainty probably explains México's problems with many countries. Figure 4.5 shows the annual number of treaties in effect for six important countries in Latin America from 1815 to 1913. México led the region in cooperation during the 1820s and 1830s, a period coinciding with its federalist Republic of 1824–1836. When it turned to a central system, it fell back to last place in the trade treaty standings until the 1880s. This reflected the political disorder of these years in México, which ended only under President Porfirio Diaz. Elected president in 1872 and again in 1876, Diaz yielded the presidency to a close colleague, General Manuel Gonzalez, in 1880–1884, before being elected six more times in succession. This period, known as the *Porfiriato*, marked the consolidation of the Mexican political system and a time of relative prosperity (Krauze 1997). Porfirio's dominance of the political system brought greater stability and predictability, and doubtless made it easier to anticipate legislative approval of treaties. Indeed, the number of Mexican treaties in effect

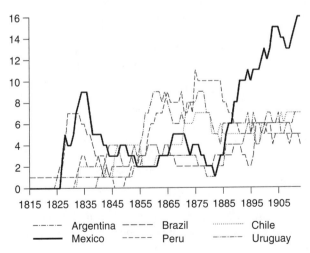

Figure 4.5   Trade Treaties in Effect: Six Latin American Countries, 1815–1905

jumped dramatically.[6] Mexican nonratifications also became much rare, occurring only once during the *Porfiriato* (see table 4.2)

The number of Mexican treaties in effect therefore seems to be well explained by variation in domestic political stability. In contrast to the other countries discussed here, domestic uncertainty also seems to explain intertemporal variation in México. By extension, the same uncertainty may be at work elsewhere in the Americas. Again, it is uncertainty and *not* the mere presence of a veto actor seems to inhibit cooperation.

Yet even if we accept this argument, the relatively high rejection rates in France and the Netherlands—though still small by any reasonable standard—remain unexplained. In the rest of Europe, in contrast, treaties were rarely rejected. This implies that incomplete information about the ratifier's preferences mattered in only a few countries, mostly in the western hemisphere. Furthermore, the rejection rate does nothing to help us understand how divided government might affect the status quo and thus have systematic effects on the likelihood of cooperation. I turn to this task in the next section.

Puzzles for the Ratification Perspective

The ratification perspective also faces serious anomalies. Indeed, anomalous countries may be as numerous as those countries that the ratification story seeks to explain. To see this, consider two seriously divided policies, the dual monarchies of Austria–Hungary and Sweden–Norway.

It has long been recognized that institutional constraints, such as domestic ratification rules, may be important even if their powers are never used. For example, the threat of nonratification may keep the executive from signing treaties even if no treaties are ever rejected. Assessing these institutions therefore requires some way to consider those treaties that are never signed. In other words, we need a measure of international cooperation that is valid across countries, so that we can determine which countries cooperate more or less than expected.

To identify countries that cooperate more or less with others, I use the total number of countries with which a given state has a trade treaty in effect in a given year. (A weighted count, weighing a treaty with, say, France more heavily than one with Portugal, would yield essentially the same results because almost all states sign treaties first with larger states.) Because this measure provides a single number for each country in a given year, it is well suited for cross-national and intertemporal comparisons. This measure varies substantially between 1815 and 1914.

Returning to figure 4.4, we can see the number of treaties that Austria-Hungary had in effect in each year, in comparison with other large countries.

They show that divided government in the dual monarchies provides a striking puzzle for the conventional wisdom on divided government. Contrary to the conventional wisdom, divided government made Austro-Hungarian trade cooperation in trade affairs much *more* likely from 1867.[7]

The Dual Kingdom of Sweden–Norway, whose treaty counts are shown in figure 4.6, shows no such pattern. It seems that Sweden was more likely to cooperate with other countries after Norway broke away in 1905, that is, after the dual monarchy came to an end.[8] Interestingly, Norway shows no such effect after independence (see figure 4.6). Though I will not explain it here, there is also a marked increase in Bulgaria's level of cooperation after it achieves full independence in 1908 (see Crampton 1997: Chapters 5–6), making Norway's lower willlingness to cooperate more puzzling in comparative perspective.

We can imagine several variables other than divided government that might account for the cross-national variation in the figures, such as country size.[9] Figures 4.4 and 4.6 compare the dual monarchies to other European countries of similar size. These data show that Austria went from being a relatively low cooperator among the great powers to being a high cooperator. The transition occurred in the late 1860s and early 1870s, that is, after the *Ausgleich* introduced permanent divided government. Because all the great powers were exposed to the same external stimulus, namely the wave of treaties resulting from the Cobden-Chevalier treaty, domestic differences provide a likely explanation for this variation.

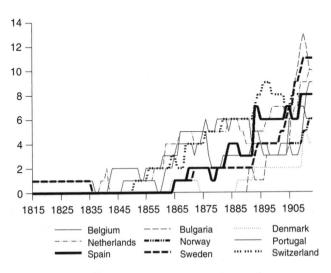

Figure 4.6   International Cooperation by Small European States

We can use the data in figure 4.6 to compare Sweden with the smaller trading states of Europe. As the figure shows, Sweden–Norway cooperated less than most other small states into the 1890s. After Norwegian independence in 1905, Sweden rapidly became the most active cooperator among the small states. Norway, in contrast, lagged behind other small states. This shift in Sweden's rank among the small powers rules out other plausible explanations for Sweden–Norway's earlier low levels of cooperation, such as a more isolated geographical position.

In short, the cross-national evidence suggests that these states do differ from their peers depending on the presence or absence of divided government. However, the evidence shows no systematic relationship between divided government and international cooperation because the figures exhibit all three imaginable effects of divided government on cooperation: divided government made cooperation more likely in Austria–Hungary, less likely in Sweden, and had no effect in Norway.

Part of the explanation for this difference is the institutional difference between these countries: the Hungarian Diet had the power to establish a separate tariff by itself,[10] while the acts of the Norwegian parliament would require approval of the Swedish King-in-Council. As Hug and König point out in chapter 4, institutional criteria alone provide a very problematic measure of the degree of divided government. Understanding the difference between these outcomes therefore requires a fuller study of the reversion points in these two countries. The following sections develop a theory that examines the differences between a status quo set by the executive and one set by the legislature (as in Hungary).

The Prenegotiation Stage

Divided Government and Reversion Points in Two Dimensions

Though either the executive or legislature may control the reversion point, negotiating with foreigners is almost always a prerogative of the executive. This fact serves as the foundation for the theory of "two-level games" (Putnam 1988), which examines how chiefs of government may negotiate an international agreement subject to approval by one or more domestic actors. Many have applied this approach to the European Union (Milner 1997; Moyer 1993; Pahre 1997; Schneider and Cederman 1993; for supranational actors, see Garrett and Tsebelis 1996; Tsebelis 1994). This section develops a two-level theory in which either the executive or legislature may control the reversion point in a divided polity. After this, I examine how increasing the degree of divided government affects cooperation.

Figure 4.7 follows Milner (1997) and other two-level presentations of trade policy problems in two dimensions (Mansfield, Milner, and Rosendorff 2000; see also Milner and Rosendorff 1996). In this case, each of the two countries (A and B) chooses an autonomous trade policy. B is a unitary actor while A has both an executive and a legislature. Each actor's ideal foreign tariff is zero, and each favors a positive home tariff because of protectionist lobbying. The legislature L has the ideal point $\{t_A^L, 0\}$, the executive E has the ideal point $\{t_A^E, 0\}$, and B has the ideal point $\{0, t_B\}$. I limit attention to cases when $t_A^L > t_A^E$, that is, cases in which the legislature is more "hawkish" than the executive.[11]

When setting the agenda, each actor will choose her ideal domestic tariffs, so the noncooperative Nash equilibrium is $N_L = \{t_A^L, t_B\}$ for a legislative agenda setter, $N_E = \{t_A^E, t_B\}$ for an executive agenda setter. Figure 4.7 shows these reversion points.

Because each country's tariff imposes externalities on the other, there are mutual gains from joint action. E and B can negotiate some cooperative agreement C, subject to ratification by L. The possible outcomes of this game are the win-set, agreements that E and B could rationally make when they anticipate L's ratification constraint. For simplicity in the comparisons here, I reduce the win-set to a unique point rather than modeling the negotiation process directly.[12] I assume that the legislature must ratify any agreement reached, which must also be acceptable to the executive in A. For simplicity, I allow the executive in B to set the negotiating agenda, that is,

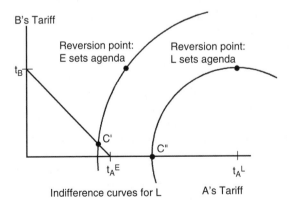

Figure 4.7   The Reversion Point and Cooperation in Two Dimensions

to propose some point subject to the constraint that it be acceptable to both actors in country A; I also require that this point be on the contract curve between the two executives if this is possible.[13] The cooperative points in figure 4.7 illustrate these two possibilities. This solution concept yields a unique outcome, making the comparative statics much easier.[14]

As the legislature becomes more distant, the reversion point becomes less attractive for both E and B.[15] The win-set also changes. In figure 4.7, moving the legislature's ideal point from t_A^L to $t_A^{L'}$ shifts the win-set onto the x-axis at t_A^E. As the legislature moves rightward, foreigners find cooperation less and less attractive. The executive finds the cooperative points increasingly attractive until they reach t_A^E, and then less attractive from t_A^E to the right.

This analysis differs from the conventional two-level analysis in that the legislature affects both the reversion point and the outcome of negotiations. Existing theory usually takes the status quo as exogenous and then examines how moving the ratifier's ideal point changes the ratification constraint on negotiators (see, for example, Hammond and Prins, chapter 2). As I have shown, modeling these reversion points explicitly affects the incentives to cooperate. I use this fact to derive explicit hypotheses about agenda setting, the degree of divided government, and international cooperation in the following section.

Divided Government in a Repeated-Play Model

With complete information in single play, the spatial model predicts that cooperation always occurs with the types of preferences shown. Because the probability of cooperation is always one, this model cannot yield propositions about the conditions that make cooperation more or less likely. This simple prediction reflects the fact that many complications important in actual international negotiations have been left out. The most salient of these complications is the problem of enforcing cooperation in an anarchic world (Axelrod 1984; Oye 1986; Taylor 1976/1987).[16] Two players will fail to achieve even a welfare-improving agreement if the sanctions against cheaters are too weak to deter defection.

The standard analysis finds that cooperation will occur only if the state's preferences meet the Taylor-Axelrod condition $(T-R)/(T-P) \geq w$.[17] In this condition, R represents the payoff from mutual cooperation, P the payoff when cooperation breaks down, T the temptation to defect, and w the discount factor or "shadow of the future." In country A, either the legislature or the executive could be in charge of implementing this punishment, so I examine the Taylor-Axelrod condition for both of them.

Because the discount factor is unobservable, we cannot determine *ex ante* whether the conditions for cooperation are met. Instead, I look at the payoffs P, R, and T in the spatial model, and then see how changing these payoffs affects the Taylor-Axelrod condition for cooperation. This synthesis of spatial models and repeated-play enforcement mechanisms makes cooperation probabilistic, allowing me to conduct comparative statics on the conditions that make cooperation more or less likely. Lowering the reversion point (P), raising the rewards of cooperation (R), or lowering the temptation to defect (T) makes this condition more likely to hold.

Consider first what happens when the legislature controls the reversion point (as in figure 4.7). If L were to move to the right, the reversion point would grow worse for both E and B. This makes cooperation more likely for both. The rewards of cooperation have a more ambiguous effect: for some range the cooperative outcome (R) would move toward the executive's ideal point, making cooperation more likely. After this, R would move rightward away from t_A^E along the x-axis, making cooperation less likely. Throughout, this shift in R always makes cooperation less likely for B.

Since the legislature might decide to defect from any agreement, we must also consider L's Taylor-Axelrod condition. The utility of noncooperation is unchanged from as t_A^L moves, since L receives its ideal home tariff and an identical foreign tariff in either case. Given the narrow definition of the win-set used here, B will always propose an agreement that leaves L indifferent between it and the reversion point, so R is also unchanged. The temptation to defect T must also be unchanged if E and R are unchanged. As a result, an increasing degree of divided government has no effect on the legislature's Taylor-Axelrod condition.

In this institutional context, then, divided government makes cooperation more likely for the president until the win-set reaches the president's ideal point. Thereafter, it has ambiguous effects that will depend on the precise location of the various points in this figure. It has no effect on the legislature's willingness to accept international cooperation. Divided government at home always has ambiguous effects on foreigners' willingness to cooperate, making both the reversion point and the rewards from cooperation less attractive. This analysis means that the effects of divided government on international cooperation are anything but clear when we consider the reversion point.

The effects of divided government on cooperation differ when the executive, not the legislature, controls the reversion point. The executive might control the reversion point either because it set the status quo, or because it has authority to threaten a reversion point if a treaty is not ratified, regardless of the status quo before negotiations. If the executive, not the legislator, chooses the autonomous tariff, the noncooperative outcome is $N = \{t_A^E, t_B\}$. Moving the legislature rightward does not affect this, so the reversion point (P) does not depend on the legislature's preferences (see figure 4.7). However, divided government does affect the win-set. As L moves to the right, it will accept fewer agreements on the contract curve between E and B. This makes the rewards for cooperation greater for E but lower for B. With P unchanged, only these changes in R will affect the inequality $w \geq (T-R)/ (T-P)$. Divided government raises R for the president, making cooperation more likely. However, it lowers R for foreigners, making them less likely to cooperate. Because both must consent to cooperate, the net effect on international cooperation is unclear.

These changes make the legislature more likely to cooperate when E controls the reversion point. As divided government increases, L's utility from noncooperation (P) goes down because t_A^L becomes increasingly distant from the executive's ideal point. The reward for cooperation goes down by the same amount because, again, B leaves L indifferent between cooperation and noncooperation. Lowering both the denominator and numerator of $(T-R)/(T-P)$ by the same amount reduces the ratio because it is less than one. This change makes cooperation more likely. The temptation to defect (T) also goes down, as it must given the fact that R and P have decreased. This also makes cooperation more likely. As a result, L becomes less likely to reject cooperation as divided government increases, even though L's utility from both cooperation and noncooperation decreases. This follows because L is happy to have any concession from B that the executive can obtain, and will not reject cooperation if that leads to an undesirable reversion point.

When the executive controls the reversion point, then, divided government makes cooperation more likely for the executive and for the legislature. The effects are less clear for foreigners, but divided government will certainly make cooperation less likely after some range.[18] Divided government therefore has various effects on international cooperation when we model the reversion point explicitly. Institutions as well as preferences matter, especially the institutional control over the reversion point. Any case study should analyze the effects of divided government on the reversion point as well as on ratification, effects that depend heavily on both preferences and institutions.

Testing the Reversion-Point Claims

Reversion Points and International Cooperation in Austria–Hungary

Testing my claims about divided government requires comparable cases that exhibit variation in the independent variables of divided government, and ratifier or negotiator control over the reversion point. I have chosen three divided polities whose internal structures coincide with systematic differences in preferences. Austria–Hungary was divided from 1867 through the first world war, Sweden–Norway from 1814 to 1905. The German customs union (*Zollverein*) provides a third case, with structural characteristics different from the dual monarchies and providing further variation in preferences. Though with some qualifications and some variation over time, we can say that the legislature controlled the reversion point in Austria–Hungary, both the executive and the legislature controlled the reversion point in Sweden–Norway, and the "executive" (Prussia) controlled the reversion point in the *Zollverein*.

Because they had complementary economies with fairly strong commercial ties, a breakdown of cooperation could have been devastating for Austria–Hungary. The economies of Sweden and Norway were more likely to compete with each other, which meant that noncooperation might actually have been beneficial for key export groups.

Divided government in Austria dates to the *Ausgleich* (compromise) of 1866, which took effect in 1867. This agreement, which had to be renewed every ten years, replaced the Habsburg dynasty's unified absolutist empire with two states, the Kingdom of Hungary and the Austrian Empire.[19] While each was nominally independent and could set its own trade policy, these states were unified in the person of the King-Emperor Franz Joseph I, and shared a common currency, imperial bank, tariffs and many indirect taxes, railroads, army, and foreign policy. Joint ministries responsible to the Crown handled common affairs, with foreign economic policy falling under the authority of the foreign minister (Brauneder and Lachmayer 1980; Kann 1974; May 1951; Szíjartó 1994). When negotiating these trade treaties, the foreign minister consulted the two commerce ministers, and any treaty required ratification by both parliaments. This meant that the ratifier, the Hungarian Diet, had control over the reversion point because it could establish a separate tariff on its own authority. The theory predicts that this control would make cooperation more likely at least in some range.

While Austrian Germans had hoped that the Dual Monarchy would give Hungarian nationalists a greater stake in the empire, the Hungarians continued to differ with the Austrians on many issues (see Eddie 1972, 1977; Huertas 1977; Hunt 1974; Matis 1973: 41–45; Somogyi 1984 for overviews). On trade policy, for example, Hungary favored lower tariffs, looked to Germany for export markets, and saw agricultural producers such as Serbia and Romania as potential threats. Several important trade disputes hung on the fact that Hungary always wanted a strong veterinary convention with Germany to secure that export market, while seeking to deny Serbian hogs the same treatment in Austria. Austrian Germans generally favored higher tariffs, looked down the Danube for export markets in which they would not have to compete with west European industries, and feared competition in manufactured goods from Germany. The Viennese market also imported large quantities of livestock, meat, grains, and fruits from southeastern Europe, all of which competed with Hungarian trade in the same products.

Prior to the Austro-Prussian War (1866), Austrian trade policy was subordinated to foreign policy, especially in Germany (Vomáčková 1963). This lost war not only led to the *Ausgleich* but also freed economic policy from serving a lost cause in Germany. Austria had already begun to join the French trade treaty system by signing a treaty with France in 1862 and one with England in 1865. With the *Ausgleich* this tendency gained momentum. Austria signed treaties with Belgium (February 23, 1867), the Netherlands (March 26, 1867), Italy (April 23, 1867), Prussia (March 9, 1868), and Switzerland (July 14, 1868). This post–*Ausgleich* flurry exceeds Austria's activity in the wake of Cobden-Chevalier, so presumably the *Ausgleich* and not the Cobden-Chevalier treaty network provided the essential difference in context.

Because the two halves of the empire retained the right to impose an independent tariff, negotiations with foreigners were always linked to implicit and explicit threats to reimpose a tariff boundary (*Zwischenzolllinie*) between Austria and Hungary. Hungary typically threatened to reinstall the old customs boundary if its concerns in agricultural trade were not given greater weight in negotiations with outsiders. The resulting demands on foreigners also led to occasional trade wars, which therefore coincided with the decennial *Ausgleich* renewals (the "economic compromises" in popular parlance). As a result, a causal link to the *Ausgleich*, and not the French treaty system, is most likely.[20]

The first renewal came while protectionism was growing strong in Austria as a result of the economic difficulties of the 1870s. In late 1875, Austria floated the idea of letting the existing trade treaties expire without renewal. In that case, responded Hungary, it wished to end the customs union with Austria and impose its own tariff. Austria backed down and renewed the treaties. Taking advantage of its evident leverage, Hungary also consented to the increases in a new Austrian tariff only on the condition that this new "autonomous" tariff for the empire include the tariff reductions of any future treaty with Germany (von Bazant 1894: 16–17, 28–29).

While it agreed to renew the treaties in western Europe, these actions prompted Austria to pursue favorable treaties with its own natural markets in the Balkans. The most important of these was an extensive treaty with Serbia in 1881, in which the empire reduced or eliminated tariffs on many agricultural goods in exchange for Serbian reductions on most of its exports and a strong veterinary convention (Láng 1906: 289–291). A stronger link between divided government and international cooperation can hardly be imagined.

In coming years, *Ausgleich* renewals regularly coincided with tariff wars. These include a tariff war with Romania during the negotiations on the second renewal in 1887 (Hunt 1974; Láng 1906: 291–292), and with Serbia around the third (1895–1896) and fourth (1906) *Ausgleich* renewals (Lampe and Jackson 1982: Chapter 6). In short, these *Ausgleich* renewals forced both Austria and Hungary to reassess their policies not only with one another but also with third parties. The functioning of this divided polity produced not only a heightened risk of trade wars but also renewed and expanded cooperation with outsiders after each "war."

Germany, which was by far the empire's largest trading partner, played a central role in Austro-Hungarian commercial policy in a way that strengthened the ties between divided government and international cooperation. In the early 1890s, the imperial-and-royal government was divided over whether talks with Germany or the Balkan countries should be concluded first. While Hungary was ready for immediate talks with Germany, the Austrians demanded that agreements be reached first with Serbia and Romania. Both sides feared that concluding any one treaty would make later treaties more difficult (Weitowitz 1978: 55–56). This makes sense in terms of the Taylor-Axelrod condition discussed earlier, in which any agreement with a third party raises the utility that Austria–Hungary would receive in the reversion point with fourth parties, since the earlier agreement would only take place if it made both sides better off. This improvement in the reversion point (P) makes the Taylor-Axelrod condition for successful cooperation less likely to be met.

The solution to this problem lay in an informal agreement known as the "Montssche Proposition." Germany and Austria–Hungary each agreed not to negotiate any treaties without coordinating with the other state. This meant that Hungary could consent to Balkan treaties since the negotiations would be linked to Hungary's own efforts to open Germany.

In these ways, Austro-Hungarian cooperation with the outside world always had close links to divided government at home. The case demonstrates a tight link between divided government and greater cooperation stemming from an undesirable reversion point and the ratifier's control over this reversion point, both of which made cooperation more likely (at least to a point). While theoretically ambiguous, the case also suggests how increasingly divided government at home can make foreigners more willing to cooperate. Though it reduces the reward to foreigners for cooperation, divided government also makes the reversion point much worse. The tariff wars with the Balkan states show both of these effects, with one-sided treaties and dreadful reversion points. Depending on the exact payoffs in the fraction (T-R)/(T-P), this protectionism may make cooperation either more or less likely. This theoretical point has clear empirical referent in the Austro-Hungarian case.

Reversion Points and International Cooperation in Sweden–Norway

Divided government worked differently in the Kingdom of Sweden–Norway than in Austria-Hungary. Here the negotiator and the ratifier jointly set the reversion point. This institutional framework has much more ambiguous effects on cooperation. Given this theoretical ambiguity, a review of the economic structure of the Dual Monarchy is necessary to supplement the institutional analysis. Because their economies were not complementary, the reversion point of an internal tariff boundary was not unattractive for important groups in both countries. This made cooperation less likely under divided government.

The Convention of Moss (1814) unified Sweden and Norway in the person of the Swedish king. Though each country retained its own constitution and armed forces, foreign affairs and similar matters were handled jointly. With some exceptions for particular goods, Sweden and Norway had a joint tariff from 1825 to 1897, though Norway refused to extend the items covered after 1857 (Lindgren 1959: Chapter 3). Both countries' parliaments controlled the customs and excise duties. The cabinet (formally, the King-in-Council) could negotiate commercial treaties with foreign governments, subject to legislative ratification by both countries (Szijártó 1994; Verney 1957). The Swedish foreign service handled almost all negotiations, and the treaties reached were equally effective in both nations.

Unlike the complementary economies of Austria and Hungary, Norway and Sweden had very similar and even competitive economic structures (Lindgren 1959: Chapter 3). Dairy products were the mainstay of both countries' agricultural sectors, though both countries rapidly expanded into forest products from the 1870s. Later in the century, Norway developed new fishing, whaling, and chemical industries (Hodne 1983), while Sweden turned to machine industries, the steel industry, and iron ore exports. Instead of trading with one another, Sweden and Norway both looked to England and Germany for trade. Most commerce went by sea, and each country had a sizeable merchant marine active in the other's ports. Links over the mountains making up the border were virtually nonexistent until Norway's Narvik became the exit port for iron exports from the Swedish Arctic.

Both halves of the monarchy saw agitation for tariff revision in the 1870s. This ultimately produced a higher Swedish tariff in 1888. In part out of a desire to oppose the Swedes but also reflecting the importance of the shipping sector, many Norwegians favored freer trade—though the agricultural party (the *Venstre*) supported tariff increases despite opposing the Swedish union. As a result, only a narrow margin supported freer trade in the Norwegian *Storting*, just as only a narrow majority existed for protectionism in the Swedish *Riksdag*. Threats to change the reversion point would not have imposed major costs on either kingdom. As a result, such threats are not in evidence in debates over trade policy, and therefore did not encourage cooperation with outsiders.

The comparative perspective in this chapter also helps rule out constitutional instability as an inhibitor of Swedish cooperation. Sweden signed two important treaties with Germany in a period of great constitutional instability. Yvonne Maria Werner (Werner 1989: 226) argues that weak and uncertain governments hindered these negotiations; as the German negotiator, Paul von Koerner, reported home on December 1, 1905, "the changes in government have had negative effects on the negotiations."[21] Perhaps surprisingly, this constant instability did not prevent either the treaty of 1906 or 1911 (see Lindberg 1983). Because instability did not have the kind of inhibiting effect that I found in México and a few other countries above, the analysis of divided government here provides a more plausible explanation of the Swedish evidence.

The analysis here supplements the existing literature on Swedish trade policy. The historiography stresses Swedish desires to pursue an autonomous commercial policy (i.e., Werner 1989: Chapter 2), though it does not give many reasons for this choice. Like many constitutional monarchies in which the cabinet did not rely on parliamentary support, divisions between the executive and legislative branches made the cabinet hesitant to negotiate many treaties. Deep divisions in Sweden over trade policy reinforced this hesitation (Lindberg 1983). The theoretical ambiguity and the preferences of the major players suggest that the conventional wisdom's claims about divided government are not too far from the mark in the case of Sweden–Norway.

Divided Government and the *Zollverein*

Like the dual monarchies, the German customs union (*Zollverein*) was characterized by divided government. The *Zollverein* differed from the dual monarchies in that the negotiator, Prussia, also controlled the reversion point. In this institutional framework, divided government makes cooperation more likely for both the executive and the legislature.

States joined the *Zollverein* by adopting the Prussian tariff by treaty. Thereafter, Prussia negotiated treaties with outsiders subject to ratification by the two houses of the Prussian legislature and the *Zollverein* Congress.[22] In other words, Berlin set the agenda by negotiating treaties. It also had significant power over the reversion point, which was originally the Prussian tariff itself. (Eventually, *Zollverein* congresses could also revise the common external tariff.)

The other members often had different interests than the Prussians. In addition to the usual sectoral differences stemming from variation in economic structure, the South Germans favored closer political ties to Austria and thus opposed Prussian maneuvers to weaken those ties. The South Germans were also generally more protectionist than the commercially oriented states of the north and west. However, divided government meant that Prussia could propose foreign treaties that other states opposed. If they balked, Prussia could threaten an unattractive reversion point, such as higher intra-German tariffs or the creation of rival customs unions, to force the treaty through. The theory shows how divided government with negotiator control over the reversion point can make a ratifier more likely to cooperate, even if cooperation is not particularly desirable to that ratifier.

The two major crises of the *Zollverein* (1848–1853 and 1861–1864) both involved linking domestic cooperation to foreign treaties in this way. While divided government produced each crisis, in both cases the reversion point helped Prussia force reluctant members to accept the proposed treaty. The first crisis arose when Hannover, on behalf of the Tax Union (*Steuerverein*), agreed to join the *Zollverein* in exchange for union tariff reductions on coffee, tea, tobacco, syrup, cognac, and wines. By lowering effective tariffs further and strengthening traditionally free trade groups in Germany, Hannover's accession spelled the end of any possibility that more protectionist Austria might join the *Zollverein* (Henderson 1984: Chapter 6; Matis 1973; Vomáčková 1963).

Neither Hannover nor Prussia consulted the other parties of their respective unions before signing the treaty. In the *Steuerverein*, Schaumburg-Lippe and Oldenburg acceded easily. In contrast, Prussia faced significant opposition from pro-Austrian states in the *Zollverein*. It responded by denouncing the *Zollverein* in November 1851, saying that it would renew the customs union only in conjunction with the Hannover treaty. Prussia's decision forced the middle German states to choose between a more liberal *Zollverein* oriented toward the west or trying to form a new and more protectionist union with Austria.

Austria tried to exploit the situation by introducing a lower tariff and inviting all German states to discuss a commercial treaty or customs union. These efforts brought no fruit in the end. Dividing Germany into rival unions would sacrifice the gains many states had already achieved through the *Zollverein*. For example, Saxony's Minister-President Graf Beust noted that dissolution of the *Zollverein* would seriously threaten the Leipzig book trade that dominated north Germany, the Leipzig fair, and the Leipzig cigar industry, which had a large market in Prussia (Zorn 1973: 332). As a result, the Prussian threat succeeded in forcing the other states to accept the *Steuerverein* treaty.

The second crisis of the *Zollverein* (1862–1865) also ended with Prussian threats (Ashley 1926: Chapter 3; Davis 1997: Chapter 7; Henderson 1984: Chapter 8; Marsh 1999: 40–45; Zorn 1963). Only Saxony and Baden were willing to accept Prussia's 1862 treaty with France;[23] Württemberg, Hannover, Nassau and Hesse-Darmstadt all rejected the treaty at first. Some of these states feared competition, but most opposed the French treaty because they wanted to improve *Zollverein* relations with Austria first. The Prussian government said it would treat rejection of the French treaty as a desire to dissolve the *Zollverein*, and it gave formal notice of the termination of the *Zollverein* in December 1863.

Again, possible dissolution threatened the smaller states with disaster because of the high levels of economic integration achieved by the *Zollverein* (Zorn 1963, 1973). The last recalcitrants were Bavaria and Württemberg, two larger states that could seriously consider leaving the *Zollverein*. Still, King Ludwig II of Bavaria argued that even if Bavaria and Württemberg *could* go it alone, powerful economic interests would sooner or later force the government to rejoin the *Zollverein*. Northern Bavaria relied on the Prussian port of Hamburg for its trade with the outside world, and it also depended on Prussia's ally, Saxony, for cotton yarn exports and coal imports. Responding to such interests, Bavaria and Württemberg accepted the treaty in October 1864.

These cases provide further evidence that divided government can make international cooperation more likely. Because it could make the reversion point unattractive to other states, Prussia could force through treaties that most South Germans opposed. This rested on institutional powers as well as the difference in preferences. Here, the same actor controlled both the reversion point and the foreign negotiations, lacking only ratification power. As the theory would expect, this made cooperation easier.

Conclusions

Divided government has two kinds of effects on international cooperation. First, as the literature has emphasized, increasing the degree of divided government makes legislative ratification of treaties more difficult. I have argued that a few divided polities did face ratification problems, especially México. Argentina, France, the Netherlands, Switzerland, the United States, and Uruguay also faced lesser ratification problems. Taken as a group, these countries account for very little of the variation in cooperation that we observe. Only France was a key player in the cooperation network whose nonratification affected the system as a whole.

Second, and overlooked by most of the literature, divided government affects the status quo. The exact effects depend on both the degree of divided government and on the identity of the agenda-setter. In Austria-Hungary, divided government made the reversion point worse, making international cooperation more likely. Divided government had little effect on the reversion point in Sweden-Norway, so the conventional wisdom's emphasis on ratification problems is probably well-placed. Interestingly, removing the divided government constraint liberated Sweden to cooperate more extensively with others, while it had no effect on Norway's willingness to cooperate. Divided government in the *Zollverein* let Prussia manipulate both the reversion point and any agreement reached with outsiders, making cooperation easier when Prussia desired it.

These relationships between divided government and international cooperation are highly context-dependent. One would not argue, for example, that the divisions of the Dual Monarchy made Austro-Russian cooperation in the Balkans, or Austro-Serbian cooperation more likely in 1914. The reverse is, of course, true.

This context dependence makes large-n studies difficult without doing violence to the underlying theory (see also Pahre 2005). The theory of two-level games is often more easily tested with case studies in which one can obtain the information necessary for analysis.

Chapter 5

Divided Government and the Ratification of the Amsterdam Treaty
Simon Hug and Thomas König

The member countries of the European Union (EU) signed the treaty of Amsterdam on October 2, 1997. It amended the Treaty on European Union (TEU) and the three Community Treaties. The most noteworthy modifications concerned the six areas of citizenship, justice and home affairs, employment, the environment, agricultural and fishing, and a common foreign and security policy (Langrish 1998: 3). Compared to the Maastricht treaty, which formed the last addition to the reversion point, these modifications were less ambitious on European integration, because member states excluded half of the issues of the draft proposal to find consensus at the Amsterdam intergovernmental conference (Hug and König 2002). According to Moravcsik and Nicolaidis (1999: 70), governments widely circulated the draft proposal for the intergovernmental conference "to minimize the possibility of subsequent ratification failures." If this is correct, the Amsterdam intergovernmental conference (IGC) provides a powerful illustration of the influence domestic ratification constraints may have on the bargaining process of international cooperation. However, the mere existence of domestic ratification constraints at the institutional level does not tell the full story. The difference in preferences between the executives and the domestic ratifiers, that is the degree of divided government, determines whether these constraints play any effective role in shaping bargaining outcomes.

These effects of domestic ratification constraints on international cooperation have come increasingly under the theoretical scrutiny of scholars.

According to Pahre (this volume, chapter 1) two perspectives can be distinguished: Ever since Putnam's (1988) seminal article "Diplomacy and Domestic Politics: The Logic of Two-Level Games," scholars have paid more attention to studying Schelling's (1960) "Paradox of Weakness." Authors adopting this perspective (Iida 1993, 1996; Milner and Rosendorff 1996; Mo 1994, 1995; Pahre 1997; Schneider and Cederman 1994) examine whether governments, which are more restricted by domestic ratification constraints, perform better in international negotiations than their domestically less restricted counterparts. For the Amsterdam intergovernmental conference, Hug and König (2002) find that the closely restricted governments were more effective in eliminating from the bargaining table issues they liked less. Other scholars emphasize the relationship between domestic ratification hurdles and the likelihood of international cooperation. On the one hand, some authors find that the presence of more restricted governments at the bargaining table makes international cooperation less likely, because their winsets will not overlap (e.g., Karol 2000; Putnam 1988). Given overlapping winsets, others suggest that restricted governments make international cooperation more likely, because such governments have fewer possibilities to renege on agreements they might reach (Martin 2000).

In many studies that adopt one of these perspectives the notion of restricted governments refers to the presence of a divided government. The term divided government is usually reserved for presidential systems in which the president's party does not control the majority party in the legislature. Thus, many empirical analyses focus on the effect of divided government on international agreements in the U.S. context (Karol 2000; Lohmann and O'Halloran 1994). Fiorina (1992) notes a strong similarity, however, between divided government in presidential systems and coalition governments, which are the norm in parliamentary systems (Alesina and Rosenthal 1995; Laver and Shepsle 1991). Other scholars of divided government have investigated how bicameral systems, in which the second chamber can be considered as veto player (Bräuninger and König 1999; Krehbiel 1996; Tsebelis 1995), may lead to unified and divided government (König 2001; Tsebelis and Money 1997). In all these views, the party affiliations of the president and the majority of the first and/or second chamber serve as proxies for the preferences of the actors. Thus, divided government in most studies is simply a dichotomous variable. The implication then is that, for instance, divided government can make international cooperation less likely because the preferences of either the president and the legislature and/or the bicameral veto player(s) differ. Often, however, the dichotomous nature of divided government is too reductionist, and Milner (1997: 38) proposes as a continuous measure for divided government the distance in preferences between the veto players.

In the following we assess how the notion of divided government helps us in understanding the negotiations leading to the Amsterdam treaty and the subsequent ratification of the new treaty in all EU member states. We show that using partisan differences alone is not enough because some parties have similar preferences on European integration, while other parties have internal differences in this question. Instead we must look at preferences in more detail and assess the resulting degree of divided government.

Our starting point is a generally employed definition of divided government in comparative politics (Pahre 2001a: 133), namely that two or more partisan actors affect the policy game. Based on this definition we first present different criteria relying on the differences with respect to presidents, government coalitions, bicameralism, and the different parties controlling these institutions. Applying these criteria to the governments having participated in the Amsterdam intergovernmental conference and having ratified the treaty, we uncover limitations of classifications relying only on such institutional and partisan criteria. Based on these results we argue that measuring the preferences of the relevant actors is crucial to assess the degree to which a government is divided. After discussing several alternatives, we propose a specific approach for measuring the actors' preferences on the Amsterdam treaty. Since we believe that measures on pro- or anti-European integration positions are too crude for the analysis of the preferences of the Amsterdam actors, we introduce our measurement of government and ratification veto players' preferences based on information from mass surveys. Finally, we show the differences between classifications of divided government and the findings based on preference measures of the actors involved. Regarding the likelihood of international cooperation, the classification based solely on institutional and partisan criteria predicts either a failure of the Amsterdam intergovernmental conference because almost all 15 member states were constrained by divided government, or, if the winsets would overlap, member state governments should have performed equally well at the Amsterdam intergovernmental conference because all governments were similarly divided according to these classifications. However, the Amsterdam treaty was adopted and ratified without attracting public attention, and member state governments significantly differed in their negotiation performance (Hug and König 2002). Since the classification relying also on preference measures introduces much more variation in the degree to which governments were divided, we conclude that whenever possible such measures should be included in the definition of divided government. Other variables from the framework in chapter 1 do not explain variation in the bargaining outcomes, however. All of the member states had similar agenda structures in that the government of the day negotiated the Amsterdam treaty and then submitted it to domestic ratifiers. The reversion point was the same for all countries: the status quo established by the previous treaties such as Maastricht. Since these variables did not vary across member states in the European Union, they do not help explain variation in the outcome.

Divided Governments in EU Member Countries

In recent years, except for a few periods, the party affiliation of the American president has differed from the majority party in one or both houses of Congress. Thus, the notion of divided government first appeared in the literature on the American presidential system. Many scholars argue, however, that the notion of divided government has close parallels in parliamentary democracies. The close parallels come about by the fact that in many parliamentary democracies more than one partisan actor has to approve political decisions, such as adopting a bill or ratifying a treaty. The necessity for support of other partisan actors may be the result of a president wielding some power in particular policy areas, the type of government coalition, qualified majorities in parliamentary votes, the presence of a second chamber, or particular provisions for referendums. Since the notion of divided government appeared first for presidential systems, we start by discussing the role of the president in the EU member states. Then, we move on and assess for the 15 governments the partisan compositions of the various institutional actors, including the presidency.[1]

Presidents in Semipresidential Systems

Even though all member countries of the EU are parliamentary democracies, some of them have a directly elected president who in some cases has wide-ranging powers. Political systems with such presidents are often referred to as semipresidential (e.g., Duverger 1980). In his detailed study of these systems, Martinez (1999) comes to the conclusion that on basis of the constitution, the presidents in Austria, Finland, France, Ireland, and Portugal all have wide-ranging powers and in addition are directly elected. He demonstrates, however, that Austria and Ireland are only "seemingly semi-presidential," since the powers of the president have been severely curtailed by common agreement among the political parties (Martinez 1999: 20). The constitutions of the remaining countries, namely Finland, France, and Portugal also give the president control over foreign policy (Martinez 1999: 33). Consequently, the party membership of the president in these countries might lead to a type of divided government coming very close to the type present in the American presidential system. The large literature on French cohabitation, first between President Mitterrand and Prime Ministers Chirac and Balladur, and then between President Chirac and Prime Minister Jospin, indicates this important parallel.

Government Coalitions

The typical reason for more than one partisan actor to be involved in the policy game in EU member states is that the support of more than one partisan actor in parliament is necessary to pass bills. This additional support is required because the government either is a coalition or only controls a minority of seats in parliament (e.g., Milner 1997; Pahre 2001a). Thus, Pahre (2001a: 133) suggests that many studies classify governments as divided whenever they are minority or coalition governments. In table 5.1 (column 1) we report for all 15 member countries having signed the Amsterdam treaty the government's partisan composition and whether it should be considered as divided according to this criterion at the time of signature in 1997.

As table 5.1 (column 1) shows, most governments, namely 13 out of 15, were either coalition or minority governments. Only in Greece and the United Kingdom did the single government party control a majority of seats in parliament when the Amsterdam treaty was signed on October 2, 1997. The same partisan composition of the governments still existed when the various governments were able, after parliamentary and possibly referendum votes, to deposit their ratification instruments with the Italian government.[2]

Requirements for Qualified Majorities in Amsterdam Treaty Ratification

While the criterion based on the coalition status of governments gives us a broad indication whether a government is divided, in some ways it does not exhaust the criterion of whether more than one partisan actor is needed to pass a treaty. A first way, how additional partisan actors might be needed is induced by possible requirements of qualified majorities in support of a treaty for parliamentary ratification. We report in table 5.1 (column 2) for each country whether such a qualified majority requirement was present for the ratification of the Amsterdam treaty. In more than half the countries, namely eight out of 15, the constitution required qualified majorities, ranging

Table 5.1   Divided Governments in EU Member Countries[a]

Country	Government	Separation of powers	Referendum
Austria	c: SPÖ/ÖVP	(b)q:2/3	
Belgium	c: CVP/PSC/SP/PS	(b: regions?)	
Denmark	c: SD/RV	Q: 5/6	nonrequired: 1/6 of MPs
Finland	c: SDP/KOK/SEP/VIHR/VAS	q:2/3(p)	
France	c: PC/PS/Mouvement des citoyens/Radicaux de gauche/Verts	bq:3/5p	nonrequired: government/ President
Germany	c: CDU/CSU/FDP	bq:2/3	
Greece	M: PASOK	q:3/5	
Ireland	c: FF/Progressive Democrats	(b)	required
Italy	c: PDS/PPI/UD/RI/VERTS	(b)	
Luxembourg	c: CSV/LSAP	q:2/3	
Netherlands	c: PVDA/VVD/D66	(b)	
Portugal	M: PS	(p)	nonrequired: government/ President
Spain	m: PP	(b)	
Sweden	m: SD	q:3/4	
United Kingdom	M: Labour	b	

Note: [a] In the appendix (Table 5.3) we report the full names of the parties appearing in this table.

Legend: Government: government type on October 2, 1997 (signing of Amsterdam treaty) (c: coalition government, m: one-party minority government, M: one-party majority; Separation of powers (b second chamber (in parenthesis, if controlled by same parties as lower house) q: qualified majority for passage (in parenthesis if government parties control qualified majority), p: semipresidentialism (in parenthesis if president belongs to a party in government).

Sources: EJPR Political Data Yearbook 1998 (1999), European Union (1999), Martinez (1999), Hug and König (2002), and Hug and Tsebelis (2002).

from three-fifths to five-sixths of the votes, in parliament for the ratification of the Amsterdam treaty. In all these eight countries, this required the support of additional partisan actors than those that formed the government.

Thus, since in Greece a qualified majority of three-fifths was required to ratify the Amsterdam treaty and PASOK (Greek Socialist Party), the government party, controlled barely more than 50 percent of the seats in parliament, an additional party had to vote in favor of the new treaty to make a successful ratification possible. This shows that classifying governments as divided or unified solely on the basis of their coalition status can be quite misleading for studying ratification processes. As the case of Greece illustrates, a single party may well form the government and control a majority of seats in parliament, but still need the support of an additional partisan actor to ratify an international treaty. Consequently, if we also consider qualified majorities as criterion to distinguish between divided and unified governments, we also have to rule out Greece as unified government and are left with the United Kingdom as the only case belonging to this latter category.

Bicameral Votes Required in Treaty Ratification

As the American literature suggests, however, divided government may also result from different parties controlling the House and Senate, which results in one chamber of Congress being controlled by a party different from the president's party. Given that several member countries also have a second chamber, we need to assess the effect of a possible bicameral constraint on the dividedness of governments in EU member countries. Again, a majority of countries, namely nine out of 15, required positive votes in both the lower and the upper house of parliament for the ratification of the Amsterdam treaty.[3] In some of these countries, since the upper houses have a different partisan composition, the bicameral ratification of the Amsterdam treaty required the support of an additional partisan actor to the parties represented in government.[4] Thus, in France, Germany, and the United Kingdom the bicameral ratification requested the support of a party outside government. Obviously, in the case of France and Germany, the qualified majorities (either in the combined session of both French houses of parliament, or the qualified majorities in the lower house, as well as in the upper house) already required a nongovernmental party supporting the ratification of the Amsterdam treaty. Only in the United Kingdom, and here only in the sense that a negative vote of the House of Lords delays the ratification of a treaty, does the bicameral ratification add another partisan actor.

The President's Role in Semipresidential Systems

Among the EU member countries we find, as discussed earlier, three (namely Finland, France, and Portugal) that have directly elected presidents with considerable powers so that the political systems can be classified as semipresidential. In all three countries the constitution also assigns a crucial role to the president in conducting foreign policy (Martinez 1999: 33). In addition, with the exception of Finland, the presidents may trigger a referendum, either after consultation with the government (France), or after a decision by the constitutional court (Portugal), on the ratification of a treaty (Hug and Tsebelis 2002). Combined, these two sets of powers make the president another crucial player in the ratification game. As table 5.1 (column 2) shows, however, only in France did the President (Jacques Chirac) belong to a party not represented in the cabinet. Thus, only in France did an additional partisan actor need to support a treaty to ensure ratification, but obviously, this additional support is also required because of the bicameral vote with qualified majorities.

Referendums

As the discussion of semipresidential systems shows, the possibility of calling a referendum may enhance the powers of an actor. As Hug and Tsebelis (2002) demonstrate, the power to trigger a referendum and the power to formulate the question posed to the voters are crucial elements distinguishing different forms of constitutional provisions allowing for referendums. In the case of treaty referendums, we must distinguish between required and nonrequired referendums and, among the latter, determine who triggers the popular vote. As table 5.1 (column 3) shows, only Ireland can be considered as a country requiring referendums on international treaties related to the EU.[5] On the other hand, the Danish constitution envisions a referendum being triggered by a minority of one-sixth of the members of parliament, if a treaty involves transfers of powers.[6] In some countries, the constitution contains precise provisions allowing particular actors to trigger a referendum. Often the actors empowered to do so are the governments themselves. Unsurprisingly, provisions for such referendums have little notable effects on policy outcomes (e.g. Hug and Tsebelis 2002).[7] In addition, even if the constitution does not explicitly envision referendums triggered by the government, the referendums having occurred in the United Kingdom, for instance, demonstrate that all governments could probably trigger a referendum on an international treaty.[8] Thus these government-triggered referendums hardly increase the dividedness of government. For this reason we do not consider the referendums triggered by government as additional ratification constraint.

Summary

In sum, we can consider divided governments in parliamentary democracies on the basis of either the coalition status of the government, or, more precisely, in terms of whether the support of a single partisan actor is sufficient in all institutional settings to ensure the ratification of a treaty. According to the first and simpler criterion we find that only Greece and the United Kingdom were unified governments during the signing and ratification of the Amsterdam treaty. If we use the second and more accurate criterion, we either find all governments being divided, or only the United Kingdom remaining as unified government, since a negative vote of the House of Lords can only have delaying effects. Independent of this distinction we observe that there is very little variation in terms of divided governments in parliamentary democracies. Either governments in such democracies have to be considered as divided because of their coalition status, or they are divided because constitutional rules for ratification require qualified majorities, bicameral votes, presidential approval, or referendums.

Identifying Policy Positions of Partisan Actors

The systematic classification of divided government has shown little variation among the 15 member states having participated in the Amsterdam intergovernmental conference. In a strict sense, with the exception of the United Kingdom, all member states had a divided government when applying a simple partisan and institutional definition of a divided polity to the ratification process of the Amsterdam treaty. This, however, assumes that political parties diverge in their opinions on the topic of European integration, or, more specifically, of the Amsterdam treaty. To uncover whether the parties really diverged, we would need measures of their preferences covering all the issues discussed at the Amsterdam intergovernmental conference. Laver and Hunt (1992) discuss three possible instruments for measuring such preferences. The first instrument relies on document analysis of party manifestos, the second uses expert interviews, and the third explores mass surveys.

Measures on European Integration

For the identification of actors' preferences a major problem concerns the trade-off between the validity and reliability of the data. Reliability refers to the degree to which the instrument can appropriately measure an underlying factor, while validity refers to the degree to which this factor relates to the theoretical concept in question (e.g., Holsti 1968 and Ray 1999: 288). The Party Manifesto Group has collected data on preferences on various items for most European countries and political parties (Budge et al. 1987; Volkens 2001). The instrument has the advantage that it directly relies on the statements of the political parties. Although the quantitative content analysis of party manifestos is highly contingent on the coding scheme, the results are judged to be reliable. However, among the items of the Party Manifesto Group's coding scheme, there is only a single item that indicates whether a party is in favor or against European integration, and some parties do not mention the issue of European integration in their manifestos.

A similar level of information is provided by Ray (1999) who conducted an expert survey on the preferences of political parties on the dimension of European integration. Experts were identified by the European Consortium of Political Scientists (ECPR) handbook of political scientists who indicated a specialization in either the domestic political system of their nation or European politics. Luxembourg's low response rate forced the opening of the survey to newspaper editors. The experts were asked which position a political party has on European integration, what importance the issue has for the party, and to what degree there is internal dissent within each political party on the issue. The last question is helpful for assessing the unitary actor assumption on political parties because the degree of internal dissent can be used to indicate the probability for a party's vote on European integration.[9]

In the context of our analysis both instruments provide a similar level of information on a single dimension of European integration. For two reasons, however, such information can hardly uncover the preferences of the actors involved in intergovernmental conferences. First, while intergovernmental conferences and the resulting treaties mark cornerstones of European integration, we can hardly conclude that the Amsterdam treaty necessarily promoted European integration. Some progress has been achieved in particular policy domains and in procedural transparency by simplifying the range of possible legislative procedures. Except for monetary policy provisions, the cooperation procedure has been largely abolished, and the European Parliament has obtained a veto right under the (modified) codecision procedure. However, the Amsterdam treaty did not fulfill the expectations of many observers and participants alike. A preparatory Reflection Group had stated that a major aim would be to prepare the European Union's institutions for enlargement, but an agreement on the number of commissioners, the council's voting thresholds, and the member state's voting weights could not be reached. By contrast, the protocol made enlargement dependent on the European Union's ability to reform its institutions and notes compensation for member states that have to give up their second commissioner. That the European Union could not find a solution is best illustrated by the treaty's provision stating that another intergovernmental conference has to carry out a "comprehensive review" of its institutional provisions a year before the EU will exceed twenty members. For this reason, we cannot assume that proponents of enlargement (integration) were supporting the Amsterdam treaty.

Second, the analysis of Hug and König (2002) illustrates another ambiguity of the Amsterdam treaty. They find that consensus among the 15 member states was reached by excluding half of the policy issues of the draft proposal of the Amsterdam treaty. This means that the Amsterdam treaty produced many so-called leftovers, which can even lead to European disintegration. In this case, the indication on European integration cannot reveal whether a prointegrationist political party would vote for or against the Amsterdam treaty. This implies that European integration is a broad concept, which is captured by Party Manifesto document analysis and expert interviews in a reliable manner. However, these preference measures have considerable drawbacks regarding their validity for analyzing the Amsterdam treaty. Another problem relates to the unidimensionality of these data, which is constructed by design of both instruments. The Amsterdam treaty encompasses a large number of issues that can hardly be reduced to a single dimension. König and Hug (2000) show, however, that considering the Maastricht treaty in a one-dimensional policy space may mislead us in our understanding of the ratification process.

Measures on the Amsterdam Treaty

Ideally, our analysis would start with preference measures on the issues of the Amsterdam treaty of all actors involved, such as the preferences of governments and the MPs in each country. Wessels, Kielhorn, and Thomassen (1996) collected data on national MPs, but this dataset fails to cover all 15 member countries, and inferring the party's positions based on responses by the responses of MEPs proves haphazard. Another instrument is provided by mass surveys allowing us to identify the positions of political parties' electorate. Using the electorates' positions as proxies for the positions of the political parties raises the question of the reliability of this instrument. Gabel and Huber (2000) show that inferring the parties' position based on the positions of their sympathizers leads to very similar results as those obtained with other instruments.

We expect to increase the validity of the data because the Eurobarometer asked for positions on specific issues related to the Amsterdam treaty. By calculating the mean positions of the sympathizers of a particular party we aggregate these positions of respondents to the level of the political party. The Eurobarometer survey does not allow us to have preference measures for each and every issue negotiated at the Amsterdam intergovernmental conference, but we nevertheless find a series of questions in the Eurobarometer 47 that relate to six broader issue areas of the Amsterdam treaty (Langrish 1998: 3).[10] Table 5.2 shows the issue areas and preference measures that are available for the exploration of the parties' policy positions on the Amsterdam treaty.

For the identification of the policy positions of political parties in these areas, we use the mean position of their respective electorates. Since all these preferences are normalized to a scale from 0 to 1 (against, respectively in

Table 5.2   Eurobarometer Questions and Issue Areas

Issue area	Questions in Eurobarometer 47 (March–April 1997)
citizenship	– right to vote for foreigners (q22.7) – right to be candidate (q22.8)
interior	– EU responsible for matters not dealt with at national legional local level (q22.4)
employment	– workers' right (q23g) – unemployment (q23i)
environment	– protection of environment (q23b)
new policies	– agriculture and fishing policies (q23j)
foreign/security	– common foreign policy (q22.2) – defense policy (q22.3)

favor), and 1 indicating the most "integration"-prone position, values below 0.5 suggest that the party prefers no integration in a particular issue area. Hence, we are able to check whether the parties of a coalition government, the president's party, the bicameral majority, or even the popular vote of a referendum would commonly vote for or against an issue area of the Amsterdam treaty. This allows us to consider the interplay of actors' preferences and ratification provisions in all 15 member states.[11]

Preferences and Partisan Induced Divided Government

As discussed earlier, table 5.1 uses as information only the institutions and the partisan composition of the various actors intervening in the ratification of an international treaty like the Amsterdam treaty. Obviously, this partisan and institution induced classification of divided government neglects the possibility that partisan actors might have identical preferences. Thus, a two-party coalition government would appear as a divided government even though its two member parties might have identical preferences with respect to the key issues of a treaty. The same obviously might occur with respect to partisan actors whose support is necessary because of bicameralism, semipresidentialism or qualified majorities.

One way to assess the restrictiveness of the partisan and institutional induced divided government classification is to assess on the basis of our preference measures whether the members of a coalition government, a president, or the bicameral parliament disagree on the key issues of the Amsterdam treaty. Since our preference measure is scaled to an interval between 0 and 1, and 0 can be likened to the position of the status quo and 1 corresponds to the location of the Amsterdam treaty,[12] a government is most clearly divided if the ideal points of two parties whose approval is necessary for the ratification are on opposite sides of the midpoint of this interval (i.e., 0.5). We use this criterion to assess whether the 15 member countries are divided over the Amsterdam treaty. Approaching Milner's (1997) claim that divided government is a matter of degree and not a qualitative difference, we count the number of issues in which the relevant partisan actors have ideal points that are on opposite sides of the 0.5 midpoint. Since we have eight such issues, the degree of dividedness can vary for each country between 0 and 8.[13]

Table 5.3 presents our results. In the first two columns we report in a succinct manner whether a member country would appear as divided according to the simplistic classification exclusively based on the institutions and partisan composition. As discussed earlier, very little variation appears in that case among the 15 EU member countries. In column 3 of table 5.3 we report the number of issue areas over which there was disagreement in the government coalition.[14] According to this preference-based indicator of divided government, we find much more variation than with the simple institutional and partisan indicator. First, we note that many countries with coalition governments can hardly be considered as divided, since the government parties shared their views about the Amsterdam treaty. Germany and Luxembourg, for example, had coalition governments at the time of signing and ratifying the Amsterdam treaty, but on no issue was there disagreement among the coalition partners. On the other hand, in Denmark, Finland, and France, on at least three issues there was disagreement among the government partners. This preference-based dividedness, and, especially its degree, can obviously not be assessed with simple institutional and partisan indicators.

In columns 3 and 5 we also take into account whether the president in semipresidential systems or the parliamentary ratification requirements, for instance bicameralism and qualified majorities, increases the degree of preference-induced dividedness. These analyses suggest that in France, for instance, President Chirac of the RPR differed with respect to one issue on which the government was unified. The only other two countries that are affected in their degree of dividedness are Spain and Sweden. In the case of Spain, the minority status of the Popular Party led to two issues on which the majority in parliament opposed the government's view. In Sweden, the coalition government, being unified on the basis of preferences, faced division in parliament on two issues, because of the qualified majority requirement of three-fifths of all MPs.

Finally, in the last column of table 5.3 we report for the two countries that have held a referendum on the Amsterdam treaty, namely Denmark

Table 5.3 Divided Government as a Function of Coalition Status, Separation of Powers, and Policy Preferences

	Party and institution-induced divided government		degree of divided government induced by policy preferences			
	Coalition status	Separation of powers	Government	Government and president	Government president, and bicameralism	plus referendum
Austria	D	D	2	2	2	n/a
Belgium	D	D	1	1	1	n/a
Denmark	D	D	4	4	4	+0
Finland	D	D	5	5	5	n/a
France	D	D	3	4	4	n/a
Germany	D	D	0	0	0	n/a
Greece	U	D	0	0	0	n/a
Ireland	D	D	2	2	2	+0
Italy	D	D	2	2	2	n/a
Luxembourg	D	D	0	0	0	n/a
Netherlands	D	D	2	2	2	n/a
Portugal	D	D	0	0	0	n/a
Spain	D	D	0	0	2	n/a
Sweden	D	D	0	0	2	n/a
United Kingdom	U	U	0	0	0	n/a
(+ Lords)		D	0	0	2	n/a

Legend: D denotes divided governments, while U denotes unified governments. The numbers 0–9 reflect the number of nine issues related to the Amsterdam treaty on which partisan actors in government, parliament or the president had opposing views.

Sources: As table 5.1, Eurobarometer 47.1.

and Ireland, whether the population at large held a position different from government on the issues on which government was unified. Interestingly enough, in both countries the presence of the population as an additional veto player did not affect the degree of dividedness.

Our analysis comparing institutional and partisan-derived dividedness and the preference-based degree of divided government suggests the following conclusions. First, at least with respect to the ratification of the Amsterdam treaty, most of the disagreements over the different issues dealt with were already well represented in governments of the various member states. Since by definition one-party governments are not divided with respect to their preferences,[15] this lends some credence to the institutional partisan approach to classify coalition governments as divided. However, as the cases of Germany and Luxembourg demonstrate, coalition governments are not a sufficient condition for divided government. Similarly, majority governments, such as Greece and Britain are obviously unified if we take into account only the government level. If we consider only the government level, however, then minority one-party governments, like the ones in Spain and Portugal for instance, are obviously also unified. Second, our analysis suggests that even one-party majority governments may be divided. For instance, if we consider the delaying powers of the House of Lords in the British parliament, the fact that the Conservatives controlled the upper house leads to divisions in government on two issues. Vice versa, we also find that a minority government, like the one in Portugal, may be unified on the basis of preferences, since it shares its views with the president and the majority in parliament.

Thus, studying divided government on the basis of preferences provides a much more detailed view of possible divisions in a country. Relating our measure of divided government with the gains and losses that the various governments made at the Amsterdam intergovernmental conference suggests that the degree of dividedness is positively related to bargaining gains (Hug and König 2002). Thus, France, Denmark, and Finland are among the top gainers. These three countries are all heavily divided compared to the remaining countries when our preference-based measure is used. The same three countries do not differ from most of the other 15 member countries, however, when we consider a strictly institutional and partisan measure for divided government. This very tentative exploration suggests that divided government defined at the level of preferences provides a much better indicator and predicts much better negotiation gains.

Our preference-based measure also goes some way toward providing a quantitative indicator for divided government as suggested by Milner (1997). Obviously, given the continuous preference measure we use to construct this indicator, we might also provide a much more fine-grained assessment by measuring distances between the ideal points of the relevant partisan actors. This, in our view, would put too much of a burden on our preference measures and suggest a false sense of preciseness. Nevertheless, if more precise preference measure are available with an easy way to assess the location of the status quo and the treaty proposals, this endeavor would be extremely fruitful.

Conclusion

The literature on the effects of domestic institutions on international cooperation relies on the notion of divided government, which is often measured only on the basis of institutional and partisan criterion. The main focus of these studies is to assess whether divided governments (or governments with higher ratification hurdles) perform better in treaty negotiations, and whether such governments make international cooperation more likely. The theoretical literature has come up with contradictory answers to these two important questions. The empirical literature, not surprisingly, has also come to ambiguous conclusions (e.g., Evans et al. 1993).

In this chapter we eschewed the theoretical debate and focused on the way in which divided government is operationalized in empirical research. Starting off by employing the traditionally used criterion to distinguish between divided and unified governments, we found that almost all EU member states participating in the Amsterdam intergovernmental conferences were divided. Given that the negotiations, as well as the ratification, of this treaty succeeded, this might be taken as indication that divided government does increase the likelihood of international cooperation, as suggested by Martin (2000). On the other hand, the fact that almost none of the negotiating governments was unified suggests that no country could exploit its weakness as Schelling's (1960) Conjecture would predict. However, Hug and König (2002) show that issues dropped from the Amsterdam treaty benefited some countries much more than others.

This suggests that a strictly institutional and partisan based classification by unified and divided government is hardly sufficient. A government may well be formed by two different parties and not be divided, since both parties are ardent supporters of issues discussed at the Amsterdam intergovernmental conference. Thus, classifications relying solely on institutions and partisan distinctions can be seriously misleading.[16] We were able to demonstrate this by resorting to information on preferences over issues discussed in Amsterdam gleaned from survey responses of party identifiers. Using this information suggested that much fewer governments were deeply divided over the Amsterdam treaty than the simple partisan and institutional classifications suggested. Under this angle, the international cooperation achieved at Amsterdam seems to have relied much less on the presence of divided governments. Similarly, the variation in the degree of divided government across countries relates closely to the gains achieved in the negotiations. Hence, a more preference-based analysis indicates that Schelling's (1960) "Paradox of Weakness" explains the outcome of the Amsterdam treaty negotiations (Hug and König 2002).

These more nuanced insights are only possible because we assessed whether a government was divided or unified on the basis of preferences over issues discussed at the international conference. This shows that preference measures permit much better informed assessments of the effect of divided government on international cooperation and on advantages at the bargaining table.

Appendix

In table 5.4 we first report the full names of the parties appearing in table 5.1. Then we report the exact wording of the questions we used to infer the positions of the political parties. We also provide some additional detail on the procedures employed to calculate these positions.

Table 5.4 Party Abbreviations

Country	Party abbreviation	Party name
Austria	SPÖ	Austrian Socialist Party
	ÖVP	Austrian People's Party
Belgium	CVP	Christian-democratic Party (Flemish)
	PSC	Christian-social Party (Francophone)
	SP	Socialist Party (Flemish)
	PS	Socialist Party (Francophone)
Denmark	SD	Social-democratic Party
	RV	Liberal Party
Finland	SDP	Social-democratic Party
	KOK	National Rally
	SEP	Swedish People's Party
	VIHR	Green Party
	VAS	Left League
France	PC	Communist party
	PS	Socialist Party
	Mouvements des citoyens	Citizen's movement (left)
	Radicaux de gauche	Leftist radicals
	Verts	Green Party
Germany	CDU/CSU	Christian-democratic/Christian-social Union
	FDP	Liberal Party
Greece	PASOK	Socialist Party
Ireland	FF	Fianna Fail
	Progressive Democrats	Progressive Democrats
Italy	PDS	Social-democratic Party
	PPI	Italian People's Party
	UD	Democratic Union
	RI	Italian Renewal
	VERTS	Green Party
Luxembourg	CSV	Christian-social Party
	LSAP	Labour Party
Netherlands	PVDA	Labour Party
	VVD	Liberal Party
	D66	Democrats 66

Continued

Table 5.4 Continued

Country	Party abbreviation	Party name
Portugal	PS	Socialist Party
Spain	PP	People's Party
Sweden	SD	Social-democratic Party
United Kingdom	Labour	Labour Party

Q.22. What is your opinion on each of the following proposals? Please tell me for each proposal, whether you are for it or against it.

2. The Member States of the European Union should have one common foreign policy toward countries outside the European Union.

3. The European Union Member States should have a common defence and military policy.

3. The European Union should be responsible for matters that cannot be effectively handled by national, regional, and local governments.

7. Any citizen of another European Union country who resides in (OUR COUNTRY) should have the right to vote in local elections.

8. Any citizen of another European Union country who resides in (OUR COUNTRY) should have the right to be a candidate in local elections.

Q.23. Some people believe that certain areas of policy should be decided by the (NATIONAL) government, while other areas of policy should be decided jointly within the European Union. Which of the following areas of policy do you think should be decided by the (NATIONAL) government, and which should be decided jointly within the European Union?

b) Protection of the environment
g) Workers' rights vis-à-vis their employers
i) The fight against unemployment
j) Agriculture and Fishing policy

Source: Melich (1999)

To infer the positions of the political parties we selected all individuals who responded to the questions listed and who stated a preference for a political party. Weighing the observations according to the weights provided for the national samples, we then calculated the mean position the sympathizers of all political parties. We report the resulting mean positions for all parties (as well as the number of seats the parties controlled in the upper and lower house at the time of signing the Amsterdam treaty in a file at http://www.ipz.unizh.ch/personal/hug/dgov/.

Chapter 6

Divided Government and the Resolution of Territorial Disputes

Todd Allee and Paul Huth

For scholars studying international conflict and war, the idea that domestic political institutions might affect patterns of military conflict has gained considerable acceptance over the past decade. The most prominent body of work linking domestic politics to conflict patterns is known broadly as the "democratic peace" literature.[1] The overarching proposition advanced by scholars working in this area is that democracy exerts a pacifying influence in international politics, although debates continue over both the nature of this finding (i.e., monadic versus dyadic), as well as the theoretical explanation for the lack of democratic bellicosity (i.e., structural versus normative).[2] Nevertheless, the literature to date continues to focus on an important but narrow aspect of the relationship between domestic politics and international behavior: the relationship between democracy and war.

We believe that much more work can and should be done to link domestic political institutions to international behavior. Of the many possible areas worthy of exploration, in this chapter we attempt to extend the literature in two broad directions. The first concern we have is that existing work focuses primarily on a relatively limited dependent variable—the onset of war. Yet the absence of war and the resolution of a dispute are two very different phenomena. In this chapter we consider the conditions under which state leaders might actively cooperate with one another to resolve a disputed issue, thereby reducing or even eliminating the possibility of war. In other words, we look to see when leaders will successfully pursue diplomatic efforts to settle disputes, not simply when they will manage to avoid taking up arms over a disputed issue. Our second goal is to push the agenda on the independent variable side. While existing work has theorized about differences in international conflict behavior *across* different regime types, we also believe that salient differences should exist *within* a given regime type. Among democratic leaders, for example, we should expect to find important differences in international behavior under different domestic institutional arrangements. Our overall argument in this chapter is that the degree to which the polity is divided should have a significant impact on the willingness of democratic leaders to make concessions to resolve existing disputes. In this chapter, then, we set out to link the divided government literature, which to date has looked primarily at international economic cooperation, with the international conflict literature, which thus far has largely ignored the issue of how state leaders might cooperate to resolve international disputes.

In particular, we examine the behavior of state leaders during bilateral rounds of talks over disputed territory and test hypotheses about whether the degree of divided government affects leaders' decisions to make concessions in these rounds of talks. Our dataset comprises 1,528 rounds of rounds talks drawn from 348 territorial disputes that span the period 1919–1995.[3] Each of the disputes in our dataset has the same basic structure. In each dispute there is a challenger state that has a standing claim to some piece of territory and desires to change the territorial status quo, as well as a target state that currently possesses the disputed territory. Furthermore, when engaged in negotiations over the disputed territory, both states ultimately decide to make either: (1) no concessions, (2) limited concessions, or (3) major concessions. For each round of talks, then, we code the level of concessions made by both the challenger and target state.

Looking at territorial disagreements provides a number of advantages. For one, all territorial disputes share a common structure and present a similar set of options to the states involved. By looking at disputes over territory, we control for the influence of possible conflating factors. Furthermore, territorial issues typically are of considerable interest to members of the legislature or parliament, as well to citizens broadly. Thus leaders who are negotiating over territory must be sensitive to the anticipated domestic political reactions to their negotiating decisions. As a result, negotiations over disputed territory constitute a particularly useful way to probe the impact of domestic political institutions on international cooperation.

Negotiations over disputed territory also share many of the features of a two-level game (Evans, Jacobson, and Putnam 1993; Putnam 1988). The two state leaders (executives) go to the bargaining table at Level I and both ultimately put forward proposals regarding the level of territorial concessions they are willing to make. Both leaders must consider the domestic political consequences of their concession decisions, as well as the chances of any agreement being ratified by the legislature or parliament at Level II. Furthermore, both leaders must consider the domestic constraints faced by their counterpart across the bargaining table.

One of the primary advantages of our research design is that we are able to examine whether divided governments are more or less likely to make concessions themselves, as well as whether such divided governments are likely to extract concessions from their bargaining adversary. These two areas of inquiry, in fact, correspond to the two most prominent propositions regarding the impact of divided government on interstate cooperation (see Pahre, chapter 1). The first claim is that the existence of divided government—conceptualized in a variety of ways—makes international cooperation less likely (O'Halloran 1994; Lohmann and O'Halloran 1994; Milner 1997, Milner and Rosendorff 1996, 1997; Putnam 1988). While others in this volume consider the conditional effects of divided government on international cooperation (Hammond and Prins, chapter 2; König and Hug, chapter 5; Pahre, chapter 4), our arguments and findings—which consider the unconditional effects of divided government on cooperation— lend support to this first general claim. For our purposes, when executives face strong domestic opposition in the legislature, they are less likely to make concessions in talks over disputed territory. These constrained leaders are unable or unwilling to move toward a cooperative solution when they are highly accountable to domestic opposition for fear of the ramifications associated with the making of unilateral concessions.

The second claim, which as König and Hug (chapter 5) note has become quite popular over the past decade, is the idea that leaders whose "hands are tied" by strong domestic constraints are able to induce more concessions from a bargaining adversary (see Iida 1993; Milner and Rosendorff 1996, 1997; Mo 1994, 1995; Putnam 1988; Rosendorff, chapter 3; see also Tarar 2001). This proposition is typically traced to the work of Thomas Schelling (1960) and is referred to as the Schelling Conjecture. Coupled with the first idea, this second claim maintains that while cooperation may be difficult if an executive is constrained by domestic actors, any agreement reached is likely to be is on terms favorable to the constrained executive. The idea is that foreign leaders know and understand the precarious situation of the home country executive and thus are more willing to accommodate many demands by making substantial concessions. Nevertheless, we are relatively unconvinced by this logic as it applies to territorial negotiations. Since most territorial disputes are settled through reciprocal concessions made by both sides, we expect to find that states are only willing to bear the costs of "cutting a deal" when they believe their adversary is also in a position to reciprocate concessions and ultimately to ratify any agreement that is reached. This is what our empirical evidence ultimately suggests. Leaders are more likely to make concessions when their adversary is in a strong, as opposed to weak, domestic political position.

When testing our hypotheses, we utilize a more continuous measure of divided government, whereas most other studies conceptualize divided government as a dichotomous variable (e.g. König and Hug, chapter 5; Milner 1997). While the general distinctions between minority versus majority government and single party versus coalition government are important ones, we choose to consider divided government in a manner that captures variation in the degree of institutional division.[4] Therefore, our measure of divided government is a continuous as well as a "structural" one, as we look at the level of support the executive has in the legislature or parliament. This variable not only provides more variation than any of the typical dichotomous conceptions of divided government, but also matches our theoretical arguments quite nicely. In precise operational terms, our measure of divided government is a variable that captures the percentage of seats in the primary legislative body held by the party or parties in government.

The level of parliamentary or legislative support for the executive is perhaps the most important domestic institutional feature that leaders must consider when negotiating over disputed territory. This is because the degree to which political opposition can hold leaders accountable for the policies they adopt is a defining feature of democratic political systems. Leaders who are accountable for their policies risk the loss of political authority and influence, if not removal from office, for policy setbacks or for pressing ahead with unpopular programs. The distribution of power within the legislative or parliamentary arena is a key factor that determines the means and opportunities available to opposition groups for challenging and contesting governmental policies. In situations in which the executive has limited support in the legislature or parliament, the domestic political consequences of pursuing failed or controversial foreign policy actions can be substantial. As a result, foreign policy leaders who face strong political opposition should be more attentive to potential foreign policy setbacks and should be more hesitant to launch diplomatic initiatives that are likely to be controversial. The making of territorial concessions is often such a controversial policy, as we detail in the next section.

We begin by putting forward several theoretical premises about incumbent leaders, political opposition, and the dynamics of domestic political competition, followed by a series of specific arguments about the impact of divided government on the propensity of leaders to resolve territorial disputes cooperatively.

Theoretical Framework for Analyzing Domestic Political Competition

Premise 1—The Primacy of Retaining Office for Incumbent Leaders
A critical goal of incumbent leaders is to maintain their position of political leadership and to protect their hold on office from political opposition. The importance of staying in power can reflect a variety of motivations: a personal drive for political power and leadership status, the attempt to secure financial and material gains, or the desire to achieve certain public policy goals by means of legislation and governmental programs. In sum, the maintenance of political office can advance personal as well as broader public policy goals for leaders. As a result, political leaders should be strategic in their pursuit of both domestic and foreign policies and try to anticipate the domestic political responses to various policies they might adopt. Leaders should not be expected to choose policies that entail significant political risks and may produce high costs; they should instead prefer policies that will more safely improve their political standing.

Premise 2—The Strategic Behavior of Political Opposition
In all political systems there are political elites who seek to remove the current leadership from office and to assume positions of political power themselves. Opposition elites, however, are strategic in deciding when to challenge incumbents and seek their removal.

Elites who aspire to positions of national leadership recognize that an incumbent's political vulnerability varies over time. They are more likely to challenge leaders at a time when they are more confident of political support from other groups and when the incumbent's supporting coalition is fractured (e.g., DeNardo 1985; Hardin 1995; Huber 1996; Laver and Schofield 1998; Lichbach 1995; Lupia and Strom 1995). Unsuccessful political challenges against an incumbent can be costly for leaders of the opposition. At a minimum, they risk the loss of political standing among potential allies. There is also the potential for a political counterattack by the incumbent.

An implication of Premise 2 is that counterelites and political opposition will be more active in challenging incumbents when the latter's policy initiatives have failed or proven controversial. The policy performance of a given democratic government on domestic and foreign policy issues plays an important role, therefore, in determining when incumbent leaders will encounter strong political opposition (e.g., Aldrich, Sullivan, and Borgida 1989; Bueno de Mesquita and Siverson 1995; Bueno de Mesquita, Siverson, and Woller 1992; Bueno de Mesquita et al. 2003; Goemans 2000; Lewis-Beck 1988; Miller and Shanks 1996; Nincic and Hinckley 1991). When the policies of the incumbent leadership have failed to achieve policy goals, the opposition can argue more effectively that the current leadership should be removed because of its track record of policy setbacks and incompetency. Furthermore, policy failures in one issue area can induce opposition against regime policies in other policy domains. For example, a regime's foreign policy failures can weaken its leader's political standing and the ability to secure favorable outcomes on domestic policies (e.g. Brace and Hinckley 1992). In sum, foreign policy setbacks can not only directly threaten a leader's tenure in office, but can also weaken the ability to pursue a broader policy agenda.

However, it also follows that policy successes may have favorable political consequences within the domestic arena for democratic leaders. They may help to deter political opposition, strengthen a leader's hold on office, and increase the stock of political capital upon which leaders can draw to advance their broader policy agendas (see Brace and Hinckley 1992; Brody 1991; Edwards and Gallup 1990; Neustadt 1990). Furthermore, the successful resolution of a territorial dispute may bring about a variety of foreign policy benefits.[5] Nevertheless, given the salience of many territorial disputes and the feelings of nationalism associated with issues of territorial integrity and sovereignty, we believe that in most situations the making of territorial concessions is likely to bring about short-term domestic political costs to the incumbent leadership.

Premise 3—The Domestic Political Incentives to Withhold Territorial Concessions
The final point in our discussion of Premise 2 leads directly to Premise 3. In territorial disputes the policy preferences of opposition elites and groups are characterized by what we term a "pragmatic nationalist bias." Opposition groups, as well as the public at large, typically will advocate a relatively firm stance regarding its state's territorial claims. Therefore, incumbent democratic leaders are unlikely to encounter strong and consistent political pressures to pursue moderate diplomatic actions or to offer unilateral concessions intended to break a deadlock over disputed territory. For incumbent leaders continued diplomatic stalemate and the maintenance of a tough stance is a less risky course of action than the adoption of a policy of accommodation and unilateral concession-making. It is typically quite convenient, particularly in the short term, for incumbent leaders to refuse concessions to an adversary during a given round of talks because such a

policy is less contestable domestically. Opposition elites are highly unlikely to challenge the government for protecting national interests and territorial sovereignty through the refusal of concessions. On the other hand, these opposition elites are quite willing to capitalize on the foreign policy failures of incumbent leaders, as we discuss in Premise 2. The course of action that is most likely to be utilized against the incumbent is the apparent weakness associated with making significant territorial concessions.

This pragmatic nationalist bias also implies that among the general public there typically will be a politically significant amount of support for relatively hawkish preferences when it comes to territorial claims.[6] Thus, even if incumbent leaders make the case to the general public that there are potential benefits to a negotiated settlement of the territorial dispute, the prevalence of pragmatic nationalist views among the public means that territorial agreements containing concessions will generally provoke criticism and controversy that opposition elites will seek to mobilize. As a result, due to the nationalist bias in the preferences held by the mass public and some opposition elites, incumbent leaders should be quite sensitive to the risks associated with accommodative diplomatic policies.

Premise 4—Differences in Domestic Political Institutions Are a Source of Variation in Political Accountability
The political accountability of state leaders varies across different political systems, and more importantly for our purposes, also varies within democratic political systems. These differences in political institutions both across and within political systems affect the ability of opposition groups to contest government policies.

First, the level of accountability for state leaders is typically higher in democratic political systems. Institutions such as well-organized and independent political parties, regular competitive elections, and independent political legislatures enable the political opposition to challenge the government more effectively.[7] As a result, political opposition is generally more capable of derailing policy programs and removing leaders from power in democratic regimes, while opposition groups in nondemocratic regimes are typically afforded fewer opportunities to challenge incumbent leaders and are often forced to threaten or use violence as the means by which to challenge nondemocratic incumbents.

More importantly here, however, is the idea that the vulnerability of democratic leaders may vary across countries, as well as over time within one country. The political vulnerability of democratic leaders at a given point in time may depend upon a number of factors. For one, elections provide a regularized means for the public to hold leaders accountable for their policies, including the decisions they have made in negotiations over contested territory. The threat of being removed through elections may be a very powerful political threat if presidential or general national elections are coming up within a few months. However, if those elections are several years away, electoral defeat is a less pressing concern for incumbent leaders.[8] Furthermore, for presidents and prime ministers, the dependence upon coalition partners to form a working majority adds a degree of vulnerability. For instance, a prime minister who assembles a coalition government to form a working majority is more vulnerable to votes of no confidence, the breakup of coalition cabinets, and calls for early elections (e.g., Alt and King 1994; Laver and Schofield 1998; Lupia and Strom 1995; Powell 2000; Warwick 1994).

All democratic leaders, however, must deal with legislatures regarding the ratification of international treaties (Lohmann and O'Halloran 1994; Martin 2000; Milner 1997; Milner and Rosendorff 1997; Putnam 1988). The key factor that affects whether executives are able to achieve ratification of treaties they submit is the level of support they have in the legislature or parliament. In cases in which the executive's party commands majority support, whether alone or with coalition partners, opposition forces are less capable of blocking ratification.[9] Ratification becomes more certain as the percentage of seats held by the governing regime continues to increase, since the presence of a large majority guards against the defection of party members or coalition allies. On the other hand, executives who head minority governments are in a more precarious situation. These leaders face a more credible threat of legislative rejection of a treaty that is not favored by opposition parties.

An implication we draw from this discussion is that while democratic institutions provide greater opportunities for political opposition to exercise its influence, the degree of political accountability for democratic leaders also varies considerably. In the next section we argue that the degree of legislative support for the executive is a key factor that affects both whether leaders are willing to make territorial concessions, and whether their negotiating adversaries are willing to offer such concessions.

Divided Government Hypotheses

Hypothesis 1   As the percentage of seats held by the ruling government in the legislature or parliament increases, political leaders are more likely to offer concessions to adversaries in talks over disputed territory.

We conceptualize the degree of divided government in a continuous and unconditional manner, since we focus on the relative institutional strength of the ruling government vis-à-vis opposition parties. We argue that the presence of strong opposition forces in legislatures and parliaments increases the possible costs associated with failed negotiations. When political opposition is sizeable, incumbent leaders face an increased chance of ratification failure, as well as a multitude of possible domestic costs associated with the making of concessions. Therefore, incumbent leaders are unlikely to offer concessions in negotiations when they face significant domestic political opposition. Conversely, the relative lack of political opposition allows leaders to pursue more controversial foreign policy initiatives. An incumbent leader therefore is more likely to take the riskier step of offering territorial concessions as his level of support in the legislature or parliament increases.

As we mentioned earlier, the political influence of opposition parties in legislatures can stem from their ability to constrain executives in several ways, such as failing to support the ratification of treaties, forcing the downfall of governments through votes of no confidence and the dissolution of coalition cabinets, and blocking the passage of legislation. Scholars working in a wide range of areas have found that the political power of opposition parties should be stronger when the government is divided in some way (Alesina and Rosenthal 1995; Binder 1999; Cox and Kernell 1991; Edwards, Barrett, and Peake 1997; Fiorina 1992; Lohmann and O'Halloran 1994; Mayhew 1991; Milner and Rosendorff 1997; Warwick 1994; also see Bond and Fleisher 1990; Edwards and Wood 1999; Peterson 1994; Wood and Peake 1998). For our purposes, the degree of division in the polity is captured by the relative legislative strength of the executive's party and coalition members compared to opposition political parties. When opposition forces are in a position of relative strength, the executive is unlikely to pursue policies that entail considerable risk, such as a bold diplomatic initiative in which significant territorial concessions are offered. Such a policy may fail if the territorial adversary fails to reciprocate concessions. Even if an agreement is reached, the terms of the agreement might still be perceived as unfair or biased to the advantage of the adversary. Recall that holding firm during negotiations and failing to make concessions is generally a safe policy for democratic leaders and that a hard-line stance is unlikely to entail serious domestic political costs. A policy of concessions, however, may provide the opposition with a number of ways to discredit the incumbent leadership and to charge it with weakness and foreign policy incompetence.

When opposition parties are in a position of strength, they are better able to use the incumbent's decision to make territorial concessions to their political advantage. First of all, a strong political opposition is able to use a number of procedural tools against the government. The most obvious means by which the opposition can flex its muscle is by failing to ratify any territorial agreement. The ratification of treaties presents a situation in which an executive must gather a majority, or at times a supermajority, to ensure ratification of the treaty. Getting the majority needed for ratification is difficult when the executive must call upon those from outside his coalition. He may need to make costly side-payments to other individuals or parties. In some situations those outside the governing coalition simply will choose not to ratify the agreement. In these situations, opposition leaders can use the failure of the treaty and allegations of "selling out" to discredit the incumbent regime. As a result, leaders should be more likely to conclude territorial agreements that contain concessions when they have strong support in the legislature or parliament. In this scenario the executive typically can call upon fellow party members and coalition allies to achieve ratification without the aid of political opposition.

Political opposition may capitalize on an incumbent leader's decision to make concessions in additional ways. In a more general sense, when the incumbent leader is relatively weak he is more dependent upon the cooperation of opposition forces to pass legislation and to retain power. A foreign policy setback, such as ratification failure or the apparent weakness associated with the offering of unilateral concessions, would make the incumbent leader even more vulnerable. He could face the loss of support from coalition partners, as well from members of his own party, if they view association with the executive as detrimental to their political goals. Furthermore, a prime minister might face a vote of no confidence in the aftermath of a failed foreign policy agenda. For all leaders, then, the pursuit of a potentially costly foreign policy is unlikely if they face strong domestic political opposition. On the other hand, a president or prime minister is much more likely to take risks such as offering territorial concessions when he has strong support in the legislature or parliament. Not only is any agreement more likely to be ratified, but in the event of ratification failure the executive is much more likely to maintain majority support and retain his grip on power.

In sum, the general political problem for any executive is that territorial concessions are likely to be controversial. On the other hand, a policy of firmness in negotiations is unlikely to provoke harsh criticism from any large segment of domestic society. While concessions in a territorial dispute always entail some political risks for a democratic leader, the possible costs of failed negotiations are not as great when the leader's governing party or coalition has a firm grip on power in the legislature or parliament. When the percentage of seats held by the governing coalition is large, executives are both more confident of ratification success, and more likely to withstand criticism and maintain power in the event of ratification failure or calls of irresolution and foreign policy weakness.

A parallel line of argumentation also applies to *Hypothesis 2*. In this next hypothesis we claim that secure democratic governments are more likely to be the recipients of territorial concessions from a negotiating adversary based on the expectation that they are better able to offer concessions and to secure ratification of any treaty that is concluded.

Hypothesis 2   A state is more likely to make territorial concessions to a democratic adversary as the ruling government in the adversary attains a stronger position in its legislature or parliament.

In addition to considering their own domestic political standing, leaders also consider whether the leadership of a democratic territorial dispute adversary is in a position of domestic political strength or weakness. The leadership of the adversary should be hesitant to offer concessions if it faces strong political opposition, but should be more likely to take the riskier step of offering concessions if domestic opposition is relatively weak. Our primary point is that leaders look to bargain with and make concessions to negotiating adversaries who have the capacity to reciprocate concessions and to achieve ratification of an agreement in their respective legislative or parliamentary body. It follows, then, that adversaries will view secure democratic governments as more politically capable partners for trying to achieve a negotiated settlement.

As we have argued already, concessions in negotiations are almost always controversial. One-sided agreements, in which leaders expect their territorial adversary to make a series of unilateral concessions, are therefore quite unlikely (see table 6.1). As a result, the more important task for a country's leaders is to gauge the right time to put offers of concessions on the negotiating table that can be reciprocated by their negotiating partner. Leaders do not want to incur the political heat at home for offering concessions unless they believe that their negotiating partner can also withstand the same type of domestic political pressure and secure ratification of any agreement. Put differently, government leaders are unlikely to make the difficult choice to offer concessions unless they expect that negotiations will produce an agreement that their adversary can secure support for at home. If leaders expect

Table 6.1   Concession Decisions by Challengers and Targets

	Target Behavior		
	No Concessions	Limited Concessions	Major Concessions
No Concessions	847	90	27
Challenger Behavior Limited Concessions	93	308	57
Major Concessions	39	48	19

a negotiated agreement to unravel due to domestic opposition in the other country, then they have few incentives to expose themselves politically to charges of selling out from their own domestic opposition.[10]

Extending the Theoretical Analysis to Include International Politics

We now spend some time discussing several variables that relate to the international political and military environment in which leaders interact. We spend relatively little time on the following premises and hypotheses since we have discussed them at length elsewhere (see Huth and Allee 2003: chapters 3 and 8).

Premise 5—State Leaders Are Charged with the Responsibility of Pursuing Territorial Claims in the Context of International Anarchy
We argue that state leaders generally prefer to rely upon their own country's resources to counter threats and to achieve foreign policy goals so as to avoid problems of entrapment and reliance on allies (e.g., Snyder 1997; Stein 1990: Chapter 6). Nevertheless, foreign policy leaders at times do conclude that they cannot achieve foreign policy goals without the assistance and cooperation of other states. As a result, various forms of security cooperation between states, ranging from formal alliance ties to close alignment, are signals that states value the ally's support so highly that they are willing to accept or risk some loss of autonomy over their own foreign policies.

Premise 6—The threat or use of military force is a critical source of bargaining leverage for state leaders in territorial disputes
Relative military strength is important even during rounds of negotiations, since bargaining strategies should be affected by: 1) anticipated future interactions in the event of negotiation failure, and 2) whether military force is a credible alternative to reliance on negotiations.

Hypothesis 3   When common security ties and interests exist between states, political leaders are more likely to make concessions in negotiations over disputed territory.

Given the security benefits that allies can provide, we expect that in disputes between states that share cooperative security ties and interests, both parties should be inclined to make concessions in pursuit of a settlement. Diplomatic and possible military conflict over disputed territory, in contrast, would put at risk the cooperation of one's ally in countering security threats from third parties.

Hypothesis 4   As a country's relative military strength increases state leaders are less likely to make concessions in negotiations over disputed territory.

A military advantage should decrease the willingness of leaders to make concessions. This is because the possible alternatives to a diplomatic solution—the use of coercive pressure and the possible initiation and escalation of military conflict—are more attractive to militarily stronger states. Leaders whose states possess a military advantage have the luxury of adopting more intransigent negotiating positions. If the adversary fails to make concessions, this more powerful state can then initiate and escalate a militarized dispute, anticipating either that the opponent will make concessions under the threat of war, or, if the target refuses to back down diplomatically, that victory will follow in an armed conflict.

Hypothesis 5   When state leaders claim territory of strategic value, they are less likely to make concessions in negotiations over disputed territory.

The logic behind this hypothesis is that securing strategically valuable territory should be a highly salient goal for policy makers in a territorial dispute. Given the high value placed on securing such territory, leaders should be less willing to offer substantial concessions in negotiations since territorial concessions would entail losing or forsaking control over highly valued territory.

Hypothesis 6a   When a state engaged in a territorial dispute is also currently involved in militarized conflicts with other countries, its policies in the territorial dispute will shift toward inaction and risk avoidance. As a result, state leaders will be more likely to make concessions in negotiations over disputed territory.

A similar logic applies to the behavior of states whose territorial dispute adversary is simultaneously involved in other military conflicts.

Hypothesis 6b   A state whose territorial dispute adversary is involved in one or more militarized conflicts with other countries is less likely to make concessions in negotiations over disputed territory.

When a dispute has escalated to the point of military threats and armed conflicts, the leaders of the states involved are likely to focus diplomatic and military efforts at managing the threatening situation in that particular dispute. Therefore, states should be more accommodative if they enter into negotiations in another territorial dispute so that this territorial adversary does not consider resorting to military force as a result of stalemated talks. In *hypothesis 6b* the analysis shifts to the behavior of states that observe that their territorial dispute opponent is involved in military conflict with other countries. The strategic course of action for leaders in this scenario is to withhold concessions and to apply more diplomatic pressure to see if their opponent will offer concessions in order to avoid another potential crisis or military conflict.

Operational Measures for Empirical Testing

In the following section we describe the operational measures used to test each of the hypotheses. In a few cases we create multiple operational indicators to measure a given theoretical concept. However, only one operational measure for each concept is included in the empirical model. We simply substitute one measure for another to check the robustness of our results.

To test *Hypotheses 1* and *2*, we first must identify those countries that are democratic, before collecting country-specific data on the legislative strength of the president or prime minister's party and its coalition allies. We utilize the *POLITY III* and *POLITY 98* datasets to classify countries as democratic (see Jaggers and Gurr 1995). The *POLITY* data produces a net-democracy score variable, which ranges in value from -10 to $+10$. This 21-point net-democracy variable is created by subtracting each state's autocracy score (which ranges from 0 to 10) from its democracy score (which also ranges from 0 to 10). For purposes of testing these two hypotheses, each territorial disputant is considered democratic if its net-democracy score is greater than or equal to $+6$ (on the -10 to $+10$ scale) and is considered nondemocratic if its net-democracy score is less than or equal to $+5$ (also on the -10 to $+10$ scale). The democracy dummy variables serve not only to identify those challenger and target states that are democratic, but the inclusion of these control variables separates territorial dispute challengers and targets into democracies and nondemocracies and allows us to properly test the two divided government hypotheses.

To actually test *Hypotheses 1* and *2*, we then collect additional data on the strength of the ruling party and its coalition partners in the primary legislative or parliamentary body. More precisely, in presidential or mixed systems in which the president is responsible for foreign policy decisions, we collect data on the percentage of seats held by the president's party (and its coalition allies, if applicable) in the upper house of the legislature, since this body typically holds effective treaty ratification power. In parliamentary or mixed systems in which the prime minister is in charge of foreign policy, we assemble data on the percentage of seats held by the ruling party (or ruling coalition, if applicable) in the lower house. This data is drawn from general sources (*Annual Register*, Bidwell 1973, *Europa World Year Book, Keesing's*, Mackie and Rose 1991, and *Political Handbook of the World*) as well as country-specific works. In addition, we consult numerous country-specific sources on the political history of countries when these basic sources do not contain all of the needed information. Our final operational measure, then, can be thought of as the percentage of legislative or parliamentary seats held by the ruling government—which includes the lead party, as well as any coalition partners it may have.

We construct two alternative measures for common security ties to test *Hypothesis 3*. We first consider whether the challenger and target share alliance ties. We record a value of one for our military alliance indicator if the challenger and target have a defense pact or entente military alliance at the time of the negotiations, and record a value of zero if they simply have a nonaggression pact or do not share a military alliance. The updated Correlates of War (COW) dataset on interstate alliances is used to code this variable. The second measure is whether the challenger and target currently face a common territorial dispute opponent. A value of one is recorded if both are embroiled in separate territorial disputes with a common adversary during a given round of negotiations. The data is taken directly from our full dataset on territorial disputes (see Huth and Allee 2003).

To test *Hypothesis 4* we construct a short-term military balance variable that measures the military capabilities of each state relative to its territorial dispute adversary. We take the average of three different ratios of military capabilities to come up with an overall measure of the short-term military balance. Our final measure is an average of the two states: (1) relative military personnel, (2) relative military expenditures, and (3) relative expenditures per soldier.[11] In calculating each of these three individual ratios, we adjust the capabilities of each state for distance if the territorial dispute is located overseas from the state's homeland territory (see Bueno de Mesquita 1981: 105). We also include the military capabilities of a target's ally as part of the capabilities of the target if the ally's military forces are stationed on the target's territory and the ally has a defense pact with the target.[12] In operational terms, each of the three component ratios, as well as the final average ratio, is translated to a continuous scale that ranges from 0 to 1. Logically, the ratios for the challenger and target sum to 1. Values above .5 indicate that a state possesses a military advantage, values near .5 indicate that a state is near military parity with its adversary, while values below .5 indicate the state is at a military disadvantage.

The primary source for data on these three indicators is the COW data set on national capabilities, which contains annual data for countries through 1992. For the years 1993–1995 and for missing data prior to 1993, information on military capabilities is collected from several additional sources (i.e., Banks Cross-Polity Data Set, *The Military Balance*, *SIPRI Yearbook*, *World Military Expenditures and Arms Transfers*).[13]

We construct a dummy variable to measure the strategic value of a piece of territory in order to test *Hypothesis 5*.[14] This dummy variable is equal to one if the territory is strategically located or if it contains (or is believed to contain) natural resources that are used by the state in the production of military weapon systems. The definition and sources relied upon to code for strategic location of territory as well as strategic natural resources are taken from Huth (1996: 256 and 1988: 65).

To test *Hypotheses 6a* and *6b* we collect data on the beginning and end month and year of any war or militarized dispute in which either the challenger or the target was involved, other than the territorial dispute between them. We then construct two dummy variables—one for the challenger and one for the target—with a value of one indicating that the challenger (target) is simultaneously involved in a military campaign elsewhere during the territorial negotiations in question. The primary data sources are the COW data set on militarized interstate disputes during the period 1816–1992, as well as our data set of military confrontations over disputed territory (Huth and Allee 2003). Additional coding sources, consulted to cover the years 1993–1995 as well as prior years, include Bercovitch and Jackson (1997), Brecher and Wilkenfeld (1997), Tillema (1991), and Wallensteen and Sollenberg (1996).

Issues of Estimation and Model Specification

Once again, the behavior we wish to explain is the decision of state leaders to offer concessions in rounds of talks over disputed territory. Recall that the level of concessions made by both the territorial dispute challenger and the territorial dispute target can be grouped into three categories: (1) no concessions, (2) limited concessions, or (3) major concessions. The choice of no concessions represents a very firm and unyielding bargaining position in which state leaders refuse to make any changes in policy. In some cases this policy may reflect an equally intransigent negotiating position by the other party, yet in other cases the refusal to make any concessions may have been maintained despite concessions by the other side. Limited concessions implies that the challenger or target either proposed or actually made concessions regarding (1) nonterritorial issues that are part of the talks, or (2) a small amount of the disputed territory. Once again, these limited concessions may or may not have been reciprocated by the other party. Finally, the outcome of major concessions by one party implies that it acceded to many, if not all, of the territorial demands of the other party. In some cases it is possible that both sides make major concessions over different sections of disputed territory.

The raw data on concession decisions exhibits a number of interesting patterns (see table 6.1). First of all, the prevailing policy of both challengers and targets is to refrain from offering concessions in a given round of talks. Challengers offer some form of concessions, either limited or major, in only 37 percent of the cases (564/1528), while targets offer at least some concessions only 36 percent of the time (549/1528). In fact, the most prominent outcome of a round of talks is a situation in which neither state offers any concessions (847 of 1528, or 55 percent of rounds of talks). The second interesting pattern is that the two states typically reciprocate, at least to some degree, the concessions offered by their adversary (see table 6.1). When the challenger offers limited or major concessions, the target, too, offers concessions nearly 77 percent of the time (432 out of 564 rounds of talks). Similarly, when the target offers some form of concessions the challenger also offers concessions in nearly 79 percent of cases (432/549). The second most likely outcome of talks, in fact, is that both sides will make limited concessions.

Certain combinations of choices by the two leaders are likely to lead to particular "overall" outcomes for the round of talks. For example, the territorial dispute is very likely to end if one or both parties makes major concessions. Limited concessions by the target, however, are unlikely to settle the dispute. In this case the challenger has to consider whether to pursue further negotiations, turn to military force, or accept the revised status quo for the time being. Similar decisions have to be made by the challenger in the event that the negotiations end in deadlock with neither side making concessions.

Nevertheless, we want to make it clear that we do not analyze rounds of talks dyadically; that is, we do not attempt to code or explain a "joint" outcome for a pair of states. While certain combinations of challenger and target concession decisions are likely to produce certain outcomes, each state makes its own decision regarding the level of concessions to offer in talks over disputed territory. Therefore we code a separate outcome for both the challenger and target and attempt to explain each state's decision to offer concessions. This allows us to understand how particular variables affect the decision making calculus of each state.

However, we are unwilling to ignore the fact that the concession decisions of the challenger and target are often linked. Our challenge, then, is to find a way to consider challenger and target decisions separately, yet to incorporate the fact that the two states' decisions are related (Smith 1999).[15]

We believe that a bivariate probit model provides a useful way to estimate the separate but interrelated decisions of two states engaged in negotiations.[16] In fact, the bivariate probit model allows the researcher to specify unique equations for the two states, yet incorporates the correlation between the disturbances of the two states' equations and provides an estimate of the magnitude of this relationship.[17]

Most bivariate probit models analyze simple dichotomous choices made by actors, but since the states in our analysis have three concession options (which are ordered in a clear manner), we turn to a model that is appropriate for the nature of our dependent variable. Therefore, we estimate a bivariate ordered probit model to examine the behavior of both challengers and targets during rounds of talks.[18] The precise methods are described in detail in Kohler and Rodgers (1999).[19] The model follows the normal latent variable structure of the ordered logit and ordered probit models. In our application of the model, a latent variable indicating the level of concessions offered by a state is represented by: $y_{ij}^* = x_{ij}\beta + \varepsilon_{ij}$, where i equals rounds of talks 1, . . ., N and $j = 1, 2$ signifies the challenger and target, respectively, in each round of talks. Furthermore, x_{ij} is a $1 \times K_I$ vector of covariates. The observed variable y_{ij} is translated to the latent y_{ij}^* in the following manner:

$$
\begin{aligned}
y_{ij} &= 0 \text{ (no concessions)} &&\text{if} &&-\infty \leq y_{ij}^* < \tau_1 \\
y_{ij} &= 1 \text{ (limited concessions)} &&\text{if} &&\tau_1 \leq y_{ij}^* < \tau_2 \\
y_{ij} &= 2 \text{ (major concessions)} &&\text{if} &&\tau_2 \leq y_{ij}^* < \infty
\end{aligned}
$$

The added twist of the bivariate ordered probit model is that the error term (ε_{ij}) is a normally distributed error term that is assumed to be independent across observations but correlated within the two states in a given observation. The parameter rho (ρ), which ranges from -1 to 1, represents the estimated correlation of the errors between challengers and targets engaged in a round of talks. A statistically significant and positive rho indicates that the unmeasured factors that affect the outcome of the challenger equation also affect the outcome of the target equation in a similar way. A statistically significant and negative rho, on the other hand, indicates that common unmeasured factors affect the outcomes of the two equations in an opposite manner.

We should note a few additional issues regarding the operationalization and estimation of our model. Since conditions may change during the course of a lengthy round of negotiations, the data included in our observations is drawn from the last month of any round of talks. Our measurement is thus more precise than it would be using annual data, and we capture the influence of factors at the time in which some final offer is on the table. An additional point is that the analysis of outcomes of talks raises possible concerns with selection bias, since a challenger's decision to offer concessions could be linked to its initial choice to propose or call for talks in the first place.[20] As a result, we also estimate a Heckman or "censored" probit model for the challenger to examine whether factors that affect a challenger's decision to call for talks are linked to its subsequent decision regarding whether to make concessions in talks (Heckman 1979). In the end we find there is no clear evidence that a selection model is necessary based upon the results of this censored probit model.[21] Furthermore, none of the conclusions we draw about the validity of our hypotheses is called into question by this check for selection bias. Finally, we also estimate separate ordered probit models for both challengers and targets, as well as a standard, dichotomous bivariate probit model for the two states. In all cases the conclusions we draw from the bivariate ordered probit model are robust to these different specifications.

Results

The bivariate ordered probit results are presented in table 6.2. The first thing to note is that we do find support for the use of a bivariate model. The

Table 6.2   Bivariate Ordered Probit Results for the Decision to Offer Territorial Concessions

	Coefficient	Standard Error	Z-Statistic
Divided Government Hypotheses			
H1: Legislative Support for Government	.0042	.0021	1.19**
H2: Adversary Government Legislative Support	.0025	.0021	1.19
Democracy Dummy Variable	−.189	.131	−1.45
Adversary Democracy Dummy Variable	−.124	.131	−.94
International Politics Hypotheses			
H3: Common Security Ties (Military Alliance)	.180	.068	2.65***
H4: Military Balance	−.033	.060	−.55
H5: Strategic Value of Territory	−.009	.052	−.17
H6a: Involvement in Other Militarized Dispute	.040	.051	.78
H6b: Adversary Involvement in Other Militarized Dispute	−.020	.051	−.39
Constant	−.438	.058	−7.59+++
Rho	.699	.021	32.86+++

Note: N = 1528

*p<.10, **p<.05, ***p<.01 (one-tailed tests)

+p<.10, ++p<.05, +++p<.01 (two-tailed tests)

Log Likelihood = −2292.59

Wald Test of Model Significance:

   Chi Square Statistic (1df) = 7.02

   p-value = .01

estimate of rho is nearly .70, and this estimate is strongly statistically significant. This finding indicates that the decisions of challengers and targets engaged in rounds of talks do indeed exhibit some positive correlation.

On the substantive side, our arguments about divided government are generally supported. The most striking finding is for *Hypothesis 1*, which posits that leaders who are in a stronger domestic position are more likely to offer territorial concessions to an adversary. In table 6.2 we see that as a government's support in the legislature increases, it becomes more likely to offer territorial concessions. The coefficient for this variable is positive and significant at the .05 level. Phrased differently, our results for *Hypothesis 1* suggest that executives are less likely to offer territorial concessions when they are in a weak domestic position. Therefore, our results confirm earlier findings that divided government makes cooperation less likely.

There are numerous examples from our dataset that highlight this pattern of stronger governments making concessions, and conversely, of weaker governments resisting the making of concessions. For example, Ecuador does not offer any concessions to Peru in five rounds of talks held between 1982–1994, and during this period the ruling coalition in Ecuador controls a minority of legislative seats on four of five occasions (it holds a mere 54 percent in the other case). In contrast, during the period 1919–1935 Belgian governments offer concessions in five rounds of talks in three different disputes, and in each case the governing coalition in Belgium controls over 90 percent of the seats in parliament.

The substantive impact of an increase in legislative support is also quite striking. For instance, in previous simulations we found that leaders in challenger states were substantially more likely to offer concessions as their level of legislative support increased (see Huth and Allee 2003). In particular, leaders were nearly 69 percent more likely to offer some type of concessions (either limited or major concessions) when their ruling coalition in the legislature shifted from controlling 40 percent to 80 percent of the seats. The increases in the likelihood of concessions were sizeable and consistent as legislative support increased within this range. The change from 40 percent to 50 percent support brought about a 15 percent increase in the likelihood of some type of territorial concessions, while the change from 50 percent to 60 percent led to an additional 14 percent increase in the probability of concessions. As support climbed from 60 percent to 70 percent and then from 70 percent to 80 percent, states became 13 percent and 12 percent more likely to offer territorial concessions, respectively.

Our next notable result is for *Hypothesis 2*, which claims that governments should be less likely to offer concessions to adversaries who are in a weak position domestically. We also find some support for this claim. While the estimate for the *Adversary Government Legislative Support* variable is indeed positive, it does not quite reach conventional levels of statistical significance. Nevertheless, we take this as suggestive evidence in support of *Hypothesis 2*. At a minimum, these results cast serious doubt on the logic of the Schelling Conjecture and the efficacy of a strategy of tying hands. In other words, we find absolutely no evidence that state leaders are able to use their domestic constraints as a way to induce concessions from a negotiating adversary.

Nevertheless, some additional evidence bolsters the suggestive finding for *Hypothesis 2*. For one, in previous work we found that territorial dispute targets were more likely to make concessions to challenger governments that had strong legislative support (Huth and Allee 2003: Chapter 8). This positive relationship was statistically significant at the .01 level. Previous simulations also highlight the substantive effect that a position of domestic weakness has on the likelihood that one's adversary will offer some form of territorial concessions. In previous work we found that leaders in target states were about 54 percent less likely to offer concessions to democratic presidents or prime ministers in challenger states when those democratic leaders were in a weak position to secure domestic support and ratification for any negotiated agreement (see Huth and Allee 2003).

Furthermore, the negotiating behavior of British territorial dispute adversaries provides a nice illustration of this pattern. On only four occasions, all in the 1920s and early 1930s, is there a minority government in power in Britain. Yet in all four rounds of talks over disputed territory in this period the Labour-led government of Ramsay MacDonald is unable to secure concessions from the negotiating adversary. Taking this pattern a bit further, we see that British governments with slim majorities also find it difficult to secure concessions from a territorial dispute adversary. During rounds of territorial talks between 1919 and 1995, British governments with less than 60 percent support in parliament garnered concessions only 33 percent of the time (in 7 of 21 rounds of talks). Meanwhile, British governments with strong majorities of 70 percent or more of the seats in parliament secured concessions 68 percent of the time (17 of 25 rounds of talks). These additional results, then, bolster our claims that a strategy of "tying hands" is unlikely to be very successful.

As a group, the various international politics hypotheses fared quite poorly. This is consistent with our findings elsewhere that international political and military variables fare poorly as explanations for decisions to pursue negotiations and decisions to make concessions in rounds of negotiations (Huth and Allee 2003). The only supportive result is for *Hypothesis 3*, which posits that states that share common security ties are more likely to make territorial concessions to one another. Our findings from table 6.2 suggest that allied states are much more likely to make concessions to one another. The variable for *Common Security Ties* is positive and statistically significant at the .001 level.[22] On the other hand, we find no evidence that the military balance, strategic value of the territory, or either state's involvement in an outside conflict affect decisions to offer concessions.[23]

Finally, it is worth noting that our results are quite robust to a number of different model specifications. None of the findings discussed above (for Hypotheses 1–3) is seriously called into question based upon the results of alternative econometric models. We noted earlier that we failed to find evidence of selection bias as a general problem for our results. In a more specific robustness check, *Hypothesis 1* continues to have strong support when we estimate a Heckman probit model to account for the challenger's decision to pursue talks in the first place. The coefficient for the *Legislative Support for Government* variable remains positive and is significant at the .01 level as an explanation for concession decisions in the Heckman probit model. In addition, alliance ties still exert a positive affect on concession-making, even after the impact of alliance ties on the decision to hold talks in the first place is taken into account. We also estimate a standard ordered probit model for all individual states engaged in rounds of talks and find continued support for *Hypotheses 1* and *3*.[24] Once again, we find that a government's level of legislative support exerts a positive and statistically significant impact on its propensity to make concessions. Alliance ties also continue to increase the likelihood of concessions. Finally, we estimate a bivariate (unordered) probit model to examine challenger and target decisions to offer any form of concessions. In this case we collapse the dependent variable into two categories: no concessions and concessions (either major or limited concessions). The results of this model continue to support *Hypothesis 1* and *3*, and this time we also find additional support for *Hypothesis 2*. In fact, we find that territorial dispute targets are much more likely to make concessions to challenger governments with strong legislative support, as this result is now statistically significant at the .025 level.

Conclusion

Our results suggest two important effects of divided government on the propensity of state leaders to cooperate and resolve potentially deadly disputes. The first, and most conclusive result, is that divided governments are less likely to behave cooperatively during rounds of negotiations over disputed territory. We find that leaders are more likely to offer territorial concessions when they have substantial support in the legislature or parliament, and are less likely to offer concessions when opposition forces are in an increasingly strong position. As we discussed in detail, democratic leaders who face strong domestic opposition are highly accountable for their actions. Therefore, such leaders are unlikely to make the concessions necessary to conclude territorial agreements due to concerns with both ratification failure and the ability of the opposition to portray the leadership as weak and ineffective.

Our second result, while less clear-cut than the first, calls into question the logic of the Schelling Conjecture. In other words, we find no evidence to suggest that divided government yields bargaining advantages, as others have claimed (see also König and Hug, chapter 5; Rosendorff, chapter 3). In fact, we find that governments in positions of domestic strength are more likely to be the recipients of concessions. This is because nearly all international agreements—particularly those regarding disputed territory—require some form of mutual concessions by both states. Thus, leaders do not want to make potentially risky concessions in order to reach an agreement unless their bargaining adversary is in a strong enough position both to make concessions itself, and to secure ratification of any agreement that is concluded.

Finally, our results highlight a more general point. To understand when and why state leaders are likely to cooperate in negotiations, we must turn to domestic-level explanations. We find that explanations focusing on international politics and the broader strategic environment are not good predictors of behavior in interstate negotiations. In fact, only the presence of common security ties helps to explain whether territorial concessions will be offered. This suggests that future studies of international cooperation will need to focus on several of the factors at the domestic level that might affect the prospects for international cooperation.

We also feel that our study adds to the literature on divided government in many ways. We not only shed additional light on the two primary claims of the divided government literature, but our endeavor suggests a number of new directions for future research. First, along with all other chapters in this volume, we push the concept of divided government beyond simple dichotomous measures. We utilize a more continuous measure of divided government that is clearly linked to our theoretical arguments. A related point is that we undertake one of the few large-n, statistical analyses of the impact of divided government on international cooperation.

Most of the existing conclusions about divided government, while quite insightful, are based largely on formal models and individual case studies. We view statistical analysis as an additional, useful tool for adding to our knowledge of the impact of divided government on international cooperation. Furthermore, we employ a unique statistical estimator that is well suited to the nature of our data, and we perform a number of checks to test for the robustness of our results.

Finally, most arguments about the impact of domestic politics on international cooperation are examined in the context of international economic relations. Our study, however, looks at an important question in another sphere of international politics. Most other studies in the area of international military conflict neither address the issue of dispute resolution, nor investigate particular domestic institutional features that might affect the resolution of contentious disputes. Yet our study points out that there are many reasons to expect divided government to be an important explanatory factor for the study of many types of international behavior.

Chapter 7

Conclusion: Democracy and Foreign Policy

Robert Pahre

On April 2, 1917, President Woodrow Wilson told Congress that the United States must enter the war then raging in Europe because "The world must be made safe for democracy." He sought not only safety for democracy in the United States, but the spread of democracy and self-determination throughout the world. Wilson presumed that many good things, from peace to wealth, would flow from success in this endeavor, cemented by a community of democracies joined in the League of Nations.

Wilson's faith persisted after his death. Even as the storm clouds of war gathered in 1938, General Jan Smuts of South Africa claimed that the League of Nations Covenant "simply carries into world affairs that outlook of a liberal democratic society which is one of the great achievements of our human advance" (cited at Carr 1939: 38). Elements of this outlook included a belief in "open" (i.e., public) foreign policy making and peaceful conflict resolution.

Wilson and Smuts were not alone, either then or now, in extolling the benefits of democracy for international affairs. Six decades later, President Bill Clinton (1994) said in a speech at the United Nations that his administration sought to enlarge "the community of market democracies" because "democracies rarely wage war on one another." He continued that

> Democracies, after all, are more likely to be stable, less likely to wage war. They strengthen civil society. They can provide people with the economic opportunities to build their own homes, not to flee their borders.

> Our efforts to help build democracies will make us all more secure, more
> prosperous, and more successful as we try to make this era of terrific change
> our friend and not our enemy.

Political scientists, economists, historians, and many others have made
similar arguments about the benefits of democracy (see especially Mueller
2001). For example, some have argued that democracies grow faster than do
other countries (Barro 1996 but Olson 1982),[1] fight fewer wars (Russett
1993 but Gowa 1999), and extract fewer resources from their society
(Ferejohn 1986; Lake and Baum 1998; North 1984). A variable for democracy
routinely appears in quantitative studies of international relations, whatever
the effect being examined.

Most of this literature makes claims about democracy that are unconditional and unidirectional: democracy is said to have a certain effect under all
conditions. For the most part, the contributions to this volume have made
less unidimensional claims, and more conditional claims, with democracy's
effects contingent upon the presence of some other cause. Having a divided
polity has various effects depending on the degree of divided government
and the identity of the agenda-setter, for example.

These more nuanced results should not surprise us, for democracy is a
multidimensional concept. Democratic political systems are characterized
by a large number of logically distinct features, such as government
accountability, polyarchy, multiparty systems, minority rights, and usually a
formal constitution. Though not essential elements of democracy, many
systems also have multicameral legislatures and/or federalist structures (see
Lijphart 1984 for overview). We would also expect a stable democracy to
have a democratic political culture of some kind (Almond and Verba 1963;
Rogowski 1974). This volume has examined only the more formal, institutional characteristics among these many characteristics.

If we cannot expect any simple answer to the question of how democracy
affects foreign policy, we may nonetheless make our understanding of this
relationship more precise. The contributors examined these contexts in
terms of preferences and institutions. This is especially evident in Hammond
and Prins' chapter, whose analytic simplicity and generality make the point
clearly. The degree of divided government in a democracy may have every
possible kind of impact on international cooperation: it may help or harm
the executive's interests, make agreement altogether impossible or it
may have no effect at all. Which outcome occurs depends on the relationship between preferences, the institutional context, and the location of the
status quo.

Without claiming that these features are exhaustive, this volume has
explored three different aspects of democracy that affect foreign policy

making—divided polity, the degree of divided government, and agenda-setting. Each feature plays a role in traditional democratic theory, but often under a different name or with a slightly different meaning. The usage here reflects the empirical nature of the project, and the contributors' decisions to focus on aspects of democracy that might be measured or observed.

Appreciating its complexity should condition our normative evaluation of democracy, and shape the role of promoting democracy in American (or any other) foreign policy. For example, if many of democracy's effects are conditional, institutional design presents a greater challenge than is generally realized. We may take as an example Henry Kissinger (1994), who now favors promoting democracy abroad. He may wish to think about what kind of democracies he prefers: parliamentary or presidential systems, unitary or federal, strong parties or weak, and so on. Not all aspects of democracy have similar effects, and some features of democracy will better serve American interests than others.

Variation among Democracies

Seeing democracy as a multifaceted concept immediately points the contributors to the question of how democracies differ from one another. This focus on variation among democracies stands in contrast to much of the literature on foreign policy and international relations. For example, the neo-Realist theories that dominated several decades of political science research argued that all domestic political systems could be treated as essentially similar. External pressures were so great that all states had to respond in similar ways or be eliminated (see especially Mearsheimer 2001; Waltz 1979; compare Bull 1977).

Another literature grew up in reaction against this, arguing that domestic political differences affected foreign policy in important ways (i.e., Mueller 1973; Milner 1997; Nincic 1992b; Page and Shapiro 1992). The most widespread claim in this literature argued that democracies differed systematically from nondemocracies in being more peaceful or more willing to trade with other nations.

Powerful as its claims were, this literature on the domestic foundations of foreign policy tended to minimize the differences *among* democracies. This was even true in the formal two-level literature, in which one might expect a greater sensitivity to institutional differences. Many, such as Helen Milner (1997) and her coauthors, have minimized the differences between presidential and parliamentary systems, arguing that divided government has similar effects in both (but Karol 2000; Pahre 1997; Tarar 2001). Allee and

Huth's chapter lies closest to this approach, looking at the size of the executive's majority across political systems.

Normative theories of democracy also assume uniform democratic values, with Presidents Wilson, Clinton, and G. W. Bush advocating the spread of democracy without giving much attention to the details. For example, President Bush's State of the Union addresses of 2003–2005 make reference to democracy in Afghanistan, Iran, Iraq, Palestine—and, in 2005, the US Supreme Court—as if this were a single ideal. He also presents al-Qaeda and other foes as single-minded opponents of an undifferentiated "democracy" (see texts at http://www.whitehouse.gov/stateoftheunion). Interestingly, the word did not appear in his 2002 address, a few months after the terror attacks of September 11, 2001, when terrorism, and not democracy, dominated the speech.

In contrast to this simple view of a single "democracy," the contributors to this volume insist that there are significant differences among democracies. Not only do presidential systems differ from parliamentary systems, but parliamentary systems vary considerably. Hug and König show that even "unified" parliamentary governments hide many veto actors, including coalition members, upper houses of the legislature, and federal actors. Such differences are at the center of how democracy works. The contributors also show variation over time within a single type of democracy. For example, Allee and Huth show that the size of an executive's majority affects its willingness to make, and its ability to receive, concessions. They also show that this is true across different types of democracies. Presidential systems, in which the executive need not have a majority to remain in office, will naturally have smaller majorities.

Like policy makers, the major databases of the discipline have downplayed the differences among democracies, tending to emphasize variation between democracy and nondemocracy. The contributors here have shown the important variation found from one democracy to another, and many have collected data to test their arguments. Their focus on the various features of democratic government represent a promising agenda for future research.

A focus on variation should affect not only our research agendas and data collection strategies but also how we think about foreign policy. We should not assume that all these democratic features have mutually reinforcing effects on foreign policy. For example, many people argue that partisan competition and accountability make policy outcomes more congruent with public preferences, and also encourage international cooperation (see inter alia Rosendorff, chapter 3). Others argue that polyarchy, multicameralism, and federalism make cooperation more difficult by adding veto actors (see inter alia Hug and König, Chapter 6).

It might be tempting to see this as a "debate" over whether democracy promotes or inhibits cooperation. This volume's focus on the institutional variability of democracy points in a different direction. Democracy normally includes some features that promote cooperation (such as competition and accountability) and others that inhibit cooperation (notably veto actors, which make up an essential part of federalism and bicameralism). Seen in this way, "democracy" per se has no single effect on international cooperation. Instead, certain features of democracies make international cooperation more likely, while other features make cooperation more difficult. Some features of democracy promote desirable outcomes, while others present challenges to good policy.

The Stages of Cooperation

While looking at how democracies differ from one another, this volume has used a particular facet of foreign policy, international cooperation, as its primary dependent variable. Though a large literature has grown up examining "international cooperation" as a relatively undifferentiated concept, it too needs to be seen as more complex than previously realized. The contributors to this volume point us to examine different *stages* of the process of cooperation, and in particular, variation in the agenda-setting function at each stage. I discuss four phases found in most cooperation: the prenegotiation stage, the negotiation stage, the ratification stage, and the implementation stage. Across these stages, the contributors also improve our understanding of the dimensions of democratic foreign policy making in the realm of international cooperation.

The prenegotiation stage determines the status quo or reversion point. As Pahre showed in chapter 4, divided government may make the reversion point less attractive than it would be under unified government. This effect on the reversion point makes cooperation more likely. The welfare effects of this cooperation are unclear, however, for cooperation may just recoup the welfare costs of a divided polity in Pahre's model. Rosendorff's chapter presents a more optimistic view, in which democracy produces an attractive, freer trade reversion point as well as making cooperation more likely. In that model, the welfare gains are unambiguous and accrue to each actor in the model.

Agenda-setting plays an important role at this prenegotiation stage. An executive who set the status quo will have less of an incentive to change policy through negotiation than an executive who has the ability to change policy established by the legislature. The effect of agenda-setting on the prenegotiation status quo also increases with the degree of divided government.

The greater the differences between actors' preferences, the more it matters who sets the agenda. As a result, a legislature that sets the prenegotiation status quo in a country that gives negotiation authority to an executive with significantly more dovish preferences will likely see high degrees of cooperation. As it turns out, this configuration characterizes many countries in trade policy, notably the United States.

The second, *negotiation stage*, of cooperation sees two governments negotiate with each other. This has attracted significant attention in the nonformal literature on negotiations (see Odell 2000 inter alia), which focuses on bargaining tactics and negotiation strategy. Even so, much work remains to be done, for tactical questions in international negotiations remain understudied in the theoretical literature, especially when we consider the effects of domestic politics. In many cases, tactical choices provide an actor with significant agenda-setting abilities, in ways that seem to benefit the agenda-setter, but the theoretical foundation of these advantages are unclear.

The formal literature has not given this stage much attention. Much of the formal literature treats the negotiation stage as merely a question of what assumptions to make about the final outcome, using take-it-or-leave-it (TILI), split-the-difference, Nash bargaining solution (NBS), or Rubinstein solutions. None of the formal models takes the problem of bargaining process (or tactics) seriously at a level comparable to the bargaining literature. These solution concepts in the formal literature differ in terms of agenda-setting power, that is, who makes initial offers and the conditions under which they are accepted or amended. Connecting agenda powers in the bargaining stage with agenda powers in the prenegotiation stage would provide a natural extension of the framework here.

Interestingly enough, the formal literature—and much of the nonformal literature—has assumed that the most interesting feature of the negotiation process is the executive's anticipation of the third, or *ratification stage* of international cooperation. The problem has proved itself so amenable to formal analysis that one might infer that this anticipated ratification is virtually the only two-level question simple enough to model formally. As we have seen, much of this literature argues that divided government makes cooperation more difficult because any ratifiers may have preferences differing from the executive's preferences, leading to rejection of agreements at the ratification stage (for the general veto player argument, see Tsebelis 1999). A similar concern characterizes the traditional foreign policy literature, which worries that a multiplicity of veto players contributes to inertia in the American political system (Hoffman 1962; Key 1961; but Waltz 1967).

In addition to blocking potential cooperation, anticipating of the ratification affects the distribution of gains from cooperation. Thomas Schelling famously argued that executives who can credibly tie their hands could refuse to grant concessions in bargaining, and might more easily extract concessions from their interlocutors. This claims stands in contrast to some traditional indictments of democratic foreign policy. For example, some have argued that democracies are generally dovish, implying that they make too many concessions to other states. Still others believe that democratic constraints on the executive make it harder for them to make concessions, even when these concessions are in the national interest. Scholars also disagree about democracies' ability to extract concessions from others. For some, democratic foreign policy is incoherent and disorganized, incapable of the kinds of consistent foreign policy necessary to drive a good bargain with other states. In contrast, the democratic peace literature suggests that democracies find it easy to make reciprocal concessions to each other in order to resolve disputes nonviolently.

Allee and Huth provide evidence confirming the conventional claim, grounded in the logic of the veto player hypothesis, that divided government makes it harder to reach cooperative settlements to disputes. At the same time, their evidence does not support the distributional claim that divided governments make fewer concessions to their interlocutors. Their explanation emphasizes the interaction between two states more than the ratification constraint within one country. Each executive wants to show domestic audiences that it has obtained concessions from the other side, so cooperation is more likely when both sides offer similar degrees of concessions. In other words, Allee and Huth emphasize audience costs in a democracy more than they do institutional constraints. They suggest that democracies are more cooperative because they can both grant and receive concessions.

Rosendorff's analysis differs from Allee and Huth's, and largely follows Schelling's logic. On his account, democracies offer fewer concessions and extract more than do other countries. This conclusion differs from Allee and Huth's in its view of how domestic groups view asymmetric concessions. For Rosendorff, only one's own utility matters, while Allee and Huth assume that perceived symmetry (fairness) also matters when selling an agreement domestically. As the debate over "relative" versus "absolute" gains shows, such a debate rests on deeply grounded assumptions about human behavior (Grieco 1988; Powell 1991; Snidal 1991).

While anticipating the third stage at the second stage has played a central role in research, the third stage, ratification itself, has not attracted much attention. By delving into the ratification procedures and examining veto players' preferences in detail, Hug and König provide one of the few credible accounts of why a treaty was ratified in more than one country. It is striking that they obtain strong results within a complete information framework, even though the formal literature has increasingly focused on the ratification problem under incomplete information. Also interesting is their finding that almost every country in the pre-2004 EU—the UK is a debatable exception—is a divided polity. As a result, institutions cannot explain variation in outcomes across countries and we must turn to preferences to understand ratifications better.

Besides the simple question of ratification, this stage also raises significant *domestic* distributional questions. These questions appear in the non formal literature in the form of side payments offered to ratifiers in exchange for their consent to a treaty (Milner 1997: Chapter 4). The formal literature has not yet examined the conditions under which an executive will find it advantageous to offer such side payments. Neither formal nor the nonformal theorists of international cooperation have examined the related question of treaty amendment during the ratification process, with one partial exception.[2] Future research should apply the approach presented in this collection to these other aspects of the ratification stage.

Ratification obstacles can also have important implications for our understanding of democracy and foreign policy. Allee and Huth show that the degree of divided government affects not only cooperation but also international conflict. Divided government, even in democracies, may make the settlement of international conflict more difficult.

These analyses highlight a possible conflict between the two-level theory of international cooperation and the literature on the democratic peace. Veto players may not only block the decision to go to war, as the structural variant of the democratic peace maintains, but may also block a settlement of the conflict. As a result, we would not expect a "divided polity" to have a uniform effect on war or peace, unless we examine particular stages in the war-making process such as initiation and termination.

Our understanding of domestic regimes and war would doubtless be strengthened if research could combine the role of veto players at both the initiation and the ratification stage, and perhaps at other stages as well. One avenue of synthesis might be to examine whether democracies with important veto players are associated with enduring rivalries that linger between peace and war for long periods, with neither hot wars nor a real settlement. Something of the sort may characterize relations between Greece and Turkey, for example, both of which have had democracies for long periods but seem to approach war only when nondemocratic.

These various possibilities become still richer as we consider interactions between autonomous policies and international cooperation. For example, Rosendorff suggests that democracies are autonomously dovish, choosing unilateral policies of freer trade that benefit other countries. The extant literature gives various answers to the question whether this dovishness makes reciprocal concessions more or less likely. Having chosen policy favorable to foreigners, democracies may be unwilling to go further; on the other hand, the kind of polity that chooses liberal policies in the first place may find it relatively easy to liberalize still further (see Pahre 2001c). These concerns will also likely affect the anticipated problem of ratification.

The fifth and final stage comes after ratification, in which we see the implementation of an agreement. The contributors to this volume give this question only incidental attention, which has recently been treated elsewhere (see especially Martin 2000). Here too more work needs to be done, for example in examining the strategic incentives for executives who know that agreements will be only partially implemented (see Mertha and Pahre 2005; Wu and Axelrod 1995). Allee and Huth's finding that an executive needs a large majority to settle a territorial conflict may be grounded not only in the bargaining and ratification stages but also at the implementation stage, since a domestically strong leader will be in a better position to implement an agreement fully, making it a better bargaining partner for other countries.

Thinking about the different stages of cooperation helps clarify some of the debates about implementation problems and cooperation. For example, the legislature may be an obstacle to the executive's foreign policy at the ratification stage because it can reject a treaty. At the implementation stage, in contrast, the legislature may be a partner for the executive, making the executive's foreign policy commitments more credible abroad (Martin 2000; Waltz 1967). At the prenegotiation stage, an increasing degree of divided government may make later cooperation easier, while at a later stage it complicates ratification. If one wishes to evaluate the overall effects of democracy on foreign policy, the separate effects of each stage are important.

Finally, looking at the effects of multiple features of democracy across five stages helps clarify two issues running through the literature on democracy and cooperation: the Schelling Conjecture and the problem of credibility. I examine these in the next two sections, after which I turn to a summary assessment of democracy and foreign policy.

The Negotiation and Ratification Stages: Schelling Revisited

The conventional analysis emphasizes the ways in which democracy may hamper an effective foreign policy. This clearly overlooks the advantages of a democratic constraint. Most notably, the Schelling Conjecture highlights how domestic opposition can limit the range of concessions that an executive can make. Schelling originally conjectured that an executive might want to tie his hands, telling his interlocutors that he could make no further concessions because of domestic constraints. This has sometimes, but wrongly, been interpreted as an *unconditional* claim that *all* executives will *always* seek to tie their hands.[3] As such, the claim is clearly false (see Evans 1993).

Schelling offered his conjecture more conditionally, suggesting that *some* executives *might sometimes* tie their hands. Hammond and Prins (this volume, chapter 2) demonstrate that this weaker claim is true. Their analysis reflects the folk wisdom of the formal modeling community, though this has not appeared in print and its conclusions (perhaps for that reason) seem unfamiliar to most nonformal scholars. Even formal theorists may be surprised by just how few preference orderings will produce the conditions are under which the veto player and Schelling hypotheses hold. The basic conditions are that (1) the home executive must be more hawkish than the foreign executive, that is, located closer to the status quo; (2) the home legislature must be more hawkish than the home executive; and (3) the legislature must prefer the executive's ideal point to the status quo (Pahre 1994).[4] As such, the Schelling Conjecture provides a good example of some complexities surrounding any effort to make unconditional claims about democracy and foreign policy, even in a relatively narrow area.

Hammond and Prins's analysis does not assume that any particular set of preferences is more or less likely than any other. Their analysis is intentionally theoretical, leaving empirical studies to build on their findings. When we turn to real-world polities, preference orderings are presumably patterned to a greater or lesser degree. Finding these patterns is an important research agenda. These analyses are central to the question whether Schelling's Conjecture is *substantively* important, that is, whether these conditions are often met in practice. These particular conditions may be found everywhere or nowhere, and this distribution matters.

The contributors approach this question in two ways. Rosendorff, echoed by Pahre, takes a deductive approach to this question. He argues that legislatures are generally more attuned to particularist interests than are executives (see also Mansfield and Busch 1995; Rogowski 1987). This makes legislatures more hawkish on the question of free trade, so they view the status quo more favorably. In addition, the home executive is more "hawkish" than the foreign executive, seeking lesser concessions on the home tariff dimension. Because these are exactly the conditions under which the Schelling Conjecture holds, executive hand-tying should be common in trade policy.

While this analysis represents a near-consensus view of trade policy preferences, there is no deductive framework that would help us make similar generalizations about other issue areas. Legislatures and publics seem to be somewhat less willing to make concessions in some settings. Allee and Huth suggest that the public will normally be more hawkish than the executive in the case of territorial disputes, so that only a leader with broad support will be able to "sell" concessions to them. The pattern of preferences is significantly more complex in the study of European integration, where it was long standard to argue that the executive (European Commission) and one legislative chamber (the European Parliament) were more dovish (prointegration) while the other legislative chamber (the Council of Ministers) was more reluctant to integrate more deeply (i.e., Schneider and Cederman 1993; Tsebelis 1994 inter alia). However, further advances in integration have tended to make disagreements over the substance of policy more evident, shifting more debates into a traditional Left-Right dimension (see Hooghe et al. 2002; Tsebelis and Garrett 2000).

The second approach makes no general claims about the frequency of the Schelling conditions in the real world. Instead, scholars such as Hug and König or Allee and Huth test the Schelling Conjecture in a large-n setting. If the conditions are found sufficiently often in the real world, these tests will yield rightly signed and statistically significant estimates. If these conditions are not common, statistical tests will reject the claim.

We must note that the large-n approach cannot falsify the Schelling Conjecture in its proper, conditional form. If the population of cases includes many without the proper preference orderings, statistical methods will obscure any relationship that hold only for a subset of observations. Case study methods could illuminate these, as could statistical tests using measurements of relative hawkishness, as found in the three conditions for the conjecture to hold. The large-n findings of Allee and Huth must be interpreted cautiously in this light. As Hammond and Prins point out in a different setting, the importance of preference orderings in a spatial model makes it difficult to derive unconditional claims about behavior and to interpret empirical generalizations about that behavior.

Allee and Huth add another claim to the literature on the Schelling Conjecture, an insight that finds resonance in several other chapters. If a high degree of divided government makes concessions more difficult, this affects the process of reciprocal concessions found in many bargaining settings. Governments prefer to offer concessions that will be reciprocated, and some bargaining strategies rely on this (see also Larson 1989). This reciprocity is difficult for a domestically divided policy, which will therefore have trouble eliciting concessions. In contrast, a unified government may find it easier to elicit concessions.

Drawing on Allee and Huth, then, we should think of the Schellingesque argument as encompassing two claims: first, that a nation with a high degree of divided government will find it difficult to *make* concessions, giving it a bargaining advantage; and second, that such a nation will also find it difficult to *elicit* concessions, giving it a bargaining *dis*advantage. Two polities, each with a high degree of divided government and a hawkish legislator, will therefore find concessions difficult.

Any consideration of democracy and foreign policy will therefore have to consider two issues. First, with whom is a given democracy negotiating? The literature on the democratic peace has emphasized the dyadic nature of its claims (but Rousseau et al. 1996) and we should consider whether similar dyadic effects exist in political economy. Second, we must examine the distribution of power and preferences inside every democracy. This determines whether a country has divided government at all, the degree of divided government, and the location of agenda-setting powers.

In short, future research examining the Schelling Conjecture should not merely be more precise in specifying the conditions under which an executive's hands are tied, making it difficult to offer concessions. We should also examine the ability of a constrained executive to solicit concessions, which means looking explicitly at a two-democracy setting (as in Leventoğlu and Tarar 2005 inter alia).

Considering the two-democracy setting also raises interesting normative problems. Normatively, the Schelling Conjecture focuses on each country doing better at the expense of the other, a goal that seems appropriate for a one-country foreign policy analysis. However, it does not seem to be an appropriate normative goal in international relations, in which we should seek outcomes that make all participants better off instead of those outcomes that make one democracy better off at the expense of one another.

The Stages of Cooperation and the Credibility of Democratic Foreign Policy

The different effects of democracy in each stage of cooperation are also evident in the problem of credibility. One of the challenges posed by international cooperation is that it requires a government to make commitments today that may contradict the popular will tomorrow. In other words, states anticipate problems at the implementation stage when they bargain at the negotiation stage.

The alleged inconstancy of democratic politics played an important role in the thinking of those who argued that democracy made foreign policy making more difficult. These concerns enjoy a long history, and are especially common among policymakers and those close to them (see inter alia Kennan 1984; Lippman 1922, 1925). Kenneth Waltz (1967: 9) reports such worries in the thinking of Lord Salisbury:

> Lord Salisbury's policy of "splendid isolation" reflected less an estimate of what was desirable in policy than a conviction that with increasing Parliamentary control long-term commitments could not be made. German governments of the 1890s doubted the value of an executive agreement with England. Parliamentary ratification was necessary to give some assurance of continuity. Even so, Salisbury thought: assurance of continuity would not be achieved. There was another hazard: the next Parliament might undo what the last had done.

Others with experience in foreign policy making have echoed these concerns. Two parts of this concern are amenable to analysis through the public choice framework here. First, a democratic executive supposedly finds it difficult to make foreign policy because any commitments to other countries are always conditional, and could be rejected or undone by the legislature. Second, any agreement made today, even if approved by the current legislature, could easily be undone by next year's government. In both cases, the credibility of a democratic executive suffers, and this effect would grow worse with divided government and an increasing degree of divided government.

This volume has examined both preferences and institutions in democracies, a focus that we may apply to the credibility question. The first claim, that executive credibility suffers because legislatures may reject their foreign policy commitments, is related to the veto player hypothesis examined in this book. As we have seen, the contributors doubt that divided government systematically makes cooperation either more or less likely. Some executives may find that democracy makes foreign policy more difficult while others will not. When cooperation occurs, of course, it represents a commitment to a given policy. For example, trade policies locked in a reciprocal trade treaty are less changeable than unilateral trade policies (Pahre 2001c).

The second concern, that tomorrow's legislature can unmake the commitments of today, must be evaluated in light of the first point. If it is indeed difficult for the executive to obtain the legislature's approval for its commitments, it must be equally difficult to get the legislature to unmake commitments once made. The hallmark of a democratic system with multiple veto players is, after all, alleged to be inertia. This inertia means that divided government, and an increasing degree of divided government, can actually make foreign policy commitments more credible (see Martin 2000; Waltz 1967).

A lack of such credibility characterized semidemocratic Slovakia under Prime Minister Vladimír Mečiar before 1998. Mečiar's various undemocratic practices made it easy for him to change policy direction, and slowed progress toward membership in the European Union and NATO. Slovakia did not meet the EU's Copenhagen criteria of democratization until after the formation of the 1998 Dzurinda government, and lacked NATO's requirement of democratic political credibility at the 1997 Madrid Summit. Slovakia's partners simply could not trust its commitments because they lacked the credibility afforded by a democratically realized domestic consensus. One high civil servant notes simply that "We were not trusted, and it is our fault that we were not trusted."[5] As the Dzurinda government demonstrated its commitment to democracy, Slovakia moved toward membership in both NATO and the EU.

The difficulty democracies face in unmaking prior commitments may not only make them better treaty partners but also give them a more attractive business environment. For example, Bergara et al. (1998) have shown that having divided government encourages incoming foreign direct investment, and that the more veto players a country has, the greater the investment that occurs. Investors realize that divided government makes it more difficult for a country to renege tomorrow on the commitments that it makes today.

We can also see the economic effects of democratic commitments in financial rating agencies, which are concerned with whether a country can keep its commitments to banks, foreign corporations, and credibly maintain a given policy direction. Again, Slovakia after independence provides an interesting example. Both Moody's and S&P's raised Slovakia's credit rating as the Dzurinda government consolidated democracy, and both cited the possibility of a Mečiar victory in September 2002 as a brake on those ratings. After a country visit in October 2000, Moody's suggested that a better rating depended on Slovak reforms reaching a stage that would be irreversible even for a future antireform government, and did not depend only on the 2002 elections. Chief analyst Jonathan Schiffer stated that "We are very cautious about giving Slovakia a better rating that would pull the country out of the speculative category. This holds especially true in light of the coming elections [of fall 2002]"[6] (Nalevanko 2001 in *Sme*, June 16, 2001).

These interactions between a country's political system and the actions of international business often lead to criticism. Certainly one may read the ratings agencies' evaluations not as rewarding democracy but limiting it—like NATO and the EU, the international business community pressured Slovaks not to give Mečiar's Movement for a Democratic Slovakia (HZDS) a parliamentary majority in September 2002 (Kaiser 2002). US NATO ambassador Nicholas Burns even said that HZDS participation in government would be "a fundamental obstacle to Slovakia's accession to NATO" (cited in Mudde 2002: 2). European Union Commissioner for Enlargement Günther Verheugen called the elections "the most important election in the history of the country," arguing that "Slovakia needs a government that is trusted in Europe and is able to lead Slovakia into the EU, while guaranteeing the continuation of the process of political, economic, and social change" (cited at Mudde 2002). These forces would also have disapproved of a government in which Anna Malíková and the far Right Slovak Nationalist Party (SNS) were to play a role. Foreign governments and foreign business may also have looked with skepticism on a government led by Robert Fico of the party *Smer* (Direction), despite his support for the Euro-Atlantic direction of Dzurinda's foreign policy. These external pressures are especially important because Fico continues to be the most popular politician in the country, and Mečiar is second. Slovakia's credibility as a democracy, it seems, depends on its voters using their powers in a highly constrained way. The fact that these constraints are imposed from outside, as opposed to constraints that a country imposes on itself through a constitution, makes them more objectionable.

Paradoxically, then, international pressure and a network of international cooperation, by constraining democratic choice, may also help consolidate democracy. Jon Pevehouse (2002) has recently shown that membership in regional international organizations helped consolidate democracy in the post–1945 era. These organizations help bind both winners and losers through commitments, establishing a credible commitment to political reform.

The relationships between democracy, divided government, credibility, and cooperation thus run in multiple directions. Democracy in general seems to enhance credibility but this comes at the cost of forgoing some less credible policies. Veto players may make ratification more difficult but this fact makes ratified treaties more long-lived.

This issue too has normative implications. A treaty is a commitment to do something, and not to do something else. If it is to be meaningful, it precludes some democratic choices. For example, Germany cannot dismantle its system of agricultural subsidies and price supports, for this is bound up with the European Union's Common Agricultural Policy (CAP). This may be an extreme example, but the basic issue was recognized by the framers of the U.S. Constitution, who made international treaties legally binding but also made them require a supramajority in the Senate for ratification. In this way, today's democracy can only tie the hands of a future democracy by meeting a higher, supramajoritarian standard. A similar concern may lie behind the supramajoritarian requirements for EU treaty ratification analyzed by Hug and König.

In these cases, the democratic public loses control of its own foreign policy, though this loss of control reflects the choices of a previous incarnation of that same public (compare Elster 1994). Whether a country will be willing to do this depends in part on the preferences of the democratic public, a question to which I turn in the next section.

Divided Government and the Delegation of Democratic Foreign Policy

To examine the normative issues raised by the contributions to this book, we must consider not only the complexity of democracy and the various stages of cooperation but also the complexity of society. Ultimately, society determines both the rules of the game in a democracy and the preferences of the actors in that game. In the terms of this book, the public decides whether it wants a divided polity and, once that polity is established, the public determines both the distribution of agenda-setting powers and the degree of divided government at any given moment.

I do not consider here the conditions under which a public decides to establish a divided polity (see inter alia Rogowski 1974) but simply assume that it has done so. Instead, I focus primarily on the public's choice of the executive and legislature, treating the public as a principal who chooses one or more agents (for a review of principal-agent theory applied to international relations, see Hawkins et al. 2006). This differs somewhat from most of existing theory about foreign policy delegation, which tends to analyze an intergovernmental principal-agent problem, examining how a legislative principal delegates to an executive agent. If the executive and legislature are selected separately—as in the United States, the European Union (with caveats), and presidential systems in many Latin American countries—we need to know whether the executive or legislature better represents the public's preferences before we can make a full evaluation of how well the public's preferences are carried out.

We should note in passing that it makes good sense for the public to delegate foreign policy tasks to agents such as an executive and/or legislature for, as a large literature has shown, the public usually has little interest in, or knowledge about, foreign policy. Even a salient issue such as Northern Ireland affects British politics only intermittently, and that lack of interest usually means that public opposition does not usually reduce the executive's discretion (Trumbore 1998). It is important to note that the public's lack of knowledge is fairly rational, since there is no incentive for every citizen to become a foreign policy expert (i.e., Page and Shapiro 1992; Russett 1990a); the citizenry can instead delegate day-to-day policymaking to specialists with expertise in the area.

Though the topic is underresearched, there is some evidence that foreign policy officials view themselves as delegates. As part of a broad review of the topic, Powlick (1991: 623) quotes one deputy assistant secretary of state who phrases his position in a particularly apropos way

> on the one hand, you can't simply read the morning newspapers in order to figure out what sort of policy decisions you should make that day, because

you're called upon to exercise your special knowledge or to exercise leadership, so that you are not just a mirror for public opinion. At the same time,
you cannot depart fundamentally from some of the basic values or elements
that shape the consensus that allows the system to continue.

In other words, while diplomats are selected for their expertise and given
discretion to use that expertise, they are nonetheless accountable to a democratic public, and this accountability is evident in the limits within which
they may exercise their discretion. Powlick's study of the foreign policy elite
suggested that diplomats believed this public scrutiny of their role to be a
good thing.

Of course, the public might delegate foreign policy making in various
ways. Broadly speaking, there are two types of divided polities that are relevant for the foreign policy issue area. The first is a parliamentary system in
which the public chooses a legislature who then chooses the executive, in
other words, the public chooses the legislature directly and the executive
indirectly. The second is a presidential system in which the public chooses
both the legislature and the executive directly, but separately. These two systems are shown schematically in figure 7.1.

These two systems are sometimes characterized as differing in terms of
whether the legislature or the executive dominates foreign policy making
(see Martin 2000 for review). This "dominance" might take the form of
who sets the agenda, as the contributors to this volume have examined.
Alternatively, dominance may be a matter of who selects whom. For example,
legislative scholars tend to assume legislative dominance, with the executive

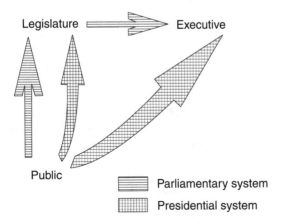

Figure 7.1 The Structure of Delegation in Parliamentary and Presidential Systems

acting as an agent ultimately responsible to Congress. Our focus on divided government shifts the view here, emphasizing the way that both executive and legislature are ultimately responsible to the public as principal.

These schematic representation helps highlight an important puzzle in any theory of divided government: how is it that a single principal might choose two agents with different preferences? That is, if the public chooses both the legislature and the executive, why would we ever see divided government?

This question is perhaps most puzzling in the case of parliamentary government, in which the legislature chooses the executive. Normally, the executive's preferences would be the same as those of a legislative majority, since the majority chooses the executive. In some cases, however, no majority can be formed and the legislature will choose—or acquiesce in—a minority government. Because this minority government does not command, and was not chosen by, a legislative majority, it will normally have preferences that differ from that majority (see Pahre 1997).

A parliamentary system may also see divided government when it has some supramajoritarian features, as Hug and König point out in chapter 5. In such cases, a legislative majority chooses the executive but a legislative supramajority is necessary for ratification of certain of the executive's actions. Under these conditions we will normally see some degree of divided government between the executive and the supramajority of the legislature.

The question of divided government is somewhat less puzzling in a presidential system. These systems usually choose the legislature and an executive on different bases, effectively giving each citizen's votes different weight across the two elections. For example, presidential elections in the United States reward candidates who can appeal to enough of the political center to win a majority. In contrast, the gerrymandered district boundaries in the House of Representatives mean that the party label of each representative is almost fixed; a candidate wins by appealing to a majority of their party. A party majority will lie to the left of the political center among the Democrats, to the right of the political center among the Republicans. As a result, members of the House of Representatives are likely to be more ideologically polarized than either the president or members of the Senate. These differences create the political foundation for divided government, since a typical president from either party will want to restrain the more ideological members of his own party in the House.

Similarly, it has become common to claim that consumer interests in the United States are better represented by the presidency whereas producer interests are better represented by the House of Representatives (Mansfield and Busch 1995; Rogowski 1987).[7] Agricultural interests are overrepresented in the Senate, since less populated rural states such as South Dakota have the same representation as densely populated urban states such as New Jersey. These kinds of structural differences in preferences lay behind several of the cases in Pahre's chapter, and are central to Rosendorff's model, among others.

The existence of actors selected on different foundations may be seen not only in presidential systems but also in federal systems, even those with parliamentary forms of government. For example, Australia and Canada have an upper house of the legislature that is selected very differently from the lower house, and whose majority is systematically different from the lower house that chooses the prime minister. When the upper house has ratification power over the prime minister's acts, a significant degree of divided government is common. Similarly, the German upper house reflects the political balance in the states and not in the country as a whole. Again, this tends to be systematically different from the majority in the lower house, and these differences matter whenever the upper house's approval is necessary (as in an increasing number of EU issue areas).

A third reason for divided government may occur in either a parliamentary or presidential system. Under some circumstances, a principal may choose agents to perform different roles, and expect the interaction of these agents to produce a particular kind of outcome. For example, the member states of the European Union have designed a political system in which they choose a Commission to serve as a motor of European integration, while the Council of Ministers serves as the brakes. As part of this constitutional design, the Commission was given agenda-setting powers while ratification powers remained with the Council and, under some conditions, the European Parliament as well. The idea behind this structure is to encourage deeper integration while retaining a more skeptical actor who will prevent this integration from going too far. As a result, we should normally see some degree of divided government between the Commission and the Council (and the Parliament, where relevant).

In a broader sense, this kind of strategy by the principal probably lies behind some of the constitutional rules that generate divided government in either a parliamentary or presidential system. The principal may have designed a supramajority ratification institution in parliamentary systems so as to give the agenda-setting executive a different role that the supramajoritarian ratifier, directly analogous to the motor-and-brakes model of the European Union. Similarly, the public may see a partisan House as a useful constraint on an executive whose centrist position makes it tend toward more compromise in international negotiation that hardliners in one or both parties would prefer.

These kinds of divisions between the executive and the legislature may be fairly common. Many literatures find that there are systematic differences in preferences between the legislature and the executive that reflect their different electorates. As I have noted earlier, theorists of trade policy typically argue that the executive better represents the national interest than the legislature. In the United States, in particular, legislators are elected from a narrow constituency and therefore tend to have more particularist interests, such as strong support for the district's major industry. The president is responsible to a national constituency and therefore worries about aggregate growth rates as well as consumer interests in lower prices.

In contrast, students of military conflict often assume that the legislature better represents the national interest. Because of the rally-round-the-flag effect (Mueller 1973), executives can gain popularity from military action abroad. Legislatures might restrain the executive, especially if it needs legislative authorization to declare or fight a war (Bueno de Mesquita and Lalman 1992; Bueno de Mesquita et al. 1999; Doyle 1986; Smith 1998; see also Martin 1993).

Presumably, each of these arguments has force for some issue areas but not for others. Whatever the issue, our normative analysis can begin with an account of the executive's and legislature's preferences, and the relationship between these preferences and the *vox populi*. This is, then, the degree of divided government.

It may not be obvious at first, but each of the explanations for divided government discussed so far in this chapter requires that the public's own preferences not be very homogenous. A homogenous public would always produce a legislature majority in a parliamentary system, and thus indirectly select an executive with the same preferences as that majority. A homogenous public in a presidential system would lack the kind of differences necessary to generate a House, Senate, and/or president whose preferences differ significantly from one another. A homogenous public would also find it unnecessary to assign different roles to different agents in either system, since it would choose a unified government that accurately reflects its preferences.

This kind of heterogeneity among social groups and the institutions that represent them, sometimes called "polyarchy" (Dahl 1971), has long been an important feature of liberal democracies, and has given its name to a leading interpretation of U.S. politics. It plays a more quiet role in this volume, usually behind the scenes but occasionally appearing on the stage. For example, Rosendorff builds his model on groups of exporters, import-competers, and consumers that disagree over trade policy. Hug and König analyze political systems with many relevant players, most importantly parties and (implicitly) the groups making up each party's support coalition. When each of these groups has formal representation in the political system, pluralism may also produce a divided polity, with multiple actors having influence over policy outcomes.

Focusing on social groups highlights the conflictual, distributional side of democracy. Not everyone can be satisfied at the same time, so politics has winners and losers. The most interesting question for foreign policy in this respect is that some groups have interests aligned with foreigners' interests. Exporters and consumers will benefit from lower tariffs at home, but so will foreign exporters whose goods will be more lightly taxed. These common interests set the stage for crossnational coalitions, which may be either explicit or implicit. Trade agreements, for example, effectively represent a meeting of minds between exporters and consumers in the two signatory countries, at the expense of import-competing industries in both (see Pahre 1998). In two-level theory, those groups whose preferences are closer to foreigners are normally labeled "doves" while those more distant from foreigners are "hawks" (Evans, Jacobson, and Putnam, eds. 1993).[8]

This kind of a heterogenous public is a necessary condition for divided government. Such heterogeneity is not sufficient, since a unified, nonfederal parliamentary system such as the classic Westminster model of government may produce unified government even if the electorate is divided. When institutions such as federalism or separation of powers permit it, however, a heterogenous public is necessary for us to observe any significant degree of divided government. This observation matters for any normative evaluation because if we see two branches of government blocking one another's actions, we must consider the preferences of the public that chose these actors in the first place. I turn to this task in the next section.

The Effectiveness of Democratic Foreign Policy

If a heterogenous public delegates foreign policy to agents with a high degree of divided government, can the foreign policy of such a government ever be effective? Such a situation would seem to define the worst nightmare of scholars who have criticized the effectiveness of democratic foreign policy making (see Nincic and Hinckley 1991 for review and discussion).

Scholars of foreign policy have traditionally had a low opinion of democratic foreign policy making. For example, Carr (1939: Chapter 3) criticized the nineteenth-century belief that public opinion was not only correct—perhaps following the principle *vox populi, vox dei*—but that this opinion would always prevail in the long run. As Carr (1939: 34) notes, this belief lay behind the League of Nations' reliance on votes critical of aggressors, for it "was unthinkable that a unanimous verdict of the League should be defied."

These criticisms of public opinion also reflect the weaknesses of the first U.S. presidents to appeal directly to their publics, such as Woodrow Wilson. Wilson's approach to foreign policy attracted considerable criticism from classic Realist authors such as E. H. Carr (1939) and Hans Morgenthau (1949). Wilson's call for "open covenants, openly arrived at," flew in the face of the diplomatic practices that Realists have traditionally advocated (for a model of publicity in foreign policy making, see Leventoğlu and Tarar 2005).

Of course, the verdicts of the League of Nations were in fact defied, despite being supported by democratic public opinion. The economic sanctions used to give these verdicts teeth also failed to stop aggressors in the 1930s. As a result, postwar thinkers argued that public opinion was not a reliable guide to foreign policy making.

On this view, legislatures were also obstacles to effective foreign policy because they represented the public's unstable and uninformed views. Reflecting this position, Henry Morgenthau (1949: 530–531) argues that democracies should reduce the role of the public, instead delegating foreign policy making to a skillful executive.

Behavioral research in the 1950s and 1960s would seem to confirm the wisdom of this advice, for it showed that public opinion was uninformed, not coherent over time, and as a result quite volatile. For these reasons, the conventional wisdom held that public opinion was harmful to a stable and effective foreign policy (see Holsti 1992 for review).

From this standpoint, democratic foreign policy making presents two challenges. First, an uninformed public may make unreasonable demands on foreign policy makers, harming foreign policy effectiveness. These demands may be impractical, may fail to consider trade-offs among several goals, or be time-inconsistent in that they do not anticipate the effects of today's demands on tomorrow's policy choices. Second, a legislature, which many assume is closer to the voters that elected it than an indirectly chosen executive, may also block the executive's efforts to pursue an effective and coherent foreign policy. Though our findings are different, the possibility that these concerns are valid is consistent with the approach of this volume, which allows for the possibility that a domestic ratifier can block cooperation that other actors in the political system desire.

Even so, the analysis of divided polities and divided government in the previous section calls both of these claims into question. First, under many conditions the public's preferences will be relatively homogenous and therefore the degree of divided government relatively low. In such cases, public support for the executive's policy can only strengthen its position, and by definition the low degree of divided government means that the legislature will not prevent effective action. Such conditions resemble the cases discussed

by Marra, Ostrom and Simon (1989), in which public approval of a president's foreign policy contributes to his freedom of action. This is especially
true if, as a revisionist literature suggests, public opinion is in fact coherent
and stable over time on many issues, changing in predictable ways in
response to events (see Nincic 1992b; Page and Shapiro 1992). Similarly,
more recent studies have raised the scholarly view of legislatures, emphasizing
how legislatures could influence policy productively, and help the nation
make consistent commitments to policies (Martin 2000).

At other times, foreign policy becomes a divisive issue. In this environment,
the public's preferences will be heterogenous and, if the rules of the polity
allow it, we would expect an increased degree of divided government.
Under some conditions, as the contributors to this volume have shown, this
increasing degree of divided government will make international cooperation and other forms of foreign policy problem-solving more difficult.
However, we should not be quick to criticize democracy for blocking effective foreign policy making in such cases. Recall that these circumstances
depend on a public being divided on foreign policy matters. Why should we
prefer higher levels of international cooperation if a large segment of the
public opposes this kind of policy? Key hardliner segments among the
public may even choose divided government strategically in order to
increase the executive's bargaining strength (as in Pahre 1997, Tarar 2001a).

The contributors to this volume also show that divided government
may, in some cases, make international cooperation *more* likely. In these
cases, public divisions over foreign policy hamper the ability of the executive and legislature to work together on foreign policy. To pursue its own
foreign policy interests—and presumably also the interests of the public
that chose it—the executive may cooperate with foreign executives to solve
problems that it cannot solve at home. This makes cooperation more likely.
Here too it seems unreasonable to criticize a democratic public's involvement in foreign policy, since it (paradoxically) creates conditions that make
it easier for the executive to work with other countries.

Viewed in this kind of strategic analysis, the argument about effective
foreign policy making longs for a homogeneity in public preferences that
does not exist, for the public (or legislature) will only make foreign policy
less effective when its preferences are not homogenous. In this environment,
actions to make foreign policy more "effective" really mean taking the side of
one part of the public over another, and trying to reduce the ability of dis-
senting groups to object. While entirely appropriate as foreign policy advo-
cacy, such a position does not make a persuasive theory of how democratic
foreign policy making does (or should) generally work.

This criticism of democratic foreign policy ineffectiveness is itself subject to
important normative criticisms. First, by whose standards are we claiming

that a policy is undesirable? In a democracy, any major policy will likely be controversial. Criticizing something as bad policy is obviously appropriate, but it is harder to criticize the process that produced that policy. After all, the policy probably has a significant number of supporters, and the process clearly empowered them to obtain the policy they thought best. Kenneth Waltz (1967: 299), normally associated with a hardline Realist position, summarized the issue succinctly in his major book on democratic foreign policy: "The question of the coherence and adequacy of policy, since those attributes cannot be measured objectively, resolves itself into a further question: namely, who decides that some policies are better than others?"

This volume's focus on divided government constrains the answers to this question a bit. If both the executive and the legislature are agents of the public principal, then it would be difficult for an analyst to decide that either the executive's preferences or the legislature's preferences should be given greater weight. However, presumably some (convex) combination of those two actors' preferences does enjoy broad support among the public and would be normatively defensible in any foreign policy analysis. In more traditional terms, any outcome of the "invitation to struggle" (Corwin 1957: 171) between the executive and the legislature would enjoy normative support.

Some might object that policy would be ineffective if the struggle to control foreign policy were not resolved at all. It is true that incoherence might result as one branch, after another snatches control over policy; as Waltz (1967: 95) notes, "When the distance between parties grows wider, concern for the continuity of policy abounds." Even so, this lack of continuity under some conditions should not be seen as a feature of democracy per se. Instead, it reflects the heterogenous preferences held by the public and its two agents. The solution would not be a less democratic foreign policy, nor delegation to a single agent such as the executive. Instead, actions to reduce the heterogeneity of preferences, perhaps through a public dialogue that might bring some social groups closer together, would be appropriate.

This kind of foreign policy incoherence might pose particular dangers in times of foreign policy crisis. Indeed, some scholars have criticized democracies for being poorly suited to act decisively in a crisis, or in other situations in which speed of decision are essential. Speed of decision is probably most valuable in a rapidly changing world such as the post–1990 international system, while policy continuity is more important in response to recurring problems where change is more gradual. Bipartisanship is often offered as a solution, but Waltz argues that it is useful only when it is not needed because the leaders are already in broad agreement.

Speed of decision has not yet been a subject of formal analysis, and the topic is poorly theorized in any case. For this reason, we must rely on empirical studies to understand the conditions under which it may or may not be important. In this context, it is certainly encouraging that Trumbore and Boyer (2000) have found evidence showing that crisis decision making does *not* take longer in democracies. All regime types, whether democratic or not, tend to develop new institutions for rapid decision making in cases of crisis. While these usually enjoy somewhat wider participation in democracies than in nondemocracies, these groups are capable of rapid decisions in either environment. It is similarly encouraging that Gelpi and Griesdorf (2001) have found that democracies are more likely to prevail in international crises because their leaders are good at choosing only those conflicts that they can win.

In short, there is no reason to believe that democratic foreign policy is any less effective than nondemocratic foreign policy. In fact, it is interesting that few scholars seem to compare democratic and nondemocratic effectiveness explicitly. The more common strategy is to analyze instances of ineffective democratic foreign policy. The framework of this book, and the research of the contributors show that under some conditions such ineffectiveness may occur in a divided polity with significant differences of opinion over foreign policy. However, the cure would probably be worse than the disease, for it would require that foreign policy makers side with one group over another, and there does not seem to be any democratic rule for doing this. Nor is there much evidence that nondemocracies would do this any better.

In fact, democracies have one major advantage even when their foreign policy is ineffective. The public can hold foreign policy makers accountable for the ineffectiveness of policy—indeed, the public may hold an executive accountable even if blame would better lie with the legislature. Leaders are also held responsible for foreign policy failures, including war (Bueno de Mesquita et al. 1992; Bueno de Mesquita and Siverson 1995). In the United States, a divided polity that usually sees a comparatively high degree of divided government, the U.S. public gives the president more freedom of maneuver in foreign policy than in most other issue areas but then evaluates his performance directly, holding him responsible for both successes and failures (Marra et al. 1990; Nincic and Hinckley 1991). In the case of a heterogenous public, each group will try to hold foreign policy makers accountable to its own view of foreign policy at the expense of one another. However, in the case of failure, even a president's supporters will hold him accountable for his failure.

In short, the standard criticisms of democratic foreign policy neglect many of the complexities of foreign policy making that the contributors to this volume have emphasized. The degree of divided government, in particular, raises important questions about "foreign policy in whose interest?"

that have not received appropriate emphasis in the literature critical of the
role of public opinion. Several empirical studies have shown that concerns
about speedy decision making in cases of crisis are probably overstated, and
the theoretical analyses in this volume.

Conclusions

With the expansion of democracy in the twentieth century, it seems that
the world has been made safe for democracy. Critics have long wondered,
however, whether democracy is safe for the world. Many of these criticisms
have focused on the roles of public opinion, a volatile electorate, and an
untrustworthy legislature, suggesting that delegation of foreign policy
authority to an expert executive makes for better foreign policy.

This volume has shown that these concerns are overblown. Particular
elements of democracy may have negative effects on foreign policies, but
other features encourage international cooperation.

Both democracy and international cooperation are multifaceted concepts.
If nothing else, the contributors to this volume show the importance of
greater specificity in both cause and effect. Rather than saying that democracy makes international cooperation more likely, for example, we should
say that, under some conditions, increasing differences of opinion between
the legislature and the executive make international negotiations more
likely but ratification of any resulting agreements more difficult.

Both our explanations of foreign policy and our normative evaluations of
these policies can be made better with a richer and more nuanced understanding of democracy. While this complexity may risk analytical chaos, using
a common framework such as the one proposed here provides a greater
coherence when examining the multifaceted nature of both democracy and
cooperative foreign policies would support this claim.

List of Contributors

Todd Allee is an Assistant Professor of Political Science at the University of Illinois at Urbana, Champaign. He is coauthor of *The Democratic Peace and Territorial Conflict in the Twentieth Century* (Cambridge University Press, 2001) and has published in the *American Political Science Review, International Interactions*, and the *Journal of Conflict Resolution*.

Thomas H. Hammond is Professor of Political Science at Michigan State University. He is coauthor of *A Zero-Based Look at Zero-Base Budgeting* (Transaction Books, 1980), and articles in the *American Journal of Political Science, American Political Science Review, Governance, Journal of Law, Economics, and Organization, Journal of Politics, Journal of Theoretical Politics, Legislative Studies Quarterly*, and other journals in political science.

Simon Hug is Professor of Political Science at the University of Zurich. He is author of *Voices of Europe: Citizens, Referendums and European Integration* (Rowman & Littlefield, 2002), *Altering Party Systems: Strategic Behavior and the Emergence of New Political Parties in Western Democracies* (University of Michigan Press, 2001), and articles in *Comparative Political Studies, European Journal of Political Research, European Union Politics, International Organization, Journal of Conflict Resolution*, and other journals in political science.

Paul Huth is Professor of Political Science at the University of Maryland. He is author of *Extended Deterrence and the Prevention of War* (Yale University Press, 1988); *Standing Your Ground* (University of Michigan Press, 1996) and coauthor of *The Democratic Peace and Territorial Conflict in the Twentieth Century* (Cambridge University Press, 2002), and articles in the *American Political Science Review, Journal of Conflict Resolution, World Politics*, and other journals in political science.

Thomas König is Professor of Political Science at the University of Speyer. He is author of *Europa auf dem Weg zum Mehrheitssystem* (Westdeutscher Verlag, 1997), *Entscheidungen im Politiknetzwerk* (Deutscher Universitätsverlag, 1992), coauthor of *Entscheidungsprozesse in der Arbeits- und Sozialpolitik*

(Campus Verlag, 1995), and author of articles in the *European Journal of Political Research, European Union Politics, International Organization, Journal of Conflict Resolution, Journal of Theoretical Politics*, and other journals in political science.

Robert Pahre is Associate Professor of Political Science at the University of Illinois at Urbana-Champaign. He is author of *Leading Questions* (University of Michigan Press, 1999), coauthor of *Trade and Political Institutions* (Edward Elgar, 2001) and coauthor of *Creative Marginality* (Westview, 1990), as well as articles in *European Union Politics, International Organization, Journal of Conflict Resolution*, and other journals in political science, library science, and linguistics.

Brandon C. Prins is Assistant Professor of Political Science at Texas Tech University. He is author of articles in *Congress and the Presidency, International Interactions, International Studies Quarterly, Journal of Peace Research, Legislative Studies Quarterly*, and other journals in political science.

B. Peter Rosendorff is Associate Professor of Politics at New York University. He is author of articles in *American Economic Review, American Political Science Review, Economics and Politics, Games and Economic Behavior, International Organization, Journal of Conflict Resolution*, and other journals in economics and political science.

Notes

Chapter 1 Divided Government and International Cooperation: An Overview

Notes to Pages 2–17

1. Bush argued, for example, that "there is a difference between responsible criticism that aims for success, and defeatism that refuses to acknowledge anything but failure" (text at http://www.whitehouse.gov/stateoftheunion/2006/index.html). This seems to acknowledge only disagreement over means, while denouncing as illegitimate any disagreement over foreign policy goals.
2. A "veto actor" is any actor who has the formal power to prevent some policy from being chosen or taking effect, that is, an actor who can veto the policy under discussion. A veto actor may or may not want to use this power, a distinction that has led to some confusion in the literature.
3. Of course, states may decide to create a rule-bound system for governing their relations in a particular issue area. See Koremenos, Lipson and Snidal 2001.
4. This claim is theoretically suspect (see Pahre 1994, 1995; Lohmann 1997). Increasing the number of players may make international cooperation more likely, not less likely, by reducing each player's incentive to break the regime apart. It also increases the number of potential sanctioners.
5. The argument parallels the analysis of veto players in domestic politics, especially in federal, presidential, and/or bicameral polities in which several actors must approve any legislation (Bräuninger and König 1999; Krehbiel 1996; Tsebelis 1995, 1999, 2002; Tsebelis and Money 1997).
6. In other words, a (potential) veto player is not the same as a veto point.
7. Another possibility, suggested by Hug and König in chapter 5, is that divided polities are so common that their presence or absence cannot explain variation in outcomes.

Chapter 2   Domestic Veto Institutions, Divided Government, and the Status Quo: A Spatial Model of Two-Level Games with Complete Information

1. The assumption that the president has pure "take-it-or-leave-it" authority might have to be modified somewhat in future work. The reason, as Blechman (1990: 65) points out, is that the Senate occasionally attaches "reservations" to treaties when it approves them, and these reservations sometimes prove so unacceptable to the president or the foreign signatories that the treaties never go into effect.

2. It would be straightforward to include a multimember veto institution in this kind of spatial model; see, Hammond and Miller (1987) or Krehbiel (1996) for examples of how this could be done. In a one-dimensional analysis, of course, one could identify the single person who can supply the final vote required for passage by the required two-thirds margin, but no such *single* critical individual necessarily exists when there are two or more dimensions. For our purposes here, it greatly simplifies matters to avoid having to deal with multimember veto institutions. Nonetheless, we suspect that models with multimember veto institutions, and even those that allow veto overrides, would generate results rather similar in general character to those we produce here.

3. In what follows we speak exclusively of a "status quo point," but our model would work just the same if instead of a status quo point there is a "reversion point," which is the policy or state of affairs that would come into existence if agreement is not reached; it is the location of this reversion point that would drive each actor's decision making rather than the location of the status quo policy.

4. To conserve space we do not show the numerous diagrams—the equivalents of figure 2.23—on which figures 2.25–2.27 are based.

5. We should note that in adding two veto institutions, in the figure 2.25 situation, we are placing them on opposite sides of $\mathbf{CORE}_{P/L}$. Were we to place the two new veto institutions on the same side of $\mathbf{CORE}_{P/L}$, the results would be similar to what happens if just one veto institution were placed there, though the location of the boundary separating the righthand regions might shift somewhat, depending on the particular locations of the two veto institutions. Similarly, in adding one additional veto institution, in the figure 2.26 situation, we are placing the new veto institution on the side of $\mathbf{CORE}_{P/L}$ opposite from the first veto institution. Were we to place the second veto institution on the same side of $\mathbf{CORE}_{P/L}$ as the first, the results would again be similar to what happens if just one veto institution were on that side, though again the location of the boundary separating the righthand regions might shift somewhat, depending on the particular locations of the two veto institutions on the same side.

6. In a sense, we are asserting that the diagrams will remain "topologically" equivalent despite changes in the ideal points' locations, as long as the overall orderings of the ideal points remain the same.

Chapter 3   Do Democracies Trade More Freely?

Thanks to Ed Mansfield and Helen Milner for many hours of conversation on this (and many other) topic(s). I also thank the participants at and organizers of the Mitsui Conference on Economic Freedom held in Tokyo in 1999, where an early draft of this chapter was presented. Lastly, thanks to the editor, Bob Pahre for his suggestions and repeated careful readings.

1. Political scientists, and to a lesser degree, and more recently, economists, have been interested in the distinctive nature of democracies, do they grow faster (Barro 1986), do they fight fewer wars (Russett 1993), have lower military expenditures (Garnkel 1994), are they less corrupt or extractive (Lake and Baum 1998)?

2. Having two actors with identical (or similar) preferences limits the consequences of the divided polity (Hammond and Pris, and Hug and König, this volume), however.

3. This paper chapter takes the contribution schedule as given and exogenous. Recent advances by Grossman and Helpman (1994) have endogenized the contribution schedule given the decision to organize. Our purpose here is to study features of democracy when political organization occurs, and we set up the simplest structure of a single lobby with an exogenous schedule.

4. Levy (1999) investigates the change in the most cooperative tariff with a change in the weight put on social welfare in the Grossman and Helpman (1994) economy with a single lobby. He finds a non-monotonic relationship.

5. A similar result is established in Milner, Mansfeld, and Rosendoff (2002), where the executive is purely extractive, in the context of periodic aggregate shocks. In that model, the international agreement limits the extractive possibilities of the executive, but provides some insurance against being evicted from office in periods of bad aggregate economic conditions. Since democrats are more responsive to the electoral process, deomcrats are more willing to buy this insurance, and are hence more willing to cooperate internationally.

6. Olsen (1993) argues that dictators are more likely to extract excessive takings from the productive assets within their domain than are Kantian republics.

7. Mas-Colell et al. (1995) note that this solution to the bargaining problem fails to be independent of the utility units.

8. The Schelling Conjecture is investigated in some detail in Milner and Rosendorff (1997) in a spatial model of divided government and international negotiations. The conjecture is shown to hold only for a limited degree of difference in the underlying preferences of the legislature and the executive. Of course, this is the same bargaining strategy used by car dealers when the dealership manager must approve any deal struck by a showroom salesperson.

9. The gravity equation has been highly successful in explaining volumes of trade offs between countries; moreover, the model is consistent with a broad set of trade-theoretic models. See Deardorff (1984), for instance.

10. While willingness to sign a common PTA is evidence of interstate cooperation, it is not immediately clear that a PTA is welfare improving. PTAs are discriminatory (they remove barriers only for members), and appear often to be motivated by trade-diversion rather than trade-creation (Bhagwati 1993). The empirical investigations here address trade within the dyad, and since the model that follows is one of a two-country world, the trade diversionary effects of the PTA are of lesser importance given the question at hand.

11. There is also likely to be interesting variation within the class of democracies. For instance, more majoritarian systems, with low costs of organizing will reward organized, mobile, import-competing factors, while less majoritarian systems with high costs of organizing will reward smaller groups engaged in active lobbying (Alt and Gilligan 1994 and Rogowski 1989).

Chapter 4   Divided Government and International Cooperation in the Nineteenth Century

1. My analysis will focus on the variables that make cooperation more or less likely. A related literature examines the design of institutions (i.e., Drezner 2003; Koremenos et al. 2001).

2. In a more elaborate model, the indifference curves would be ellipses because home tariffs are more important than foreign tariffs to each government. While the shape of the indifference curves would affect the outcome (as a point prediction), it does not affect the comparative statics that are central to the graphical analysis here.

3. The number of actors, and the complexity of the rules governing their interaction, can be varied within this framework as necessary. For an example with more than a dozen actors and a half-dozen different types of rules, see Pahre (2004).

4. This method of counting also has some theoretical foundation. A home legislature may reject a treaty because of problems with the foreign government. Without a stronger theory of nonratification it could be wrong to count, say, a Dutch nonratification of a French treaty against the Netherlands if we suspect that parliamentary uncertainty in France can cause non-French nonratifications. The logic is analogous to signaling models of the democratic peace (i.e., Bueno de Mesquita and Lalman 1992) in which peaceful democracies may nonetheless initiate conflict against nondemocracies.

5. Modern presidential systems also have more veto players than modern parliamentary systems, though most nineteenth-century parliamentary systems had monarchs, independent chancellors, and/or upper houses with much more power than their equivalents today. For a fuller treatment of veto players, see Tsebelis (2002).

6. The upswing in treaties also coincides with the spread of railroads, some foreign investment, and reforms of the commercial, mining, and banking codes (see Coatsworth 1978).

7. Figures 4.4 and 4.6 shows the total number of treaties with European countries. The picture is essentially the same if we look at the global total, which is subject to more measurement error.

8. Divided government probably did not characterize Sweden in 1905–1914, which had majority governing coalitions formed to address the constitutional crisis arising from Norwegian independence. However, Yvonne Maria Werner (1989: Chapter 8) argues that negotiators' uncertainty over legislative preferences inhibited cooperation in the first round of talks with Germany in 1906.

9. The figure also shows a secular increase in both countries regardless of divided government. Plausible explanations for this include the greater rewards of cooperation from growing trade volumes, lower transportation costs, higher discount factors, and responses to cooperation by other states.

10. This was implicit from 1866, and made explicit in 1906.

11. Because legislatures represent smaller constituencies with more particularistic interests, while executives may consider broader social interests in free trade, this assumption usually characterizes the preference ordering in real political systems (Mansfield and Busch 1995; Rogowski 1987). This assumption also captures any nontrade issue in which the legislature is more hawkish than the executive (Evans, Jacobson and Putnam 1993). It also has a theoretical justification in that the legislature is irrelevant in this game when $t_A^L > t_A^E$ (see Hammond and Prins, chapter 2).

12. See Hammond and Prins (1999) for discussion of how one might compare winsets that are larger than a single point.

13. See Dai (2002; see also Mansfield, Milner and Rosendorff 2002) for a critique of this assumption in a take-it-or-leave-it (TILI) model. However, other negotiation solutions, such as the Nash bargaining solution or the Rubinstein solution, would yield only outcomes on this contract curve, so I prefer to constrain the TILI assumption in this way as well. Both the Nash and Rubinstein solutions have difficulties of their own; see Butler (2004) for an excellent review.

14. This solution concept also makes the outcome a continuous function of t_A^L. Without the second requirement, B's utility off the contract curve $t_B t_A^E$ would be maximized by a point above the x-axis on L's indifference curve, creating a discontinuity at t_A^E; the results in the text would still follow except for points near this discontinuity. The results in the text should also follow from a broad range of other solution concepts, at a considerable loss in ease of presentation.

15. The analysis in the text is static in that B's tariff does not change in response to changes in A's tariff (compare Rosendorff, chapter 3). Many scholars would expect a trade war, in which B raises its tariff in response to A's increases. Pahre (1998) has criticized this view, arguing that B's tariff will decrease as A's tariff increases. One can imagine either type of reaction in other issue areas, depending on both preferences and the characteristics of the issue. Whichever hypothesis is correct, including these kinds of reactions would complicate the analysis considerably.

16. Another salient complication is the possibility of incomplete information, which would also yield probabilistic claims about the likelihood of cooperation (see Milner 1997).

17. I assume Grim Trigger enforcement, so that if one state cheats, the other state returns to the reversion point forever. Cooperation will occur only if the payoff from indefinite cooperation (R + wR + w²R + . . .) is equal to or greater than the one-time temptation to defect (T) plus subsequent punishment rounds (wP + w²P + w³P + . . .). Rearranging this weak inequality yields the condition.

18. It may be true that the executive and legislature jointly control the reversion point, with results intermediate between the two pure cases; see Pahre 2001a.

19. Technically, the non-Hungarian half was known as "the lands represented in the *Reichsrat* (Imperial Council)," but they were typically referred to as "Austria" or "Cisleithania."

20. Some have suggested that Austrian liberalization after 1866 also reflects a fiscal crisis stemming from the costs of the war, and the possibility of raising more revenue with lower tariffs that would encourage imports (i.e., Matis 1984: 116). However, the fiscal crisis after the war of 1859 led to no such liberalization.

21. "att regeringsskiftet inverkat negativt på förhandlingarna."

22. Full members included the middle powers such as Bavaria or Hannover but not the smaller states. This status was negotiated on each state's entry into the *Zollverein*, as were some exceptions. Hesse-Darmstadt only had the right to reject treaties with states bordering it. Baden had the right to sign a separate treaty with Switzerland. Frankfurt-am-Main was a full member but did not have the right to reject trade treaties. When the *Zollverein* was reconstituted in 1867 as a treaty between North German Confederation, Bavaria, Württemberg, Baden, and Hesse, all vetoes were eliminated and decisions made on the basis of majority rule.

23. Treaties with Belgium and Britain were submitted at essentially the same time but did not obtain the same political salience as the French treaty.

Chapter 5   Divided Government and the Ratification of the Amsterdam Treaty

Hug acknowledges the financial support through a special research grant of the University of Texas at Austin provided for this project. Helpful comments by Robert Pahre are gratefully acknowledged.

1. The first part of our analysis resembles Stoiber and Thurner's (2000, 2003) approach combining Tsebelis' (1995) notion of veto players, or more precisely veto points, with the partisan composition. In some aspects their analyses are more far reaching, namely by counting the number of partisan veto players in the Amsterdam treaty ratification, on the other it is more restricted, since the preferences of these partisan actors are not considered.

2. While several countries held elections between the signing and the ratification of the treaty (e.g., Denmark, France (change in Senate), and the Netherlands), no change in government composition occurred.

3. Here we consider the vote of the British House of Lords also as an upper house having to agree to the ratification of the Amsterdam treaty. Strictly speaking the House of Lords does only have delaying powers, in the sense that a negative vote by the upper house can be overridden by the lower house after one year (Tsebelis and Money 1997: 62).

4. Obviously, at this stage one might also consider whether in countries with both bicameral parliaments and qualified majority requirements these additional hurdles require the support of the same additional party or parties, or whether each hurdle adds a different party.

5. Strictly speaking, only international treaties implying the transfer of some powers to a supranational organization fall in this category (Hug 2002).

6. As the ratification of the Nice treaty showed, the government has some leeway in determining whether a treaty involves such transfers. To the protests of a vocal but small opposition, the Danish government decided that the treaty could be ratified under a simplified procedure, which did not allow for a referendum being triggered by one-sixth of the MPs. The Irish government, on the other hand, believed that the Nice treaty required a change in the constitution, which can only be adopted after a referendum vote, which had a negative outcome.

7. This statement certainly holds for domestic policy decisions, but the negative referendum outcomes in France and the Netherlands on the proposed EU constitution may question this. The last word, however, has not yet been spoken about the EU constitution, and second, Hug and Tsebelis' (2002) work relies on the assumption of complete and perfect information. This element hardly characterizes the decision situation of President Chirac and the Dutch government.

8. Exceptions to this are obviously countries in which the constitution explicitly prohibits referendums on international treaties (e.g., Italy).

9. The response rate of the survey was about 45% and the findings show that the meaning of European integration does not vary over time and across national contexts, but political parties become increasingly pro-European over the period 1984–1996.

10. In the appendix we reproduce the exact question wording for the variables employed in this study and explain our analysis in detail.

11. In fact, this instrument also allows for comparing how much these actors favor or oppose on the particular issue areas. However, since this instrument has certainly a lower reliability, we only consider their pro- or con- attitudes.

12. König and Hug (2006) discuss in much more detail the methodological problems of these implicit assumptions.

13. While Milner's (1997) continuous measure refers to distances between ideal points on a single dimension, such a measure becomes more problematic in multidimensional spaces with more than two actors. For this reason we refrain from relying on distances between ideal points to assess the degree to which a government is divided.

14. Obviously, by definition there can be no disagreement in one-party governments, since we cannot assess the dividedness of a particular issue inside a single party. As Milner (1997) discusses, this can be a considerable simplification in some instances.

15. Obviously, this presumes that the governmental party is not internally divided, as is sometimes the case in the main British parties and in some other parties as well when it comes to EU issues.
16. To a large degree this difference echoes the crucial distinction between "veto points" and "veto- players," which is often misunderstood in the literature.

Chapter 6   Divided Government and the Resolution of Territorial Disputes

1. Reviews of much of the literature can be found in Chan 1997; Maoz 1997, 1998; Ray 1995: Chapter 1, 1998; and Rousseau et al. 1996.
2. On the debate concerning whether democracy reduces the likelihood of war because of democratic leaders' political accountability, or the strength of nonviolent norms of conflict resolution held by democratic political elites, see Bueno de Mesquita and Lalman 1992; Bueno de Mesquita et al. 1999; Bueno de Mesquita et al. 2003; Dixon 1993, 1994, 1998; Doyle 1986; Maoz and Russett 1992, 1993; Owen 1994, 1997; Raymond 1994; Russett 1993; Schweller 1992; and Weart 1998. Those who argue for or find support for the monadic version of the democratic peace include: Benoit 1996; Bremer 1992; Hart and Reed 1999; Hermann and Kegley 1995; Hewitt and Wilkenfeld 1996; Huth 1996; Huth and Allee 2003; Leeds and Davis 1999; O'Neal and Russett 1997a, 1997b, 1999a, 1999b; Rousseau 1996; Rummel 1995, 1997; Russett and O'Neal 2001; and Schultz 2001. Those who argue for or find support for the dyadic version of the democratic peace include: Dixon 1993, 1994; Maoz 1997; Maoz and Russett 1992, 1993; Owen 1994, 1997; Small and Singer 1976; Weart 1998; Weede 1984, 1992.
3. See Huth and Allee 2003, Appendices B-F, for a detailed description of all 348 territorial disputes.
4. See König and Hug (chapter 5 this volume) and Pahre (chapter 1 this volume) for a discussion of the ways in which divided government is often operationalized.
5. States that reach a negotiated solution to a territorial dispute may benefit from a reduction in bilateral tensions. They may be able to divert military and other resources away from managing the dispute with one another and may now reap the benefits of increased trade and other cross-border exchange. Furthermore, these states will benefit if third parties and allies had been pressuring them to resolve the dispute. They may receive increased economic aid and investment, and may see the removal of any negative sanctions. Finally, the peaceful resolution of a territorial dispute may provide challenger states with the strategic or economic benefits of newly acquired pieces of territory.
6. We are not convinced that mass opinions are consistently anchored at dovish policy positions. Furthermore, we reject the idea that the foreign policy preferences we can identify in the mass public are consistently more dovish than the policy position of political elites and incumbents (e.g., Brace and Hinckley

1992; Chanley 1999; Gaubatz 1995; Hermann, Tetlock, and Visser 1999; Holsti 1996; Jentleson and Britton 1998; Knopf 1998; Mueller 1994; Nincic 1992: Chapter 2, 1997; Owen 1997; Page and Shapiro 1992; Russett 1990a: Chapter 4; Zimmerman 2002).

7. See Huth and Allee 2003, Chapter 4 for a more detailed discussion of these points.

8. Of course, in parliamentary systems in which where there is no fixed date for national elections, a prime minister is in a stronger position to determine the timing of the next election provided that his or her party commands a majority in the parliament.

9. We acknowledge that it should be easier to achieve ratification when there is a single-party majority in the legislature or parliament as opposed to a coalition majority, *ceteris paribus*. However, in most political systems coalition parties are likely to share similar preferences on issues of major importance. Thus we think the overall level of legislative support, regardless of the number of parties in the governing coalition, is the most important factor to consider.

10. Scholars such as Schelling (1960) and Putnam (1988) argue that negotiators will be sensitive to the strength of domestic opposition forces in both their own country and their bargaining adversary, and will attempt to use their own domestic constraints to their own advantage. We agree that leaders are keenly aware of the domestic politics situation in their territorial dispute adversary. However, we agree with Milner (1997) and Milner and Rosendorff (1997) that strategies of "tying- hands" make reaching an international agreement more difficult, since policy differences between the two governments are likely to be larger on average (see also Tarar 2001). Furthermore, an additional problem with the logic behind the Schelling conjecture is the fact that making unbalanced concessions over an issue as salient as territory is very risky, even when the government of an adversary faces serious domestic constraints (see *Premise 3*). Within one's own country, domestic political opposition, as well as domestic public opinion, is unlikely to be sympathetic to the constraints facing the leadership of the adversary. The domestic actors at home instead are likely to focus on the fact that one's own government has made major concessions that have not been reciprocated.

11. In rare cases where in which data on one or more of these indicators could not be calculated, the remaining available ratio(s) are used.

12. In the Middle East, British military capabilities are added to those of Iraq in 1932–1947, Kuwait in 1961–1967, Jordan in 1946–1956, and Egypt in 1922–1925. In Asia, the Soviet Union's military capabilities are added to those of Outer Mongolia in 1936–1940 and 1946–1962; British capabilities are added to those of Malaysia in 1962–1970; and U.S. capabilities are added to those of South Korea in 1953–1995. In the Americas, British capabilities are added to those of Belize in 1981–1993. Finally, in Europe, British, French, and West German military capabilities are added to those of the United States (the dispute over West Berlin) in 1955–1971 and the Soviet Union's military capabilities are added to those of Czechoslovakia 1955–1973, East Germany 1955–1972, and Poland 1955–1970.

13. In some cases missing data for selected years are filled in by extrapolating from data that were available for years prior to and after the missing data.

14. To check for robustness we also create a variable to indicate whether the territory is of economic value to the disputing states.

15. The use of "directed-dyads" is one way to analyze the behavior of two disputants, yet this type of analysis does not capture the strategic dynamics of the two states' decisions. Furthermore, the use of directed-dyads treats the two states' decisions as unrelated despite the fact that the two directional observations are not independent and the disturbances across the two observations are likely to be correlated.

16. See Greene (1997: 906–911) for a general discussion of the bivariate probit model and Smith (1999) for a detailed discussion of bivariate models and the interrelatedness of state decisions.

17. Bivariate probit and similar models are sometimes used as a method for estimating two potentially interrelated decisions of the same actor (see Reed 2000). Yet bivariate probit models work just as well, if not better, for modeling the simultaneous actions of two separate actors (see Zorn 2002).

18. The model we use was devised by Kohler, Rodgers, and Christensen (1999) to study fertility patterns among pairs of twins. Oddly enough, studies of twin behavior share many similarities to the study of pairs of states in international politics. The logic behind twin fertility studies is that each twin makes a decision regarding how many children to have, yet both twins are affected by both shared genetic characteristics, as well as characteristics specific to each twin. This is parallel to pairs of states engaged in international negotiations. Some characteristics are inherent to the pair of states, such as alliance ties. Yet many domestic political variables, such as regime type or divided government, are specific to each state.

19. We use Stata 6 to estimate our model, since the Kohler and Rodgers procedures were originally programmed in Stata 6.

20. In Huth and Allee (2003, Chapter 2) we argue extensively that challengers first consider whether and how to challenger the territorial status quo. As a result, rounds of talks over disputed territory typically follow the challenger's initiation of a diplomatic process.

21. We estimate a model that accounts for the impact of our slate of independent variables on both the challenger decision to call for talks in the first place, as well as its decision to offer concessions. This Heckman or "censored" probit model indicates that these selection and outcome models are correlated only at a magnitude of .23, and that this estimate of the correlation between the two models is not even statistically significant.

22. We also substitute into the model the alternative indicator for common security ties, the presence of a common territorial dispute opponent. The coefficient for the common dispute opponent variable is positive, but the p-value of .15 falls just short of standard levels of statistical significance.

23. We also run this model by substituting the economic value of territory indicator for the strategic value of territory indicator. Once again, the economic value of territory does not affect whether state leaders were likely to offer territorial concessions, as the z-statistic is a modest $-.24$.

24. Keep in mind that this model treats the challenger and target concessions decisions in a given round of talks as independent decisions. We simply employ this model as a robustness check and to illustrate the stability of our results.

Chapter 7   Conclusion: Democracy and Foreign Policy

The existence of this conclusion and substantial parts of its contents reflect conversations with the contributors and the insights of our discussant, Duncan Snidal, when we presented these manuscripts at the Annual Meeting of the Midwest Political Science Association.

1. Notice too that higher-income countries are more likely to be democratic (Londregan and Poole 1996 inter alia), complicating inference considerably.
2. Pahre (1997) shows that if both the legislature and executive must approve the ratification rule in advance, they will never choose a ratification rule that allows amendments.
3. Some contributors to Evans et al. 1993, for example, commit this error.
4. The second of these requirements is less robust and may depend on the bargaining solution used (see Hammond and Prins, this volume).
5. Interview, Ministry of Foreign Affairs, Bratislava, June 2002.
6. "Pri zlepšovaní ratingu, ktorým by sa krajina dostala zo špekulatívneho pásma, sme veľmi opatrní. To platí obzvlášť v horizonte do nadchádzajúcich volieb."
7. See Rogowski and Kayser (2002) for an interesting argument about the comparative representation of producer and consumer interests in modern democracies.
8. These concepts have straightforward meanings in a one-dimensional spatial theory, not in a multidimensional model. See Hammond and Pris, this volume.

References

Aldrich, John, John Sullivan, and Eugene Borgida. 1989. "Foreign Affairs and Issue Voting: Do Presidential Candidates 'Waltz' before a Blind Audience?" *American Political Science Review* 83(1): 123–41.

Alesina, Alberto and Howard Rosenthal. 1995. *Partisan Politics, Divided Government and the Economy*. New York: Cambridge University Press.

———. 1996. "A Theory of Divided Government." *Econometrica* 64(6): 1311–41.

Almond, Gabriel A. and Sidney Verba. 1963. *The Civic Culture*. Princeton: Princeton University Press.

Alt, James and Gary King. 1994. "Transfers of Governmental Power: The Meaning of Time Dependence." *Comparative Political Studies* 27(2): 190–210.

Alt, James E. and Michael J. Gilligan. 1994. "The Political Economy of Trading States." *Journal of Political Philosophy* 2: 165–92.

Annual Register 1920–95. New York: Longmans, Green and Co., 1921–58, Longman, 1959–96.

Apodaca, Clair and Michael Stohl. 1999. "United States Human Rights Policy and Foreign Assistance." *International Studies Quarterly* 43(1): 185–98.

Ashley, Percy. 1926. *Modern Tariff History. Germany—United States—France*, 3rd edn. New York: E. P. Dutton and Company.

Axelrod, Robert. 1984. *The Evolution of Cooperation*. New York: Basic Books.

Bacchus, William I. 1997. *The Price of American Foreign Policy: Congress, the Executive, and International Affairs Funding*. University Park, PA: Pennsylvania State Press.

Banks, Arthur. 1996. *Cross-Polity Time Series Data Archive*. Binghamton, NY: Department of Political Science.

Barro, Robert J. 1973. "The Control of Politicians: An Economic Model." *Public Choice* 14(1): 19–42.

——— 1996. "Democracy and Growth." *Journal of Economic Growth* 1(1): 1–27.

Baum, Matthew A. 2002. "The Constituent Foundations of the Rally-Round-the-Flag Phenomenon." *International Studies Quarterly* 46(2): 263–98.

Benoit, Kenneth. 1996. "Democracies Really Are More Pacific (in General)." *Journal of Conflict Resolution* 40(4): 636–57.

Bercovitch, Jacob and Richard Jackson. 1997. *International Conflict: A Chronological Encyclopedia of Conflicts and Their Management, 1945–1995*. Washington, DC: Congressional Quarterly.

Bergara, Mario E., Witold J. Henisz, and Pablo T. Spiller. 1998–1999. "Political Institutions and Electric Utility Investment: A Cross-Nation Analysis." *California Management Review* 40(2): 18–35 (Winter).

Bhagwati, Jagdish N. 1982. "Directly Unproductive, Profit-Seeking (DUP) Activities." *Journal of Political Economy* 90(5): 988–1002.

Bhagwati, Jagdish N. 1993. "Regionalism and Multilateralism: An Overview." in *New Dimensions in Regional Integration*, ed., Jaime de Melo and Arvind Panagariya. New York: Cambridge University Press, pp. 22–50.

———. 1998. "Democracy and Development: New Thinking on an Old Question." in *A Stream of Windows*. Cambridge: MIT Press, pp. 379–407.

———. 2004. *In Defense of Globalization*. Oxford: Oxford University Press.

Bidwell, Robin. 1973. *Bidwell's Guide to Government Ministries: The Major Powers and Western Europe 1900–1971*. London: Frank Cass & Company Limited.

Binder, Sarah. 1999. "The Dynamics of Legislative Gridlock, 1947–96." *American Political Science Review* 93(3): 519–33.

Blanton, Shannon Lindsey. 2000. "Promoting Human Rights and Democracy in the Developing World: U.S. Rhetoric versus U.S. Arms Exports." *American Journal of Political Science* 44(1): 123–31.

Blechman, Barry M. 1990. *The Politics of National Security: Congress and U.S. Defense Policy*. New York: Oxford University Press.

Bliss, Harry and Bruce Russett. 1998. "Democratic Trading Partners: The Liberal Connection, 1962–1989." *The Journal of Politics* 60(4): 1126–47.

Bond, Jon and Richard Fleisher. 1990. *The President in the Legislative Arena*. Chicago: University of Chicago Press.

Botcheva, Liliana and Lisa L. Martin. 2001. "Institutional Effects on State Behavior: Convergence and Divergence." *International Studies Quarterly* 45(1): 1–26.

Brace, Paul and Barbara Hinckley. 1992. *Following the Leader: Opinion Polls and the Modern Presidents*. New York: Basic Books.

Brauneder, Wilhelm and Friedrich Lachmayer. 1980. *Österreichische Verfassungsgeschichte*. 2nd edn. Wien: Manzsche Verlags- und Universitätsbuchhandlung.

Bräuninger, Thomas and Thomas König. 1999. "The Checks and Balances of Party Federalism." *European Journal of Political Research* 36(6): 207–34.

Brecher, Michael and Jonathan Wilkenfeld. 1997. *A Study of Crisis*. Ann Arbor: University of Michigan Press.

Bremer, Stuart. 1992. "Dangerous Dyads." *Journal of Conflict Resolution* 36(2): 309–41.

Brody, Richard. 1991. *Assessing the President: The Media, Elite Opinion, and Public Support*. Stanford: Stanford University Press.

Budge, Ian, D. Robertson, and Derek Hearl, eds. 1987. *Ideology, Strategy and Party Change*. Cambridge: Cambridge University Press.

Bueno de Mesquita, Bruce. 1981. *The War Trap*. New Haven: Yale University Press.

Bueno de Mesquita, Bruce and David Lalman. 1992. *War and Reason: Domestic and International Imperatives*. New Haven: Yale University Press.

Bueno de Mesquita, Bruce, James D. Morrow, Randolph M. Siverson, and Alastair Smith. 1999. "An Institutional Explanation of the Democratic Peace." *American Political Science Review* 93(4): 791–808.

Bueno de Mesquita, Bruce and Randolph M. Siverson. 1995. "War and the Survival of Political Leaders." *American Political Science Review* 89(4): 841–55.

Bueno de Mesquita, Bruce, Randolph M. Siverson, and Gary Woller. 1992. "War and the Fate of Regimes." *American Political Science Review* 86(3): 638–46.

Bueno de Mesquita, Bruce, Alasdair Smith, Randolph M. Siverson, and James D. Morrow. 2003. *The Logic of Political Survival.* Cambridge, MA: MIT Press.

Bull, Hedley. 1977. *The Anarchical Society: A Study of Order in World Politics.* New York: Columbia University Press.

Butler, Christopher K. 2004. "Modeling Compromise at the International Table." *Conflict Management and Peace Sciences* 21(3): 159–77.

Carr, Edward Hallett. 1939. *The Twenty Years' Crisis, 1919–1939: An Introduction to the Study of International Relations.* New York: Harper Torchbook edition, 1964.

Carroll, Holbert N. 1966. *The House of Representatives and Foreign Affairs.* Boston: Little, Brown, and Company.

Chan, Steve. 1997. "In Search of the Democratic Peace: Problems and Promise." *Mershon International Studies Review* 41(1): 59–91.

Chanley, Virginia. 1999. "US Public Views of International Involvement from 1964 to 1993: Time-Series Analyses of General and Military Internationalism." *Journal of Conflict Resolution* 43(1): 23–44.

Cheney, Dick. 1990. "Congressional Overreaching in Foreign Policy." in *Foreign Policy and the Constitution*, ed., Robert A. Goldwin and Robert A. Licht. Washington, DC: American Enterprise Institute, pp. 101–20.

Chiozza, Giacomo and Henk E. Goemans. 2004. "Avoiding Diversionary Targets." *Journal of Peace Research* 41(4): 423–44.

Clinton, William J. 1994. "Speech to UN General Assembly." September 26. Available at http://www.clintonfoundation.org/legacy/092694-speech-by-president-address-to-un-general-assembly.htm>, accessed May 25, 2006.

Coatsworth, John H. 1978. "Obstacles to Economic Growth in Nineteenth-Century Mexico." *American Historical Review* 83(1, supp): 80–100.

Codding, George Arthur, Jr. 1961. *The Federal Government of Switzerland.* Boston: Houghton Mifflin Company.

Collier, David. 1993. "The Comparative Method." in *Political Science: The State of the Discipline II*, ed., Ada W. Finifter. Washington: American Political Science Association, pp. 105–20.

Corwin, Edward. 1917. *The President's Control of Foreign Relations.* Princeton: Princeton University Press.

Corwin, E.S. 1957. *The President: Office and Powers, 1787–1957*, 4th rev. edn. New York: New York University Press.

Cox, Gary and Samuel Kernell, eds. 1991. *The Politics of Divided Government.* Boulder: Westview Press.

Crampton, R.J. 1997. *A Concise History of Bulgaria.* Cambridge: Cambridge University Press.

Crovitz, L. Gordon. 1990. "Micromanaging Foreign Policy." *The Public Interest* 100(1): 102–15.

Dahl, Robert. 1971. *Polyarchy.* New Haven: Yale University Press.

Davies, Graeme A.M. 2002. "Domestic Strife and the Initiation of International Conflicts: A Directed Dyad Analysis, 1950–1982." *Journal of Conflict Resolution* 46(5): 672–92.

218   REFERENCES

Davis, John R. 1997. *Britain and the German* Zollverein, *1848–66*. Houndmills, Basingstoke, Hampshire, UK: Macmillan and New York: St. Martin's Press, Inc.

Deardorff, Alan V. 1984. "Testing Trade Theories and Predicting Trade Flows," in *Handbook of International Economics*, ed., R.W. Jones and P.B. Kenen. Amsterdam: North- Holland, pp. 67–517.

DeNardo, James. 1985. *Power in Numbers: The Political Strategy of Protest and Rebellion*. Princeton: Princeton University Press.

Destler, I.M., Leslie H. Gelb, and Anthony Lake. 1984. *Our Own Worst Enemy: The Unmaking of American Foreign Policy*. New York: Simon and Shuster.

Diermeier, Daniel. 1996. "Rational Choice and the Role of Theory in Political Science." in *The Rational Choice Controversy: Economic Models of Politics Reconsidered*, ed., Jeffry Friedman. New Haven and London: Yale University Press, pp. 59–70.

Dixon, William J. 1993. "Democracy and the Management of International Conflict." *Journal of Conflict Resolution* 37(1): 42–68.

Dixon, William. 1994. "Democracy and the Peaceful Settlement of International Conflict." *American Political Science Review* 88(1): 1–17.

——. 1998. "Dyads, Disputes and the Democratic Peace," in *The Political Economy of War and Peace*, ed., Murray Wolfson. Boston: Kluwer, pp. 103–26.

Dixon, William J. and Paul D. Senese. 2002. "Democracy, Disputes, and Negotiated Settlements." *Journal of Conflict Resolution* 46(4): 547–71.

Downs, George W. and David M. Rocke. 1995. *Optimal Imperfection?: Domestic Uncertainty and Institutions in International Relations*. Princeton: Princeton University Press.

Doyle, Michael. 1986. "Liberalism and World Politics." *American Political Science Review* 80(4): 1151–70.

Drezner, Daniel W. 2003. *Locating the Proper Authorities: The Interaction of Domestic and International Institutions*. Ann Arbor: University of Michigan Press.

Duchesne, Erik. 1997. *International Bilateral Trade and Investment Negotiations: Theory, Formal Model, and Empirical Evidence*. Ph.D. Dissertation, Department of Political Science, Michigan State University.

Dunham, Arthur Louis. 1930. *The Anglo-French Treaty of Commerce of 1860 and the Progress of the Industrial Revolution in France*. Ann Arbor: University of Michigan Press.

Duverger, Maurice. 1980. "A New Political System Model: Semi-Presidential Government." *European Journal of Political Research* 8(2): 165–87.

Eckstein, Harry. 1975. "Case Studies and Theory in Political Science," in *Handbook of Political Science, Volume Seven: Strategies of Inquiry*, ed., Fred Greenstein and Nelson Polsby. Reading, MA: Addison-Wesley Press, pp. 79–137.

Eddie, Scott M. 1972. "The Terms of Trade as a Tax on Agriculture: Hungary's Trade with Austria, 1883–1913." *Journal of Economic History* 32(1): 298–315.

Edwards, George and George Gallup. 1990. *Presidential Approval*. Baltimore: Johns Hopkins University Press.

Edwards, George, Andrew Barrett, and Jeffrey Peake. 1997. "The Legislative Impact of Divided Government." *American Journal of Political Science* 41(2): 545–63.

Elster, Jon. 1994. *Ulysses and the Sirens: Studies in Rationality and Irrationality.* Cambridge: Cambridge University Press.

Europa World Year Book 1960–95. London: Europa Publications.

European Union. 1999. *Ratification Procedures.* <http://europa.eu.int/abc/obj/amst/ratifen.pdf>, accessed July 15, 1999.

Evans, Peter B., Harold K. Jacobson, and Robert D. Putnam, eds. 1993. *Double-Edged Diplomacy.* Berkeley: University of California Press.

Fearon, James D. 1998. "Bargaining, Enforcement, and International Cooperation." *International Organization* 52(2): 269–305.

Ferejohn, John. 1986. "Incumbent Performance and Electoral Control." *Public Choice* 50(1–3): 5–25.

Findlay, Ronald W. and Stanislaw Wellisz. 1982. "Endogenous Tariffs, the Political Economy of Trade Restrictions, and Welfare," in *Import Competition and Response*, ed., Jagdish N. Bhagwati. Chicago: University of Chicago Press, pp. 223–44.

Fiorina, Mo. 1992. *Divided Government.* New York: Macmillan.

Friman, H. Richard. 1993. "Side-Payments versus Security Cards: Domestic Bargaining Tactics in International Economic Negotiations." *International Organization* 47(3): 387–410.

Gabel, Matthew J. and John D. Huber. 2000. "Putting Parties in Their Place: Inferring Party Left-Right Ideological Positions from Party Manifestos Data." *American Journal of Political Science* 44(1): 94–103.

Garrett, Geoffrey and George Tsebelis. 1996. "An Institutional Critique of Intergovernmentalism." *International Organization* 50(2): 269–99.

Gaubatz, Kurt. 1995. "Intervention and Intransitivity: Public Opinion, Social Choice, and the Use of Military Force Abroad." *World Politics* 47(4): 534–54.

Geddes, Barbara. 1992. "Democracy and the Market—Political and Economic Reforms in Eastern Europe and Latin America." *American Political Science Review* 86(4): 1093–94.

Gelpi, Christopher. 1997. "Democratic Diversions: Governmental Structure and the Externalization of Domestic Conflict." *Journal of Conflict Resolution* 41(2): 255–82.

Gelpi, Christopher and Michael Griesdorf. 2001. "Winners or Losers? Democracies in International Crisis, 1918–94." *American Political Science Review* 95(3): 633–47.

Gilligan, Michael J. 1997. *Empowering Exporters: Reciprocity, Delegation, and Collective Action in American Trade Policy.* Ann Arbor: University of Michigan Press.

Goemans, Hein. 2000. *War and Punishment: The Causes of War Termination and the First World War.* Princeton: Princeton University Press.

Goldstein, Judith. 1996. "International Law and Domestic Institutions." *International Organization* 50(4): 541–64.

Gowa, Joanne. 1999. *Ballots and Bullets: The Elusive Democratic Peace.* Princeton: Princeton University Press.

Graham, Thomas W. 1989. *The Politics of Failure: Strategic Nuclear Arms Control, Public Opinion, and Domestic Politics in the United States, 1945–1980.* Ph.D.

Dissertation, Department of Political Science, Massachusetts Institute of Technology.

Green, Donald P. and Ian Shapiro. 1994. *Pathologies of Rational Choice Theory: A Critique of Applications in Political Science*. New Haven: Yale University Press.

Green, Donald P. and Ian Shapiro. 1996. "Pathologies Revisited: Reflections on Our Critics," in *The Rational Choice Controversy: Economic Models of Politics Reconsidered*, ed., Jeffrey Friedman. New Haven and London: Yale University Press, pp. 235–76.

Greene, William. 1997. *Econometric Analysis*. 3rd edn. Upper Saddle River, NJ: Prentice Hall.

Grieco, Joseph. 1988. "Realist Theory and the Problem of International Cooperation. Analysis with an Amended Prisoner's Dilemma Model." *Journal of Politics* 50(3): 600–24.

Grossman, Gene M. and Elhanan Helpman. 1994. "Protection for Sale." *American Economic Review* 84(4): 833–50.

Haggard, Stephan and Steven B. Webb. 1994. *Voting for Reform: Democracy, Political Liberalization and Economic Adjustment*. New York: Oxford University Press.

Hammond, Thomas H. and Gary J. Miller. 1987. "The Core of the Constitution." *American Political Science Review* 81(4): 1155–74.

Hammond, Thomas H. and Brandon Prins. 1999. "The Impact of Domestic Institutions on International Negotiations: A Taxonomy of Results from a Complete-Information Spatial Model." Paper presented at the Annual Meeting of the American Political Science Association, Atlanta, September 2–5.

Hansen, Wendy L. 1990. "The International Trade Commission and the Politics of Protectionism." *American Political Science Review* 84(1): 21–46.

Hardin, Russell. 1995. *One For All*. Princeton: Princeton University Press.

Hart, Robert and William Reed. 1999. "Selection Effects and Dispute Escalation." *International Interactions* 25(3): 243–64.

Hawkins, Darren, David A. Lake, Daniel Nielson, and Michael J. Tierney. 2006. "States, International Organizations, and Principal-Agent Theory," in *Delegation and Agency in International Organizations*, Darren Hawkins, David A. Lake, Daniel Nielson, and Michael J. Tierney, eds. Forthcoming with Cambridge University Press, Summer 2006.

Heckman, James. 1979. "Sample Selection Bias as a Specification Error." *Econometrica* 47(1): 153–61.

Henderson, W. O. 1984. *The Zollverein*. 3rd. edn. London: Frank Cass.

Henning, C. Randall. 1994. *Currencies and Politics in the United State, Germany, and Japan*. Washington, DC: Institute for International Economics.

Hermann, Margaret and Charles Kegley. 1995. "Rethinking Democracy and International Peace." *International Studies Quarterly* 39(4): 511–34.

Hermann, Richard, Philip Tetlock, and Penny Visser. 1999. "Mass Public Decisions on Going to War." *American Political Science Review* 93(3): 553–74.

Hewitt, Joseph and Jonathan Wilkenfeld. 1996. "Democracies in International Crises." *International Interactions* 22(2): 123–42.

Hillman, Arye L. 1982. "Declining Industries and Political–Support Protectionist Motives." *American Economic Review* 72(5): 1180–90.

Hodne, Fritz. 1983. *The Norwegian Economy 1920–1980*. New York: St. Martin's Press.

Hoffman, Stanley. 1962. "Restraints and Choices in American Foreign Policy." *Daedalus* 91(3): 689–90.

Holsti, Kalevi. 1996. *The State, War, and the State of War*. Cambridge: Cambridge University Press.

Holsti, Ole R. 1968. "Content Analysis," in *Handbook of Social Psychology 2nd edn*, ed., G. Lindzey and E. Aronson. Reading: Addison-Wesley.

———. 1992. "Public Opinion and Foreign Policy: Challenges to the Almond-Lippmann Consensus." *International Studies Quarterly* 36(4): 439–66.

———. 1996. *Public Opinion and American Foreign Policy*. Ann Arbor: University of Michigan Press.

Hooghe, Liesbet Gary Marks and Carole J. Wilson. 2002. "Does Left/Right Structure Party Positions on European Integration?" *Comparative Political Studies* 35(8): 965–89.

Huber, John. 1996. "The Vote of Confidence in Parliamentary Democracies." *American Political Science Review* 90(2): 269–82.

Huertas, Thomas F. 1977. *Economic Growth and Economic Policy in a Multinational Setting. The Habsburg Monarchy, 1841–1865*. New York: Arno Press.

Hug, Simon. 2002. *Voices of Europe. Citizens, Referendums and European Integration*. New York: Rowman and Littlefield.

Hug, Simon and Thomas König. 2002. "In View of Ratification: Governmental Preferences and Domestic Constraints at the Amsterdam Intergovernmental Conference." *International Organization* 56(2): 447–76.

Hug, Simon and Thomas Konig. 2006. "Divided Government and Ratification of the Amsterdam Treaty," in *Democratic Foreign Policy Making: Problems of Divided Government and International Cooperation*, ed., Robert Pahre. Palgrave, chapter 5.

Hug, Simon and George Tsebelis. 2002. "Veto Players and Referendums around the World." *Journal of Theoretical Politics* 14(4): 465–516.

Hunt, James C. 1974. "Peasants, Grain Tariffs, and Meat Quotas: Imperial German Protectionism Reexamined." *Central European History* 7(4): 311–31.

Huth, Paul K. 1998. *Standing Your Ground: Territorial Disputes and International Conflict*. Ann Arbor: University of Michigan Press.

Huth, Paul K. and Todd L. Allee. 2003. *The Democratic Peace and Territorial Conflict in the 20th Century*. Cambridge: Cambridge University Press.

Iida, Keisuke. 1993. "When and How Do Domestic Constraints Matter? Two-Level Games with Uncertainty." *Journal of Conflict Resolution* 34(3): 403–26.

Iida, Keisuke. 1996. "Involuntary Defection in Two-Level Games." *Public Choice* 89(2): 283–303.

Jaggers, Keith and Ted Robert Gurr. 1995. "Transitions to Democracy: Tracking Democracy's Third Wave with the Polity III Data." *Journal of Peace Research* 32(4): 469–82.

James, Patrick. 1988. *Crisis and War*. Montreal: McGill-Queen's University Press.

James, Patrick, and John Oneal. 1991. "The Influence of Domestic and International Politics on the President's Use of Force." *Journal of Conflict Resolution* 35(1): 307–32.

Jentleson, Bruce and Rebecca Britton. 1998. "Still Pretty Prudent: Post–Cold War American Public Opinion on the Use of Military Force." *Journal of Conflict Resolution* 42(4): 395– 417.

Kaiser, Robert G. 2002. "Moderate Reformers Win Slovak Election." *Washington Post*, September 23, p. A15.

Kann, Robert A. 1974. *A History of the Habsburg Empire, 1526–1918.* Berkeley: University of California Press.

Karol, David. 2000. "Divided Government and U.S. Trade Policy: Much Ado About Nothing?" *International Organization* 54(4): 825–44.

Kahler, Miles. 1993. "Bargaining with the IMF: Two-Level Strategies and Developing Countries," in *Double-Edged Diplomacy: International Bargaining and Domestic Politics,* edited by Peter B. Evans, Harold K. Jacobson, and Robert D. Putnam. Berkeley: University of California Press, pp. 363–94.

Keesing's Contemporary Archives 1935–86. London: Keesing's Publications.

Keesing's Record of World Events 1987–95. London: Keesing's Publications.

Kennan, George F. 1984. *American Diplomacy.* Chicago: University of Chicago Press.

———. 1993. *Around the Cragged Hill: A Personal and Political Philosophy.* New York: W. W. Norton.

Keohane, Robert O. 1984. *After Hegemony: Discord in the World Political Economy.* Princeton: Princeton University Press.

Key, V. O. 1961. *Public Opinion and American Democracy.* New York: Knopf.

King, Gary, Robert O. Keohane, and Sidney Verba. 1994. *Designing Social Inquiry.* Princeton: Princeton University Press.

Kissinger, Henry. 1994. *Diplomacy.* New York: Simon and Schuster, Inc.

Knopf, Jeffrey. 1998. "How Rational is 'The Rational Public?' " *Journal of Conflict Resolution* 42(5): 544–71.

Kohler, Hans-Peter and Joseph L. Rodgers. 1999. "DF-like Analyses of Binary, Ordered and Censored Variables using Probit and Tobit Approaches." *Behavior Genetics* 29(4): 221–32.

Kohler, Hans-Peter, Joseph L. Rodgers, Kaare Christensen. 1999. "Is Fertility Behavior in our Genes: Findings from a Danish Twin Study." *Population and Development Review* 25(2): 253–88.

König, Thomas. 2001. "Bicameralism and Party Politics in Germany." *Political Studies* 49(3): 421–37.

König, Thomas and Simon Hug. 2000. "Ratifying Maastricht: Parliamentary Votes on International Treaties and Theoretical Solution Concepts." *European Union Politics* 1(1): 93–124.

———. eds. 2006. *Policy-Making Processes and the European Constitution: A Comparative Study of Member States and Accession Countries.* London: Routledge.

Koremenos, Barbara, Charles Lipson, and Duncan Snidal. 2001. "The Rational Design of International Institutions." *International Organization* 55(4): 761–800.

Koremenos, Barbara, Charles Lipson, and Duncan Snidal, eds. 2001. *Rational Institutional Design,* special issue of *International Organization*: 55(4).

Krauze, Enrique. 1997. *Mexico: Biography of Power.* New York: HarperCollins.

Krehbiel, Keith. 1996. "Institutional and Partisan Sources of Gridlock: A Theory of Divided and Unified Government." *Journal of Theoretical Politics* 8(1): 7–40.

Lake, David A. and Matthew A. Baum. 1998. "The Rent-Seeking State: Monopoly Power and Democratic Control." *Paper presented at APSA Meetings, Boston.*

Lampe, John R. and Marvin R. Jackson. 1982. *Balkan Economic History, 1550–1950. From Imperial Borderlands to Developing Nations.* Bloomington: Indiana University Press.

Láng, Ludwig (László). 1906. *Hundert Jahre Zollpolitik.* Alexander Rosen, trans. Wien und Leipzig: Kaiserliche und königliche Hof-Buchdruckerei und Hof-Verlags-Buchhandlung Carl Fromme.

Langrish, Sally. 1998. "The Treaty of Amsterdam: Selected Highlights." *European Law Review* 23(1): 3–19.

Larson, Deborah Welch. 1989. *Origins of Containment: A Psychological Explanation.* Princeton: Princeton University Press.

Lasswell, Harold D. 1902. *Politics: Who Gets What, When, How.* New York and London: Whittlesey House, McGraw-Hill.

Lauck, W. Jett. 1904. "The Political Significance of Reciprocity." *Journal of Political Economy* 12(4): 495–524.

Laver, Michael and Ben Hunt. 1992. *Policy and Party Competition.* New York: Routledge.

Laver, Michael and Norman Schofield. 1998. *Multiparty Government.* Ann Arbor: University of Michigan Press.

Laver, Michael and Kenneth Shepsle. 1991. "Divided Government: America is not 'Exceptional.' " *Governance* 4(3): 250–69.

Layne, Christopher. 1993. "The Unipolar Illusion: Why Great Powers Will Rise." *International Security* 17(1): 5–51.

Layne, Christopher. 1994. "Kant or Cant: The Myth of the Democratic Peace." *International Security* 19(1): 5–45.

Leeds, Brett Ashley and David R. Davis. 1997. "Domestic Political Vulnerability and International Disputes." *Journal of Conflict Resolution* 41(6): 814–34.

Leeds, Brett Ashley and David Davis. 1999. "Beneath the Surface: Regime Type and International Interaction, 1953–78." *Journal of Peace Research* 36(1): 5–21.

Leventoğlu, Bahar and Ahmer Tarar. 2005. "Prenegotiation Public Commitment in Domestic and International Bargaining." *American Political Science Review* 99(3): 419–33.

Levy, Philip I. 1999. "Lobbying and International Cooperation in Tariff Setting." *Journal of International Economics* 47(2): 345–70.

Lewis-Beck, Michael. 1988. *Economics and Elections: The Major Western Democracies.* Ann Arbor: University of Michigan Press.

Lichbach, Mark. 1995. *The Rebel's Dilemma.* Ann Arbor: University of Michigan Press.

Lijphart, Arend. 1984. *Democracies: Patterns of Majoritarian and Consensus Government in Twenty-One Countries.* New Haven: Yale University Press.

Lindberg, Anders. 1983. *Småstat mot stormakt. Beslutssystemet vid tillkomsten av 1911 års svensk-tyska handels- och sjöfartstraktat.* Lund: CWK Gleerup. (Bibliotheca historica Lundensis vol. 55.)

Lindgren, Raymond E. 1959. *Norway-Sweden. Union, Disunion, and Scandinavian Integration.* Princeton: Princeton University Press.

Lindsay, James M. 1994. *Congress and the Politics of U.S. Foreign Policy*. Baltimore: Johns Hopkins University Press.

Lindsay, James M., Lois W. Sayrs, and Wayne P. Steger. 1992. "The Determinants of Presidential Foreign Policy Choice." *American Politics Quarterly* 20(1): 3–25.

Lippman, Walter. 1922. *Public Opinion*. New York: Macmillan.

Lippman, Walter. 1925. *The Phantom Public*. New York: Harcourt Brace.

Lipson, Charles. 1984. "International Cooperation in Economic and Security Affairs." *World Politics* 37(1): 1–23.

Lohmann, Susanne. 1997. "Linkage Politics." *Journal of Conflict Resolution* 41(1): 38–67.

Lohmann, Susanne. 1996. "Demosclerosis, or Special Interests R Us: An Information Rationale for Political Gridlock," in *The Political Economy of Conflict and Appropriation*, ed., Michelle R. Garfinkel and Stergios Skaperdas. Cambridge: Cambridge University Press. pp. 119–30.

Lohmann, Susanne and Sharyn O'Halloran. 1994. "Divided Government and U.S. Trade Policy: Theory and Evidence." *International Organization* 48(4): 595–632.

Londregan, John B. and Keith T. Poole. 1996. "Does High Income Promote Democracy?" *World Politics* 49(1): 1–30.

Lupia, Arthur and Kaare Strom. 1995. "Coalition Termination and the Strategic Timing of Parliamentary Elections." *American Political Science Review* 89(3): 648–65.

Mackie, Thomas and Richard Rose. 1991. *The International Almanac of Electoral History*, 3rd edn. Washington DC: Congressional Quarterly Inc.

Magee, Stephen, William A. Brock, and Leslie Young. 1989. *Black Hole Tariffs and Endogenous Policy Theory*. Cambridge MA: Cambridge University Press.

Manin, Bernard, Adam Przeworski, and Susan C. Stokes. 1999. "Elections and Representation," in *Democracy, Accountability and Representation*, ed., Adam Przeworski, Susan C. Stokes, and Bernard Manin. Cambridge: Cambridge University Press, pp. 29–44.

Mansfield, Edward D. and Marc L. Busch. 1995. "The Political Economy of Nontariff Barriers: A Cross-National Analysis." *International Organization* 49: 723–49.

Mansfield, Edward D., Helen V. Milner, and B. Peter Rosendorff. 2000. "Free to Trade: Democracies, Autocracies, and International Trade." *American Political Science Review* 94(2): 305–22.

——. 2002. "Why Democracies Cooperate More: Electoral Control and International Trade Agreements." *International Organization* 56(3): 477–514.

Maoz, Zeev. 1997. "The Controversy over the Democratic Peace." *International Security* 22(1): 162–98.

——. 1998. "Realist and Cultural Critiques of the Democratic Peace." *International Interactions* 24(1): 3–89.

Maoz, Zeev and Bruce Russett. 1992. "Alliance, Contiguity, Wealth, and Political Equality." *International Interactions* 17(3): 245–67.

——. 1993. "Normative and Structural Causes of the Democratic Peace." *American Political Science Review* 87(3): 624–38.

Marra, Robin F., Charles W. Ostrom, Jr., and Dennis M. Simon. 1990. "Foreign Policy and Presidential Popularity: Creating Windows of Opportunity in the Perpetual Election." *Journal of Conflict Resolution* 34(4): 588–623.

Marsh, Peter T. 1999. *Bargaining on Europe: Britain and the First Common Market, 1860–1892*. New Haven: Yale University Press.

Martin, Lisa L. 1992. *Coercive Cooperation: Explaining Multilateral Economic Sanctions*. Princeton: Princeton University Press.

———. 1993. "Credibility, Costs, and Institutions: Cooperation on Economic Sanctions," *World Politics* 45(3): 406–32.

———. 1998. "Evasive Maneuvers? Reconsidering Presidential Uses of Executive Agreements," in *Strategic Politicians, Institutions, and Foreign Policy*, ed., Randolph M. Siverson. Ann Arbor: University of Michigan Press, pp. 51–77.

———. 2000. *Democratic Commitments: Legislatures and International Cooperation*. Princeton: Princeton University Press.

Martinez Martinez, Rafael. 1999. *Semi-Presidentialism: A Comparative Study*. Mannheim: Paper prepared for presentation at the ECPR Joint Sessions of Workshops.

Matis, Herbert. 1973. "Leitlinien der österreichischen Wirtschaftspolitik," in *Die Habsburgermonarchie*, volume I, ed., A. Wandruszka and P. Urbanitsch, pp. 29–67.

———. 1984. "Österreichs Wirtschaft im Zeitalter Franz Josephs I," in *Das Zeitalter Kaiser Franz Josephs. 1. Teil: Von der Revolution zur Gründerzeit*, ed., Harry Kühnel and Adam Wandruszka. St. Pölten: Kulturabteilung der Niederösterreichischen Landesregierung, pp. 113–20.

May, Arthur J. 1951. *The Habsburg Monarchy 1867–1914*. Cambridge: Harvard University Press.

Mayer, Frederick W. 1992. "Managing Domestic Differences in International Negotiations: The Strategic Use of Internal Side-Payments." *International Organization* 46(4): 793–818.

Mayhew, David R. 1991. *Divided We Govern: Party Control, Lawmaking, and Investigations, 1946–1990*. New Haven: Yale University Press.

Mas-Colell, Andreu, Michael D. Whinston, and Jerry R. Green. 1995. *Microeconomic Theory*. New York: Oxford University Press.

Mayer, Wolfgang. 1984. "Endogenous Tariff Formation." *American Economic Review* 74(5): 970–85.

McCloskey, Donald N. 1985. *The Rhetoric of Economics*. Madison: University of Wisconsin Press.

McKeown, Timothy J. 1999. "Case Studies and the Statistical Worldview: Review of King, Keohane, and Verba's *Designing Social Inquiry: Scientific Inference in Qualitative Research*." *International Organization* 53(1): 161–90.

Mearsheimer, John J. 2001. *The Tragedy of Great Power Politics*. New York: W.W. Norton and Company.

Meernik, James, Eric L. Krueger, and Steven C. Poe. 1998. "Foreign Aid During and After the Cold War." *Journal of Politics* 60(1): 63–85.

Melich, Anna. 1999. *Eurobarometer 47.1: Images of Switzerland, Education Throughout Life, Racism, and Patterns of Family Planning and Work Status, March–April 1997*. Brussels: INRA (Europe), 1997. Köln, Germany: Zentralarchiv für Empirische Sozialforschung/Ann Arbor, MI: Inter-university Consortium for Political and Social Research.

Mertha, Andrew and Robert Pahre. 2005. "Patently Misleading: Partial Implementation and Bargaining Leverage in Sino-American Negotiations on Intellectual Property Rights," *International Organization* 59(3): 695–729.

The Military Balance 1970–95. New York: Oxford University Press.

Miller, Warren and Merrill Shanks. 1996. *The New American Voter.* Cambridge MA: Harvard University Press.

Milner, Helen V. 1988. *Resisting Protectionism: Global Industries and the Politics of International Trade.* Princeton: Princeton University Press.

——. 1997. *Interests, Institutions, and Information. Domestic Politics and International Relations.* Princeton: Princeton University Press.

Milner, Helen V. and Keiko Kubota. 2005. "Why the Rush to Free Trade? Democracy and Trade Policy in Developing Countries." *International Organization* 59(1): 107–44.

——. 1996. "Trade Negotiations, Information and Domestic Politics: The Role of Domestic Groups." *Economics and Politics* 8(2): 145–89.

——. 1997. "Democratic Politics and International Trade Negotiations: Elections and Divided Government as Constraints on Trade Liberalization." *Journal of Conflict Resolution* 41(1): 117–46.

Mitchell, David. 2002. "International Institutions and Janus Faces: The Influence of International Institutions on Central Negotiators within Two-Level Games." *International Negotiations* 6(1): 25–48.

Mo, Jongryn. 1994. "The Logic of Two-Level Games with Endogenous Domestic Coalitions." *Journal of Conflict Resolution* 38(3): 402–22.

Mo, Jongryn. 1995. "Domestic Institutions and International Bargaining: The Role of Agent Veto in Two-Level Games." *American Political Science Review* 89(4): 914–24.

Montgomery, John D. 1962. *The Politics of Foreign Aid: American Experience in Southeast Asia.* New York: Frederick A. Praeger.

Moravcsik, Andrew. 1998. *The Choice for Europe. Social Purpose and State Power from Messina to Maastricht.* Ithaca, NY: Cornell University Press.

Moravcsik, Andrew and Kalypso Nicolaidis. 1999. "Explaining the Treaty of Amsterdam: Interests, Influence, Institutions." *Journal of Common Market Studies* 37(1) 59–85.

Morgan, T. Clifton and Kenneth N. Bickers. 1992. "Domestic Discontent and the External Use of Force." *Journal of Conflict Resolution* 36(1): 25–52.

Morgan, T. Clifton and Sally Campbell. 1991. "Domestic Structure, Decisional Constraints, and War." *Journal of Conflict Resolution* 35(2): 187–211.

Morgenthau, Hans J. 1949. *Politics Among Nations: The Struggle for Power and Peace.* New York: Knopf.

Morton, Rebecca B. 1999. *Methods and Models: A Guide to the Empirical Analysis of Formal Models in Political Science.* Cambridge: Cambridge University Press.

Moyer, H. Wayne. 1993. "The European Community and the GATT Uruguay Round: A Two-Level Game Approach," in *World Agriculture and the GATT*, ed., William P. Avery. Boulder: Lynne Rienner Publishers, pp. 95–120.

Mudde, Cas. 2002. "Slovak Elections: Go West!" RFE/RL East European Perspectives 4(21) October 16, 2002, available at <http://www.rferl.org>, accessed January 3, 2003.

Mueller, John E. 1973. *War, Presidents, and Public Opinion*. New York: John Wiley.

———. 1994. *Policy and Opinion in the Gulf War*. Chicago: University of Chicago Press.

———. 2001. *Capitalism, Democracy, and Ralph's Pretty Good Grocery*. Princeton: Princeton University Press.

Nalevanko, Michal. 2001. "Na lepší rating treba aka do volieb." *SME* online date accessed is July 2001 <http://www.sme.sk>.

Nash, John F. 1950. "The Bargaining Problem." *Econometrica* 18(2): 155–62.

Neustadt, Richard. 1990. *Presidential Power and the Modern Presidents: The Politics of Leadership from Roosevelt to Reagan*. New York: Free Press.

Nincic, Miroslav. 1992a. *Democracy and Foreign Policy: The Fallacy of Political Realism*. New York: Columbia University Press.

———. 1992b. "A Sensible Public: New Perspectives on Popular Opinion and Foreign Policy." *Journal of Conflict Resolution* 36(4): 772–89.

Nincic, Miroslav and Barbara Hinckley. 1991. "Foreign Policy and the Evaluation of Presidential Candidates." *Journal of Conflict Resolution* 35(2): 333–55.

North, Douglass C. 1984. *Structure and Change in Economic History*. New York: Norton.

O'Halloran, Sharyn. 1993. "Congress and Foreign Trade Policy." *Congress Resurgent: Foreign and Defense Policy on Capitol Hill*, ed., Randall B. Ripley and James M. Lindsay. Ann Arbor: University of Michigan Press.

———. 1994. *Politics, Process, and American Trade Policy*. Ann Arbor: University of Michigan Press.

O'Neal, John and Bruce Russett. 1997a. "Escaping the War Trap." Paper presented at the Annual Meeting of the International Studies Association.

———. 1997b. "The Classical Liberals Were Right." *International Studies Quarterly* 41(2): 267–94.

———. 1999a. "Is the Liberal Peace Just an Artifact of the Cold War?" *International Interactions* 25(3): 213–41.

———. 1999b. "Assessing the Liberal Peace with Alternative Specifications." *Journal of Peace Research* 36(4): 423–42.

Odell, John S. 2000. *Negotiating the World Economy*. Ithaca and London: Cornell University Press.

Olson, Mancur. 1982. *The Rise and Decline of Nations*. New Haven: Yale University Press.

———. 1993. "Dictatorship, Democracy and Development." *American Political Science Review* 87(3): 567–76.

Ostrom, Charles W. and Brian Job. 1986. "The President and the Political Use of Force." *American Political Science Review* 80(2): 541–66.

Owen, John. 1994. "How Liberalism Produces Democratic Peace." *International Security* 19(2): 87–125.

———. 1997. *Liberal Peace, Liberal War*. Ithaca: Cornell University Press.

Oye, Kenneth A., ed. 1986. *Cooperation Under Anarchy*. Princeton: Princeton University Press.

Paarlberg, Robert L. 1993. "Why Agriculture Blocked the Uruguay Round: Evolving Strategies in a Two-Level Game." in *World Agriculture and the GATT*, ed., William P. Avery. Boulder: Lynne Rienner Publishers, pp. 39–54.

Page, Benjamin I. and Jason Barabas. 2000. "Foreign Policy Gaps between Citizens and Leaders." *International Studies Quarterly* 44(2): 339–64.

Page, Benjamin I. and Robert Y. Shapiro. 1992. *The Rational Public: Fifty Years of Trends in Americans' Policy Preferences*. Chicago: University of Chicago Press.

Pahre, Robert. 1994a. " 'Who's on First, What's on Second': Actors and Institutions in Two-Level Games," Institute of Public Policy Studies Research Forum on International Economics, Discussion Paper No. 352.

——. 1994b. "Multilateral Cooperation in an Iterated Prisoners' Dilemma." *Journal of Conflict Resolution* 38(2): 326–52.

——. 1995. "Wider and Deeper: The Links between Expansion and Enlargement in the European Communities," in *Towards a New Europe: Stops and Starts in Regional Integration*, ed., Gerald Schneider, Patricia A. Weitsman, and Thomas Bernauer. Boulder: Praeger/Greenwood, pp. 111–36.

——. 1997. "Endogenous Domestic Institutions in Two-Level Games: Parliamentary Oversight in Denmark and Elsewhere." *Journal of Conflict Resolution* 41(1): 147–74.

——. 1998. "Reactions and Reciprocity: Tariffs and Trade Liberalization in 1815–1914." *Journal of Conflict Resolution* 42(4): 467–92.

——. 2001a. "Divided Government and International Cooperation in Austria-Hungary, Sweden-Norway and the European Union." *European Union Politics* 2(2): 131–62.

——. 2001b. "Most-Favored-Nation Clauses, Domestic Politics, and Clustered Negotiations." *International Organization* 55(4): 861–92.

——. 2001c. "Agreeable Duties: The Tariff Treaty Regime in the Nineteenth Century," in *International Trade and Political Institutions*, ed., Fiona McGillivray, Iain McLean, Robert Pahre, and Cheryl Schonhardt-Bailey. Cheltenham, UK: Edward Elgar, pp. 29–79.

——. 2004a. "House Rules: Institutional Choice and United States Trade Negotiations." *Conflict Management and Peace Sciences* 21(3): 195–213.

——. 2004b. "The Political Economy of European Integration in a Spatial Model," in *The Political Economy of European Integration*, ed., Erik Jones and Amy Verdun. Routledge: pp. 179–90.

——. 2005. "Formal Theory and Case-Study Methods in EU Studies," *European Union Politics* 6(1): 113–46.

——. 2006a. "Divided Government and International Cooperation: An Overview," in *Democratic Foreign Policy Making: Problems of Divided Government and International Cooperation*, ed. Robert Pahre. Palgrave, chapter 1.

——. 2006b. "Divided Government and International Cooperation in the Nineteenth Century," in *Democratic Foreign Policy Making: Problems of Divided Government and International Cooperation*, ed. Robert Pahre. Palgrave, chapter 4.

Pahre, Robert and Paul Papayoanou. 1997. "Using Formal Theory to Link International and Domestic Politics." *Journal of Conflict Resolution* 41(1): 4–11.

Patterson, Lee Ann. 1997. "Agricultural Policy Reform in the European Community: A Three-Level Game Analysis." *International Organization* 51(1): 135–66.

Persson, Torsten, Gerard Roland, and Guido Tabellini. 1997. "Separation of Powers and Political Accountability." *Quarterly Journal of Economics* 112(4): 1163–202.

Peterson, Paul. 1994. "The President's Dominance in Foreign Policy Making." *Political Science Quarterly* 109(2): 215–34.

Pevehouse, Jon C. 2002. "With a Little Help from My Friends? Regional Organizations and the Consolidation of Democracy." *American Journal of Political Science* 46(3): 611–26.

Pickering Jeffrey, and Emizet F. Kisangani. 2005. "Democracy and Diversionary Military Intervention: Reassessing Regime Type and the Diversionary Hypothesis." *International Studies Quarterly* 49(1): 23–44.

Polachek, Solomon W. 1997. "Why Democracies Cooperate More and Fight Less: The Relationship Between International Trade and Cooperation." *Review of International Economics* 5(3): 295–309.

Political Handbook of the World 1926–39. New York: Harper and Row.

Powell, G. Bingham. 2000. *Elections as Instruments of Democracy.* New Haven: Yale University Press.

Powell, Robert. 1991. "Absolute and Relative Gains in International Relations Theory." *American Political Science Review* 85(4): 1303–20.

Powlick, Philip J. 1991. "The Attitudinal Bases for Responsiveness to Public Opinion among American Foreign Policy Officials." *Journal of Conflict Resolution* 35(4): 611–41.

Prins, Brandon C. and Christopher Sprecher. 1999. "Institutional Constraints, Political Opposition, and the Escalation of Interstate Disputes: Evidence From Parliamentary Systems." *Journal of Peace Research* 36(2): 271–87.

Przeworski, Adam. 1991. *Democracy and Markets: Political and Economic Reforms in Eastern Europe and Latin America.* New York: Cambridge University Press.

Putnam, Robert D. 1988. "Diplomacy and Domestic Politics: The Logic of Two-Level Games." *International Organization* 42(3): 427–60.

Ragin, Charles C. 1992. "Introduction: Cases of 'What is a Case?' " in *What is a Case? Exploring the Foundation of Social Inquiry,* ed., Charles C. Ragin and Howard S. Becker. Cambridge: Cambridge University Press, pp. 1–17.

Ratcliffe, Barry M. 1978. "The Tariff Reform Campaign in France, 1831–1836." *Journal of European Economic History* 7(1): 61–138.

Ray, James Lee. 1995. *Democracy and International Conflict.* Columbia: University of South Carolina Press.

——. 1998. "Does Democracy Cause Peace?" in *Annual Review of Political Science* 1, ed., Nelson Polsby. Palo Alto: Annual Reviews, pp. 27–46.

Ray, Leonard. 1999. "Measuring Party Orientations Towards European Integration: Results From an Expert Survey." *European Journal of Political Research* 36(2): 283–306.

Raymond, Gregory. 1994. "Democracies, Disputes, and Third-Party Intermediaries." *Journal of Conflict Resolution* 38(1): 24–42.

Reed, William. 2000. "A Unified Statistical Model of Conflict Onset and Escalation." *American Journal of Political Science* 44(1): 84–93.

Remmer, Karen. 1998. "Does Democracy Promote Interstate Cooperation? Lessons from the Mercosur Region." *International Studies Quarterly* 42(1): 25–51.

Riker, William H. and Peter C. Ordeshook. 1973. *An Introduction to Positive Political Theory.* Englewood Cliffs, NJ: Prentice-Hall.

Rodrik, Dani. 1994. "The Rush to Free Trade in the Developing World: Why So Late? Why Now? Will It Last?" in *Voting for Reform: Democracy, Political Liberalization and Economic Adjustment*, ed. Stephan Haggard and Steven B. Webb. New York, NY: Oxford University Press.

——. 1995. "Political Economy of Trade Policy," in *Handbook of International Economics, 3*, ed., Gene M. Grossman and Kenneth Rogoff. Amsterdam: North-Holland, pp. 1457–94.

Rogowski, Ronald. 1974. *Rational Legitimacy: A Theory of Political Support*. Princeton: Princeton University Press.

——. 1987. "Trade and the Variety of Democratic Institutions." *International Organization* 41(2): 203–23.

——. 1989. *Commerce and Coalitions: How Trade Affects Domestic Political Alignments*. Princeton: Princeton University Press.

Rogowski, Ronald and Mark Andreas Kayser. 2002. "Majoritarian Electoral Systems and Consumer Power: Price-Level Evidence from the OECD Countries." *American Journal of Political Science* 46(3): 526–39.

Rostow, Eugene. 1989. "President, Prime Minister, or Constitutional Monarch?" McNair Papers, No.3. Washington, DC: National Defense University.

Roth, Alvin E. 2002. "Bargaining (Economic Theories of Bargaining)." Website at <http://www.economics.harvard.edu/~aroth/barg.html>, accessed January 9, 2002.

Rousseau, David. 1996. "Domestic Political Institutions and the Evolution of International Conflict." Ann Arbor: Ph.D. Dissertation, Department of Political Science, University of Michigan.

Rousseau, David, Christopher Gelpi, Dan Reiter, and Paul Huth. 1996. "Assessing the Dyadic Nature of the Democratic Peace." *American Political Science Review* 90(3): 512–33.

Rubinstein, Ariel. 1982. "Perfect Equilibrium in a Bargaining Model." *Econometrica* 50(7): 97–109.

Rummel, R. J. 1995. "Democracies ARE Less Warlike Than Other Regimes." *European Journal of International Relations* 1(4): 459–79.

——. 1997. *Power Kills: Democracy as a Method of Nonviolence*. New Brunswick: Transaction Publishers.

Russett, Bruce. 1990a. *Controlling the Sword: The Democratic Governance of National Security*. Cambridge, MA: Harvard University Press.

——. 1990b. "Economic Decline, Electoral Pressure, and the Initiation of International Conflict," in *Prisoners of War?* ed., Charles Gochman and Alan Ned Sabrosky. Lexington: Lexington Books, pp. 123–40.

——. 1993. *Grasping the Democratic Peace*. Princeton: Princeton University Press.

Russett, Bruce and John O'Neal. 2001. *Triangulating Peace: Democracy, Interdependence, and International Organizations*. New York: W. W. Norton.

Ruttan, Vernon W. 1996. *United States Development Assistance Policy: The Domestic Politics of Foreign Economic Aid*. Baltimore: Johns Hopkins University Press.

Schelling, Thomas C. 1960. *The Strategy of Conflict*. Cambridge, MA: Harvard University Press.

Schneider, Gerald and Lars-Erik Cederman. 1994. "The Change in Tide in Political Cooperation: A Limited Information Model of European Integration." *International Organization* 48(4): 633–62.

Schoppa, Leonard J. 1993. "Two-Level Games and Bargaining Outcomes: Why *Gaiatsu* Succeeds in Japan in Some Cases but Not Others." *International Organization* 47(3): 353–86.

Schultz, Kenneth A. 1998. "Domestic Opposition and Signaling in International Crises." *American Political Science Review* 92(4): 829–44.

———. 2001. *Democracy and Coercive Diplomacy*. Cambridge: Cambridge University Press.

Schumpeter, Joseph. 1942 [1976]. *Capitalism, Socialism and Democracy*. New York: Harper Colophon.

Schweller, Randall. 1992. "Domestic Structure and Preventive War." *World Politics* 44(2): 235–69.

Simmons, Beth A. 1994. *Who Adjusts?: Domestic Sources of Foreign Economic Policy During the Interwar Years, 1924–1939*. Princeton: Princeton University Press.

Singer, J. David and Melvin Small. 1994. *Correlates of War Project: International and Civil War Data, 1816–1992*. Vol. 9905 Ann Arbor: Inter-University Consortium for Political and Social Research.

SIPRI Yearbook: World Armaments and Disarmament 1970–95. New York: Humanities Press 1970–73; Cambridge: MIT Press, 1974–77; London: Taylor and Francis, 1978–85; New York: Oxford University Press, 1986–95.

Small, Melvin and David Singer. 1976. "The War Proneness of Democratic Regimes." *Jerusalem Journal of International Relations* 1(1):46–61.

Smith, Alastair. 1998. "International Crises and Domestic Politics." *American Political Science Review* 92(3): 623–38.

———. 1999. "Testing Theories of Strategic Choice: The Example of Crisis Escalation." *American Journal of Political Science* 43(4): 1254–83.

Snidal, Duncan. 1985. "The Game *Theory* of International Politics." *World Politics* 38(7): 25–57.

———. 1991. "Relative Gains and the Pattern of International Cooperation." *American Political Science Review* 85(3): 701–26.

Snow, Donald M. and Eugene Brown. 1997. *Beyond the Water's Edge*. New York: St. Martin's Press.

Snyder, Glenn. 1997. *Alliance Politics*. Ithaca, NY: Cornell University Press.

Somogyi, Éva. 1984. "Ungarn in der Habsburgmonarchie," in *Das Zeitalter Kaiser Franz Josephs. 1. Teil: Von der Revolution zur Gründerzeit*, ed., Harry Kühnel and Adam Wandruszka. St. Pölten: Kulturabteilung der Niederösterreichischen Landesregierung, pp. 269–76.

Stahl, I. 1972. *Bargaining Theory*. Stockholm: Stockholm School of Economics.

Stein, Arthur A. 1983. "Coordination and Collaboration: Regimes in an Anarchic World," in *International Regimes*, ed., Stephen D. Krasner. Princeton: Princeton University Press, pp. 115–40.

———. 1990. *Why Nations Cooperate*. Ithaca, NY: Cornell University Press.

Stoiber, Michael and Paul W. Thurner. 2000. *Der Vergleich von Ratifikationsstrukturen der EU-Mitgliedsländer für Intergouvernementale Verträge: Eine Anwendung des Veto-Spieler Konzeptes.* Mannheim: MZES.

——. 2003. "Die Ratifikation Intergouvernementaler Verträge: Konstitutionelle Erfordernisse und Akteursspezifische Agendakontrolle," in *Die Institutionalisierung Internationaler Verhandlungssysteme.* (Mannheimer Jahrbuch Für Europäische Sozialforschung Band 8), ed., Franz U. Pappi, Eibe Riedel, Roland Vaubel, and Paul W. Thurner. Frankfurt: Campus, pp. 173–203.

Szijártó, István M. 1994. "Playing Second Fiddle: The Role of Hungary and Norway in the Foreign Policies of the Austro-Hungarian Monarchy and the Swedish-Norwegian Union: A Comparison." *Scandinavian Journal of History* 19(2): 143–63.

Tarar, Ahmer. 2001. "International Bargaining with Two-Sided Domestic Constraints." *Journal of Conflict Resolution* 45(3): 320–40.

Taylor, A. J. P. 1964. *The Habsburg Monarchy 1809–1918.* London: Penguin Books.

Taylor, Michael. 1987. *The Possibility of Cooperation.* Cambridge: Cambridge University Press. (Revised edition of Taylor, *Anarchy and Cooperation*, 1976).

Thompson, J. M. 1954. *Louis Napoleon and the Second Empire.* Oxford: Blackwell.

Tillema, Herbert. 1991. *International Armed Conflict Since 1945: A Bibliographic Handbook of Wars and Military Interventions.* Boulder: Westview Press.

Trumbore, Peter F. 1998. "Public Opinion as a Domestic Constraint in International Negotiations: Two-Level Games in the Anglo-Irish Peace Process." *International Studies Quarterly* 42(3): 545–66.

Trumbore, Peter F. and Mark A. Boyer. 2000. "International Crisis Decisionmaking as a Two-Level Process." *Journal of Peace Research* 37(6): 679–97.

Tsebelis, George. 1994. "The Power of the European Parliament as a Conditional Agenda Setter." *American Political Science Review* 88(1): 128–42.

——. 1995. "Decision Making in Political Systems: Veto Players in Presidentialism, Parliamentarism, Multicameralism and Multipartism." *British Journal of Political Science* 25(3): 289–325.

——. 1999. "Veto Players and Law Production in Parliamentary Democracies: An Empirical Analysis." *American Political Science Review* 93(3): 591–608.

——. 2002. *Veto Players: How Political Institutions Work.* Princeton: Princeton University Press.

Tsebelis, George and Geoffrey Garrett. 2000. "Legislative Politics in the European Union." *European Union Politics* 1(1): 9–36.

Vandenbosch, Amry. 1944. "Formulation and Control of Foreign Policy in the Netherlands: A Phase of Small Power Politics." *Journal of Politics* 6(4): 430–52.

Tsebelis, George and Jeanette Money. 1997. *Bicameralism.* New York: Cambridge University Press.

Verdier, Daniel. 1994. *Democracy and International Trade. Britain, France, and the United States, 1860–1990.* Princeton: Princeton University Press.

——. 1998. "Democratic Convergence and Free Trade." *International Studies Quarterly* 42(1): 1–24.

Verney, Douglas V. 1957. *Parliamentary Reform in Sweden 1866–1921.* Oxford: Clarendon Press.

Volkens, Andrea. 2001. "Manifesto Research since 1979. From Reliability to Validity," in *Estimating the Policy Positions of Political Actors*, ed., Michael Laver. London and New York: Routledge, pp. 33–49.

Vomáčková, Vera. 1963. "Österreich und der deutsche Zollverein." *Historica* 5(1): 109–46.

von Bazant, Johann. 1894. *Die Handelspolitik Österreich-Ungarns 1875 bis 1892 in ihrem Verhältnis zum Deutschem Reiche und zu dem westlichen Europa*. Leipzig: Verlag von Dunker and Humblot.

Wallensteen, Peter and Margareta Sollenberg. 1996. "The End of International War? Armed Conflict 1989–1995." *Journal of Peace Research* 33(3): 353–70.

Waltz, Kenneth N. 1967. *Foreign Policy and Democratic Politics: The American and British Experience*. Boston: Little, Brown and Company.

———. 1979. *Theory of International Politics*. Reading, MA: Addison Wesley.

Warwick, Paul. 1994. *Government Survival in Parliamentary Democracies*. Cambridge: Cambridge University Press.

Weart, Spencer. 1998. *Never at War: Why Democracies Will Not Fight One Another*. New Haven: Yale University Press.

Weede, Erich. 1984. "Democracy and War Involvement." *Journal of Conflict Resolution* 28 (4): 649–64.

———. 1992. "Some Simple Calculations on Democracy and War Involvement." *Journal of Peace Research* 29(4):377–83.

Weitowitz, Rolf. 1978. *Deutsche Politik und Handelspolitik unter Reichskanzler Leo von Caprivi 1890–1894*. Düsseldorf: Droste Verlag.

Werner, Yvonne Maria. 1989. *Svensk-tyska Förbindelser kring Sekelskiftet 1900. Politik och ekonomi vid tillkomsten av 1906 års svensk-tyska handels- och sjöfartstraktat*. Lund: Lund University Press. (Bibliotheca historica Lundensis, vol. 65, ed., Eva Österberg and Göran Rystad.)

Wessels, Bernhard, Achim Kielhorn, and Jacques Thomassen. 1996. *European Study of Members of Parliament*. University of Twente, Netherlands, Wissenschaftszentrum Berlin für Sozialforschung (WZB).

Wood, B. Dan and Jeffrey S. Peake. 1998. "The Dynamics of Foreign Policy Agenda Setting." *American Political Science Review* 92(2): 173–84.

World Military Expenditures and Arms Transfers 1970–95. Washington DC: United States Arms Control and Disarmament Agency, 1979–96.

Wu, Jianzhong and Robert Axelrod. 1995. "How to Cope with Noise in the Iterated Prisoner's Dilemma." *Journal of Conflict Resolution* 39(1): 183–89.

Yarbrough, Beth V. and Robert M. Yarbrough. 1986. "Reciprocity, Bilateralism, and Economic 'Hostages': Self-Enforcing Agreements in International Trade." *International Studies Quarterly* 30(1): 7–21.

Zimmerman, William. 2002. *The Russian People and Foreign Policy*. Princeton: Princeton University Press.

Zorn, Christopher. 2002. "U.S. Government Litigation Strategies in the Federal Appellate Courts." *Political Research Quarterly* 55(1): 145–66.

Zorn, Wolfgang. 1963. "Wirtschafts- und sozialgeschichtliche Zusammenhänge der Reichsgründungszeit (1850–1879)." *Historische Zeitschrift* 197: 313–42.

———. 1973. "Die wirtschaftliche Integration Kleindeutschlands in der 1860er Jahren und die Reichsgründung." *Historische Zeitschrift* 216(3): 304–34.

Index

accountability, 176, 178–9, 191
  electoral, 83, 86–7, 91–2, 96–7, 102,
      157–8, 176
  level of, 157
Afghanistan, 23, 178
agenda-setting, 2, 9–12, 17–18, 109, 111,
      121–2, 177, 179–80, 186, 190, 193
  agenda-setters, 10–11, 28, 95, 121, 130,
      132, 176, 180
  see also reversion point; veto actor
agreements, international, 11, 22, 26, 28,
      33, 84, 87, 91, 93, 99, 107–14, 116,
      120–7, 134, 153–4, 157, 159–61, 171,
      173, 176, 180–1, 183, 185, 187, 195,
      198, 200
  see also cooperation; treaties
al-Qaeda, 178
alliances, 110, 162, 165, 169, 172,
  see also treaties
Amsterdam Intergovernmental Conference,
      11, 14, 133–150
  Treaty of Amsterdam, 133–150
  see also European Union
anarchy, 4, 17, 84, 162
  see also Realism
Argentina, 115, 117, 132,
  see also Mercosur
Arms Control and Disarmament Agency
      (ACDA), 23
  see also United States
audience costs, 181
  see also referendums; two-level games;
      veto actors
Australia, 193
Austria, 108, 113, 115, 118–20, 124–32
  see also Austria-Hungary; European
      Union

Austria-Hungary, 108, 113, 115, 118–20,
      124–32
  Ausgleich (compromise), 119, 125–127
  Austro-Prussian War, 126
  Franz Joseph I, King-Emperor, 125
  trade policy of, 113, 121, 125–6, 129
  Zwischenzolllinie (internal tariff
      division), 126
  see also Austria; dual monarchies;
      Germany; *Zollverein*
autocracies, 1, 17, 84, 93–4, 96–100, 102,
      104, 164
  see also regimes
autonomy, executive, 17, 19
  see also regimes

Baden, 131
  see also Germany; *Zollverein*
Balkans, 126–7
Balladur, Édouard, 137
Bavaria, 131
  see also Germany; *Zollverein*
bargaining, 14, 22, 25–8, 33–5, 39–42,
      55–8, 63–71, 84, 87, 90–6, 102, 105,
      133–5, 147–8, 152–3, 162, 166, 173,
      181, 183, 185–6, 197
  Nash bargaining solution, 25, 180
  power and, 17–18, 92, 162, 180
  Rubinstein solution, 25–6, 180
  tactics in, 8, 25, 162, 180
  theories of, 25–6
  see also cooperation; equilibrium; Schelling
      Conjecture; two-level games
behavioralism, 196
Belgium, 110–11, 115–16, 119, 126, 138,
      146, 149, 170
  see also European Union

polity, divided, 83–6, 100, 102, 108, 121, 127, 141, 176–7, 179, 182, 190, 194, 199
see also government
polyarchy, 108, 176, 178, 194
see also government; polity
Popular Party (Spain), 1, 145
see also Spain
Portugal, 115–16, 118–19, 136, 138–9, 146–7, 150
see also European Union
power, 2, 9, 11–12, 19, 21, 24, 27, 81, 84, 87, 92–3, 102, 110, 112, 118–19, 130, 136, 139–40, 147, 155, 157, 159–60, 180, 193
see also separation of power
see also under bargaining
preferences, 24–30, 34, 85–8, 94, 107–8, 110, 112–14, 116–18, 122–5, 129, 131, 133–5, 141–3, 150, 156–7, 176, 178, 180–2, 184–200
see also utility
Preferential Trade Agreement (PTA), 83, 99–100
see also European Union; Mercosur; trade, international; treaties, economic
principal-agent theory, 190
see also delegation; international organizations
Prisoners' Dilemma (PD), 5, 90
"shadow of the future," 6, 122; *see also* discount rate
repeated-play in, 122–3
Taylor-Axelrod condition, 122–3
see also compliance; cooperation; conflict; defection; enforcement; game theory; implementation
property, private, 97
Prussia, 113, 115–16, 125–6, 129–32
see also Germany; *Zollverein*
public choice theory, 187
public opinion
see opinion, public

qualified majority voting, 136–41, 144–5
see also European Union

RPR (Rally for the Republic or *Rassemblement pour la République*), 145
see also France; parties, political

rally-round-the-flag effect, 194
see also conflict, diversionary theory of; domestic politics
ratification, 8, 10–11, 16–17, 22, 93, 107–8, 131, 133, 138–9, 144, 158, 162, 173, 180–83, 189, 193
bicameralism and, 8, 134, 139–41, 179
federalism and, 178–9, 195
nonratification, 108, 114–18, 132, 159–60, 173
see also referendums; two-level games; veto actors
rational choice theory, 7
see also equilibrium; game theory; public choice; utility
Realism, 21, 24, 27, 177, 196, 198
referendums, 93, 110, 136–41, 144–6
see also European Union; ratification; veto actors
regimes, political, 100
measurement of, 98–100
types, 16, 84, 88–90, 96–9, 101–2, 108, 152, 157, 199
see also autocracy; democracy
"relative" vs. "absolute" gains, 181
Republican Party (U.S.), 192
see also parties, political
research design, 153
see also methods
reversion point, 2, 7, 10–12, 16–17, 83, 95, 105, 108–9, 111–14, 120–30, 133, 136, 179
see also agenda-setting
risk avoidance, 163
Romania, 125, 127
Rostenkowski, Dan, 22
Rostow, Eugene, 22
rule of law, 97, 100
see also democracy; institutions; property, private; regimes
Russia, 113, 116, 132
see also Union of Soviet Socialist Republics

Salisbury, Lord, 187
SALT II (Strategic Arms Limitation Treaty), 22
sanctions, economic, 196
Saxony, 131
see also Beust, Graf; Germany; *Zollverein*